CLASSIC GUITARS

WALTER **CARTER**

METRO BOOKS
NEW YORK

TEXT: Walter Carter
EDITOR: Peter Chrisp
DESIGN: Paul Cooper Design

Metro Books
122 Fifth Avenue
New York, NY 10011

ISBN: 978-1-4351-1161-5

Printed and bound by Everbest Printing Co Ltd (China)

10 9 8 7 6 5 4 3 2

CONTENTS

CONTENTS

classic guitars

CONTENTS

CONTENTS

classic guitars

CONTENTS

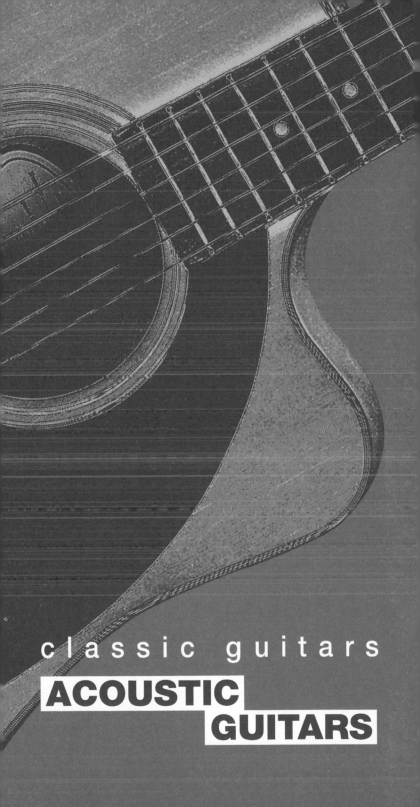

classic guitars

ACOUSTIC GUITARS

ACOUSTIC
GUITARS

Although acoustic guitars have been around since the Renaissance, and in their modern form since the mid 1800s, they didn't rise to the top of the fretted instrument world until the 1930s. And then, just as musicians started putting aside banjos and mandolins for guitars, the electric guitar emerged and went on to dominate popular culture. But even as the guitar was being revolutionized by amplification, and then taken beyond imagination by digital technology, the acoustic guitar never missed a beat.

The pure, natural quality of an acoustic guitar, along with the intimate connection that a player has with an unamplified instrument, has never lost its appeal – to guitar players or to guitar makers. It takes an artistic eye to design an acoustic guitar and a special level of craftsmanship to build one. And yet no matter how carefully the materials are chosen – whether they be wood, metal or synthetic – and no matter how beautifully designed or meticulously crafted a guitar may be, the mystique remains. Some acoustic guitars sound great and others, virtually identical, are simply not as good.

The guitars on these pages have earned the right to be called classic for a variety of reasons. Obviously, those that sound the best, look the best, or, in some other way, get the job done the best, are classics. But so are those that have made a lasting impression by being flamboyantly wild, radically innovative, or just hugely popular. These classic acoustics are the instruments that continue to inspire guitar makers and guitar players alike.

St. Louis Music, a distributor founded in 1922 by violinist Bernard Kornblum, created the Alvarez brand in 1965 for a line of Japanese import guitars. A year later the company teamed up with Kazuo Yairi, a second-generation luthier, who designed and supervised some of the most respected and innovative acoustic guitars to come out of Japan.

Yairi's models appeared in the United States under two brand names: Alvarez-Yairi on those that he supervised and personally signed, and Alvarez by Yairi on those built by his workers. He used the K. Yairi brand on models marketed outside the U.S. Yairi created a wide variety of steel-string and classical models, including this small-bodied steel-string AR300, with such distinctive features as a cedar top, rounded headstock and moustache-shaped bridge.

Such noteworthy artists as Jerry Garcia and Bob Weir of Grateful Dead, Jeff "Skunk" Baxter and Patrick Simmons of The Doobie Brothers, Carlos Santana, David Crosby, and Graham Nash have played Alvarez-Yairi instruments. Kazuo Yairi still makes guitars in the mountain region of Honshu, Japan.

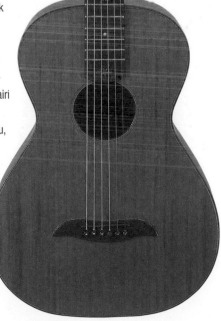

11

MODEL
K. Yairi AR300

YEAR
1983

PRODUCTION
Early 1980s

ounded by Japanese classical guitarist Shiro Arai in 1960, Aria became one of the leading makers of guitars for beginning and intermediate players by the end of the decade.

Although the company's first efforts were classical guitars, Aria's best-selling models, like those of other successful Japanese makers in the 1960s and 70s, were copies of the traditional steel-string designs of Martin and Gibson. Aria also secured its place in guitar history in 1967 for developing one of the earliest piezo transducer pickups, which was initially attached to an internal brace. In more recent years, Aria has introduced more of its own original designs and gained a reputation for stylish aesthetics as well as quality production.

Aria's Sandpiper guitars, introduced in 1998, featured onboard electronics and their own distinctive headstock shape, along with the intriguing design concept of an arched back on a flat-top cutaway body. Available in at least five different combinations of woods and ornamentation (plus a 12-string), the Sandpipers were last offered in 2004.

MODEL
Aria Sandpiper SP-99

YEAR
1999

PRODUCTION
1999

12

BENEDETTO

Born in the Bronx, New York, Robert Benedetto made his first guitar in 1968. By the end of the 1980s, he had emerged as the leading force in a new generation of archtop guitar makers who expanded on the tradition established by John D'Angelico and James D'Aquisto.

In 1982 Benedetto co-designed an instrument with jazz guitarist Chuck Wayne (who played with Woody Herman, Dizzy Gillespie and George Shearing) that would lay the groundwork for a new aesthetic for archtops. In a dramatic turn away from the opulent inlays and gold-plated hardware of traditional archtops, the new model, named La Venezia, had no body binding, no inlays, and an ebony pickguard and tailpiece. Benedetto began offering it as a regular model in 1993.

In 1999, Benedetto began consulting with Fender on archtop models for Fender's newly acquired Guild brand, and he cut back production to the occasional custom guitar. He ended the relationship with Fender in 2007, relocated to Savannah, Georgia, and returned to making guitars as an independent luthier.

13

MODEL
Benedetto La Venezia

YEAR
2003

PRODUCTION
1993 to current

BOURGEOIS

Dana Bourgeois built his first guitar in his dorm room at Bowdoin College in Maine and first gained notoriety building Martin OM-style guitars in the shop of Eric Schoenberg from 1986–90. After working with Paul Reed Smith and Gibson, he established his own shop in 1995.

Bourgeois's reputation was elevated considerably in 1997 with the introduction of a Martin Simpson signature model. The English guitarist was living in America at the time and was well-established as an eclectic artist, with a background in folk and a taste for everything from blues to bluegrass to Cajun music. The Bourgeois Martin Simpson had a large dreadnought body and a 12-fret neck for a booming sound, but it had a "fallaway" cutaway that not only made it easily recognizable but also distinguished Bourgeois from the growing field of Martin-influenced acoustic guitar makers.

In 2000, Bourgeois formed the Pantheon company with a group of investors in Lewiston, Maine, where he continues to oversee the design and production of Bourgeois guitars.

MODEL
Bourgeois Martin Simpson

YEAR
1998

PRODUCTION
1997 to 1999

The blue finish and the archtop design of this Bozo Chicagoan are not typical Bozo features, but the highly ornate trim is the unmistakable mark of Bozo (pronounced "Bo-zho") Padunavac.

Born in Serbia and raised in Belgrade, Yugoslavia, Padunavac began making instruments in the 1940s. He immigrated to Chicago in 1959 and, after working for five years in a guitar store as a repairman, he began making guitars under the Bozo brand. He quickly became known for his Bell Western model, a flat-top that featured a wide lower bout and a short, square-ish upper bout. He also gained a reputation for his 12-string models, which were played by Rev Gary Davis and Leo Kottke.

Although Bozo's reputation has always been based on his flat-tops, he was one of 22 luthiers commissioned by collector Scott Chinery to build an archtop for Chinery's Blue Guitars collection in 1996. Bozo named it after the city where he had started his American career. After relocating to California, then back to the Chicago area, he now makes guitars in East Englewood, Florida.

MODEL
Bozo Chicagoan

YEAR
1996

PRODUCTION
1996

15

BREEDLOVE

The Breedlove SC20 served notice in 1995 that the small custom guitar shop in Bend, Oregon, was reinventing itself with regular production models. Moreover, the SC20 represented a departure from the shop's emphasis on spectacular woods and inlays. It was a relatively plain guitar, built for performance – thanks to a body depth of 4⁹⁄₁₆ inches – rather than show.

Although the SC20 has a traditional non-cutaway body shape, it is hardly a traditional design. The asymmetrical peghead shape provides straighter string pull than traditional designs. The moustache bridge is part of a patented system that uses the tailblock to counterbalance the tension on the top.

Breedlove was founded in 1990 by former Taylor employees Larry Breedlove and Steve Henderson, and for its first five years the business was more of a custom shop than a production facility. Larry Breedlove left in 1994; his older brother Kim, a master luthier, now represents the Breedlove name in the business. Breedlove has continued to expand, and its offerings now include mandolins and electric guitars.

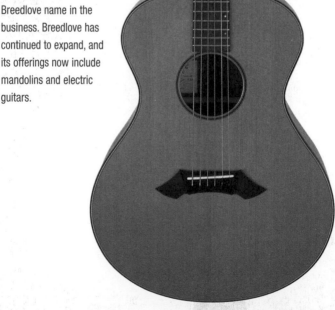

MODEL
Breedlove SC20

YEAR
1996

PRODUCTION
1995 to 2004

Brook guitars are made by Simon Smidmore and Andy Petherick in a converted barn in rural Devon, England. In keeping with the flowing water connection of the brand name, their models are named after Westcountry rivers, ranging from the tiny, parlour-sized 12½-inch Creedy to the super jumbo 17-inch Okement. The Clyst is the second smallest at 13¾ inches, slightly larger than a Martin 0-size.

Smidmore and Petherick honed their luthier skills working for Andy Manson, one of the U.K.'s best-known guitarmakers, before opening their own shop in 1995. They gained a reputation for their combination of quality and value, and their instruments have found a home with such noted musicians as innovative English fingerstylist Adrian Legg and Jethro Tull bandmembers Martin Barre and Ian Anderson.

The current Brook line includes an archtop and an acoustic bass. Their output is around 120 guitars per year, and most of them are made to order with a wait time of up to a year.

BROOK
guitars

17

MODEL
Brook Clyst

YEAR
2002

PRODUCTION
2001 to current

CAMPELLONE

Based in Greenville, Rhode Island, Mark Campellone makes archtop guitars that combine traditional basic designs with artistic ornamental touches. Not surprisingly, Campellone considered a career in art before entering the Berklee College of Music in Boston to study guitar.

Campellone began building guitars in the mid 1970s, concentrating on electric guitars and basses while he also did repair and restoration work. He completed his first archtop in 1988 and, within a few years, he had quit working as a professional musician to devote full-time to making guitars.

The Special is the most ornate of Campellone's three standard models, all of which are available with 16-, 17- or 18-inch body width. This example illustrates the combination of a traditional cutaway body style with modern artistic touches in the design of the tailpiece and headstock inlay. In 1996 Campellone was one of 22 makers commissioned by collector Scott Chinery to build an archtop guitar with a distinctive blue finish, and this Special was his contribution to Chinery's Blue Collection

18

MODEL
Campellone Special

YEAR
1995

PRODUCTION
1995 to current

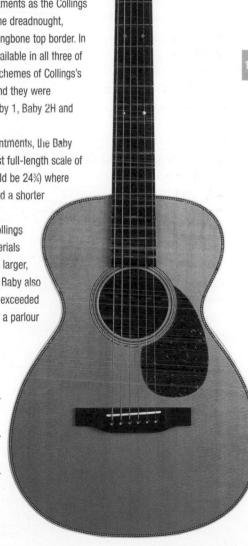

Wile most guitar makers have viewed smaller "parlour" guitars as an opportunity to introduce new designs, such as the "travel guitar" concept, or simply to lower costs with a plainer and less expensive guitar than standard-size models, Bill Collings of Austin, Texas, cut no corners when he designed the Baby Collings.

The first Baby Collings, introduced in 1997, featured the same appointments as the Collings D2H, the company's midline dreadnought, distinguishable by its herringbone top border. In 2004 the Baby became available in all three of the basic ornamentation schemes of Collings's dreadnoughts and OMs, and they were numbered accordingly: Baby 1, Baby 2H and Baby 3.

In addition to its appointments, the Baby Collings featured an almost full-length scale of 24⅛ inches (standard would be 24¾) where other makers typically used a shorter "three-quarter" scale. Consequently, the Baby Collings not only matched the materials and trim of the company's larger, standard-size models, the Baby also had volume and tone that exceeded the typical expectations of a parlour guitar.

MODEL
Collings Baby

YEAR
2001

PRODUCTION
1997 to current

19

COLLINGS

The "jumbo" shape of Gibson's classic dreadnought guitars, featuring the "slope-shouldered" lines of their upper bout, provided the model for the CJ or Collings Jumbo.

Although the CJ did not become official until 1995, Collings made one with a pearl-trimmed top in the early 1990s for longtime Collings player Lyle Lovett. (Lovett has been playing Collings guitars since 1978, when he was a college student at Texas A&M.)

The CJSB (SB stands for sunburst) illustrates how a modern guitarmaker builds on and refines a classic design. While the body shape, the pickguard shape and, on this example, the sunburst finish, make it look very much like one of Gibson's pre-World War II Advanced Jumbos or J-35s, the neck is unlike that of any Gibson. The graduated-size pearl dot inlays add a touch of elegance to the bound ebony fingerboard, and the peghead, though inspired by that of Gibson's 1920s L-5 archtop, has the offset notch that is a Collings signature feature.

MODEL
Collings CJSB

YEAR
1999

PRODUCTION
1995 to current

Bill Collings has been the most
successful of a generation of builders
whose core talent was building a Martin-
inspired guitar that was as good or better
than the high-production models produced by
the Martin company. In essence, his
dreadnought and OM models beat Martin at
their own game.

Collings made his first instruments shortly
after abandoning pre-medical studies at Ohio
University. By 1975 he had relocated to
Houston, Texas, where he repaired and built
instruments out of his apartment. After five
years and around 50 guitars he moved to
Austin, where he has become one of the most
highly respected makers of tradition-inspired
guitars and mandolins

The D3 is distinguished from the D1 and
D2 by its abalone soundhole ring and inlay-
less ebony fingerboard. Like
all Collings models, it has a
mortise-and-tenon neck
joint rather than the
dovetail design of a
Martin or Gibson. Although
that represents an
uncharacteristic break with
tradition, it was designed
to make the inevitable
resetting of the neck
less traumatic for
the repairman as
well as for the
guitar.

MODEL
Collings D3

YEAR
2001

PRODUCTION
1990 to current

21

D'ANGELICO

In his 32 years as a guitar maker, John D'Angelico went from a copier of Gibson's archtop design to become the leading – and now legendary – individual maker of archtop guitars. Born in 1905 in New York, he learned the luthier's craft from his uncle and established his own shop in 1932 to build violins, mandolins and guitars.

D'Angelico's earliest guitars were modeled on Gibson's L-5 archtop, which at the time were 16 inches wide. When Gibson 'advanced' the L-5 to 17 inches and introduced the 18-inch Super 400, D'Angelico followed suit. By the end of the 1930s he had established four standard models, topped by the 18-inch New Yorker.

This 1939 New Yorker, built for Joe Senacorin, is a transitional example that shows the Gibson influence in the "dove wing" or center-dip design at the top of the peghead. The rest of the appointments are distinctly D'Angelico, including the heavy, stairstep-design tailpiece, the multiple layers of binding, the flared peghead shape, and the engraved peghead inlay.

MODEL
D'Angelico New Yorker

YEAR
1939

PRODUCTION
1936 to 1964

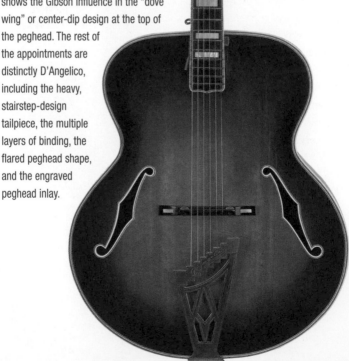

John D'Angelico recorded his first Excel model in his ledger book in 1936, and by the end of the 1940s it had emerged as his standard 17-inch model.

As the archtop guitar became the preferred style of professional players, and as more and more guitarists became virtuosos, the increased attention on the instrument resulted in two improvements, one visual and one functional. A natural finish made the guitarist stand out, and a cutaway body provided easier access to the upper register of the fingerboard. Gibson implemented both of these features by 1939, but D'Angelico lagged behind. His first cutaway did not appear until 1947.

By the time this guitar was made, cutaways were commonplace on D'Angelicos, and D'Angelico's instruments were considered by most guitar players to be the best archtop guitars available by any maker. His guitars were easily recognizable by their headstock design, which sported a cutout shape known in architecture terms as the broken scroll pediment, along with an ornamental cupola (button). D'Angelico died on September 1, 1964, after building 1,164 guitars.

MODEL
D'Angelico Excel Cutaway

YEAR
1954

PRODUCTION
1947 to 1964

D'ANGELICO

John D'Angelico never strayed far from traditional archtop designs, except in 1957 when he made this one-of-a-kind archtop guitar. The story is that Peter Girardi, whose initials are engraved in the peghead inlay where *New Yorker* would normally be, performed as a strolling troubadour in Italian restaurants, and he wanted a guitar that diners would remember. D'Angelico's former apprentice Jimmy D'Aquisto joked that the real purpose of the pointed lower bout was so that Girardi could poke the diners who didn't tip him.

This guitar was rumored to exist for some years, and when it turned up in 1993, collector Scott Chinery made headlines when he bought it for $150,000, which was three or four times the going rate for a cutaway D'Angelico. The model had initially been nicknamed the Can Opener but after Chinery bought it was more respectfully referred to as the D'Angelico Teardrop New Yorker.

In recent years, licensed replicas of the Teardrop have been made under the D'Angelico brand as well as the D'Aquisto brand.

MODEL
D'Angelico Cutaway Special

YEAR
1957

PRODUCTION
1957

James L. D'Aquisto apprenticed in John D'Angelico's shop and became the steward of the archtop tradition when D'Angelico died in 1964.

After finishing the work in progress, D'Aquisto quickly established his own distinctive style while maintaining a traditional approach to archtop design. The headstock on this guitar, for example, pays tribute to D'Angelico with its cutout and ornamental cupola, but the cutout shape is D'Aquisto's own circular design. The oval soundhole, while unusual on a post-World War II archtop, actually dates back to Orville Gibson's guitars in the 1890s and predates the introduction of f-hole archtops by a quarter-century.

The streamlined pickguard shape, the larger bridge, the solid ebony tailpiece, and the inlay-less fingerboard are more than just cosmetic refinements. They are signs of a major change in direction that lay ahead for D'Aquisto. By the late 1980s he would effectively "blow the lid off" archtop design, abandoning all but the most fundamental elements and inspiring a new generation of individual archtop makers.

25

MODEL
D'Aquisto New Yorker Oval Hole

YEAR
1973

PRODUCTION
1965 to early 1990s

D'AQUISTO

Like the works of a true artist, Jimmy D'Aquisto's archtop guitar designs evolved and changed dramatically from 1964, when his mentor John D'Angelico died, to his own death in 1995. The evolution was gradual until 1987, when he made a model called the Avant Garde that featured no celluloid and a minimal amount of metal. Bindings, peghead veneer, pickguard and tailpiece were all made of wood.

The Avant Garde marked a change in direction toward a freer, modernistic design philosophy, exemplified by this D'Aquisto Solo model from 1992. The two-segment elliptical soundholes establish a theme that is repeated in cutouts in the tailpiece and peghead. The non-cutaway body, though an older style, was relatively rare on a 1990s archtop.

The Solo was one of several models with which D'Aquisto executed his new ideas in the 1990s. At the time of his death, he was regarded not only as the finest builder of traditional archtops but also as the leader of a new modernistic school of archtop guitar design.

MODEL
D'Aquisto Solo

YEAR
1992

PRODUCTION
1992 to 1995

26

Oliver Ditson of Boston was one of the leading sellers of guitars in the northeastern U.S. in the late 1800s and early 1900s. Ditson had a well-established sheet music business when, in 1861, he set up employee John C. Haynes in a guitar-making operation that would become best known for its Excelsior and Bay State brands. Ditson also started George Lyon and Patrick Healy in business as his Chicago affiliate, and they eventually became the largest instrument maker in America.

In the early 1900s, the Haynes operation became a retail outlet and Ditson-brand instruments were sourced from other makers. This parlor-size guitar is a typical turn-of-the-century instrument, with modest rope-pattern purfling and a movable bridge, a concept borrowed from mandolins.

Ditson is most famous in guitar circles for contracting C.F. Martin to build Martin's dreadnought models in 1916. Martin continued supplying guitars to Ditson until Ditson was sold to the Philadelphia-based Theodore Presser music publishing company in 1931, not coincidentally the same year that Martin introduced dreadnoughts under the Martin brand.

MODEL
Ditson Model 261

YEAR
Circa 1906

PRODUCTION
Early 1900s

DOBRO

Los Angeles inventor John Dopyera was a founding partner of the National company, which introduced Dopyera's innovative "tri-cone" metalbody resonator guitars in 1927. A year later, after a dispute with his partners, he formed Dobro – short for Dopyera Brothers – and designed a new style of guitar that featured the resonator cone opening towards the top of the instrument.

Dopyera quickly settled his differences with National, and the two companies merged in 1932. Both resonator styles – National's rear-opening cone and Dobro's top-opening cone – retained their own loyal following, and both styles thrived until the rise of electric guitars in the late 1930s.

The basic Dobro models were plain and inexpensive, with bodies made of laminated birch or mahogany. A midline model featured what appeared to be eleborate relief-carving on the body – it was actually sandblasted. And the top-of-the line Dobros sported bodies of burl walnut, some of them with highly figured two- or four-piece bookmatched backs. Model 100 was the longest-lived of these 'custom walnut' Dobros, lasting until 1937.

MODEL
Dobro No. 100

YEAR
1935

PRODUCTION
1930 to 1937

28

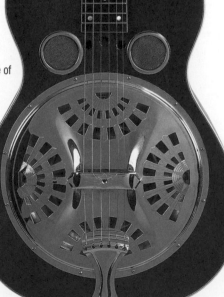

When inventor John Doypera broke away from the National company to form Dobro in 1929, he undercut National's expensive triple-cone metalbody models with less expensive, single-cone, woodbody Dobros. For the next few years, National became identified primarily with metal guitars while Dobros were strictly woodbodies.

In 1933, after the two companies had merged, National-Dobro began cross-pollenating the lines, first with woodbody National models, then a year later with a trio of metalbody guitars with the Dobro style resonator. The fanciest of the three, the Artist model (aka Model 16) featured engraving on the body and a bound fingerboard.

Although they matched the Nationals aesthetically, the metal Dobros never caught on with players. Resonator guitars had been invented to meet a demand for louder instruments, and by the late 1930s the electric guitar was taking over that role. After World War II, National (by this time reorganized as Valco) abandoned acoustic resonator guitars. The Dobro brand wasn't revived until the 1960s, when woodbodied Dobros found a home in bluegrass music.

29

MODEL
Dobro Artist 16M

YEAR
Circa 1934

PRODUCTION
1934 to 1935

DYER

The Dyer company began in 1871 when William John Dyer and his brother C.E. Dyer opened a music store in St. Paul, Minnesota. When they decided to offer instruments under their own brand, they contracted production to various makers. Although their labels claimed otherwise, Dyer harp guitars were actually made by the Larson Brothers of Chicago, who were best known for the guitars they made for performers on the WLS *National Barn Dance* radio show.

The hollow support arm, which is an integral part of the body, distinguishes the Dyer harp guitars and harp mandolins from those of other makers. The design was patented by, and licensed from, Norwegian-born Chris Knutsen, who made instruments for Dyer before the Larsons came onboard around 1902.

The harp guitar's sub-bass strings provided a wider and richer array of harmonic possibilities than the standard six-string, but few guitarists made the extra effort to master the technique. In modern times, numerous individual makers have created harp guitars, many of them in the Knutsen/Larson/Dyer style, but no major guitar maker offers a harp guitar.

MODEL
Dyer Harp Guitar No. 7

YEAR
Circa 1920

PRODUCTION
Circa 1902-39

With roots in 19th century Greece and Turkey, Epiphone emerged in the 1920s as one of the most successful makers of tenor banjos. In 1931 the New York-based company introduced a full line carved-top f-hole guitars, invading a territory that had been owned by Gibson. Gibson responded with the huge, 18-inch Super 400 model in 1934, and Epiphone topped Gibson a year later with the Emperor, which was ⅜ of an inch wider than the Gibson.

In the 1930s and early 1940s, even though electric guitars were available, large-bodied acoustic archtops were the preferred instrument of big band guitarists, and Epiphone and Gibson fought for dominance.

Gibson gained the upper hand in 1939 with the introduction of cutaway bodies. This time, however, Epiphone was slow to respond, and a cutaway Emperor did not officially appear until 1948. In the meantime, company president Epaminondas "Epi" Stathopoulo had died of leukemia in 1943, and the company never fully recovered. The guitar wars ended in 1957 when Epiphone was sold to its old archrival Gibson.

31

MODEL
Epiphone Emperor

YEAR
Mid 1940s

PRODUCTION
1935 to 1957

The body of an Epiphone Texan from the 1960s looks just like that of a Gibson J-45, and it's no coincidence. Gibson bought the Epiphone company in 1957 and gave the line a complete makeover. The new models of 1958 retained some distinctive Epiphone features, exemplified on the Texan by the pickguard and the peghead, but the Texan's "round-shouldered" dreadnought body shape and its "reverse-belly" bridge with height-adjustable saddle were unmistakably Gibson.

Gibson's goal was to create a second brand so the company could expand its dealership base while still protecting the exclusive territories of Gibson dealers. Epiphones were made in the Gibson factory in Kalamazoo, Michigan and, except for the pickups on electric guitars and the Epiphone name – which by the late 1950s no longer carried the same prestige as Gibson – Epiphones were as good as Gibsons.

The Texan, like most of the Gibson-Epiphone models, sold well until the late 1960s, when the influx of cheap imports from Japan prompted Gibson to move Epiphone production overseas.

32

MODEL
Epiphone Texan

YEAR
1964

PRODUCTION
1958 to 1969

When Gibson moved Epiphone production overseas in 1970, the brand name was cheapened even beyond the budget prices of the Japanese-made and then Korean-made guitars that bore the Epiphone logo. Not until the 1990s, with Gibson under new ownership, did Gibson take steps to elevate the quality of Epiphone guitars and to restore confidence in the brand that had once battled toe-to-toe with Gibson.

By the end of the 1990s, a new Epiphone had emerged. It was still an import line, but as the AJ-30CE illustrates, it was becoming known for affordable guitars that combined the best elements of rich tradition – especially Gibson's tradition – with features that would appeal to modern players.

The *AJ* in this guitar's model name stands for Advanced Jumbo, one of Gibson's legendary flat-top guitars of the 1930s. Epiphone appropriated it for their "round-shouldered" dreadnoughts in 1998. The "reverse belly" bridge is also a Gibson feature. The cutaway, however, has never been available on this body shape under the Gibson brand.

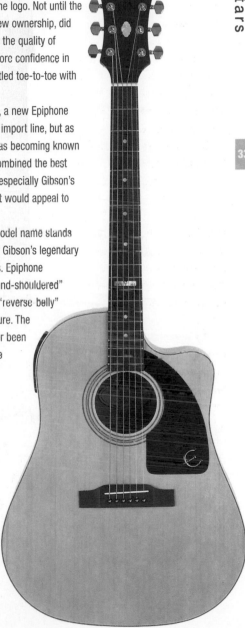

MODEL
Epiphone AJ-30CE

YEAR
1999

PRODUCTION
1998 to 2001

EUPHONON

Carl and August Larson, based in Chicago, made guitars under the Euphonon brand from the mid 1930s to the mid 1940s. Although they had a regular model line, many of their estimated 2500 instruments – including this large-bodied flat-top – fell outside any standard specifications.

The Swedish-born brothers came to the United States in the 1880s and began building instruments for music teacher Robert Maurer by the late 1890s. In 1900 August Larson and partners, who were eventually replaced by Carl, bought the shop. They made Maurer-brand instruments and later Prairie State and Euphonon, plus instruments for others under such brands as Stahl, Dyer, and Wack, but to date, no Larson-made guitar has ever been found with the Larson name on it.

Carl retired in 1940 and died in 1946. Production ended with August's death in 1944. Although the Larsons are obscure compared to Gibson and Martin, in the opinion of many collectors, their instruments rank with the best of the big companies in the 1930s.

MODEL
Euphonon jumbo body

YEAR
Circa 1940

PRODUCTION
Circa 1940

After studying guitar with Rev Gary Davis and learning guitar making from Michael Gurian, Michael Millard established Froggy Bottom Guitars as a custom shop in Newfane, Vermont, in 1970. His philosophy was to build each guitar to an individual player's personal preferences, but as his clientele and his reputation grew, some of the favorite styles emerged as a standardized line.

By the mid 1980s, the 15-inch wide Froggy Bottom H-12 model, inspired by Martin's 12-fret 000-size, had become Millard's most popular model. This Deluxe version features an abalone soundhole ring and gold-plated tuners while the Standard has a herringbone ring and nickel-plated tuners. The highest grade, Limited, sports intricate fingerboard inlays and a paua abalone top border.

Millard took on a partner, Andy Mueller, in 1996. They produce around 125 guitars a year and, although they have a variety of standard models, ranging from parlor-size to dreadnoughts, each guitar is still made to a specific order from a dealer or a customer. The H-12 remains their most popular model.

MODEL
Froggy Bottom H12 Deluxe

YEAR
2002

PRODUCTION
Mid 1980s to current

FYLDE

Fylde founder Roger Bucknall had a childhood interest in guitars and built his first one in his father's garage, but he took a roundabout path through an engineering career before devoting full-time to guitar making in 1973. His brand name was the location of his first shop – on the Fylde coast of Lancashire.

Fylde was at one time England's largest maker of acoustic guitars, but when Bucknall relocated to Cumbria in 1996, he downsized to concentrate on custom and high-end instruments. He personally hand-carves and fits every neck, builds the guitar soundboards, bends the sides and oversees the work of his four assistants. His client list is an eclectic group, highlighted by Eric Bibb, Gordon Giltrap, Ken Nicol, Pete Townshend, K.T. Tunstall, Ritchie Blackmore, and Sting.

The Fylde Alchemist is a ⁹⁄₁₀ version of the Magician, a popular model with Celtic musicians, and it was designed for those players who felt the 17-inch wide, 5-inch deep Magician was a bit unwieldy. The Alchemist is also the base model for Gordon Giltrap's signature Fylde.

MODEL
Fylde Alchemist

YEAR
2000

PRODUCTION
1999 to current

Established in 1902 in a blossoming market for mandolins, the Gibson company treated the guitar as a member of the mandolin family. Gibson guitars featured the same carved-top design as mandolins, and they were strung with steel strings (unlike any other guitars of the day except those made by the Larson Brothers).

In 1910 Gibson revamped its Style O model from a conventional guitar shape to one that was more in the image of the Gibson F-style mandolins, with a scroll on the upper bass bout. The new design, called Style O Artist, provided a cutaway on the treble side of the neck, giving guitarists clear access to the 15th fret – a highly innovative feature in an era when most guitars had only 12 frets clear of the body.

As demand for mandolins began to fade with the rise of "Dixieland" jazz after World War I, so did demand for a guitar that was uniquely associated with the mandolin, and Gibson halted production of the Style O Artist in 1925.

37

MODEL
Gibson Style O Artist

YEAR
1916

PRODUCTION
1908 to 1925

The harp guitar's extra strings provided players with additional, chromatically tuned bass tones that could enrich some of the more difficult chordings, such as Eb or Bb, and expand the harmonic possibilities of the guitar.

Gibson's first catalog of 1902 included four harp guitar models with varying numbers of sub-bass strings and degrees of ornamentation, but only Style U survived more than a few years. Catalogs featured Style U in the center spread, while catalog text touted the harp guitar as being to the standard guitar what the piano was to the harpsichord. However, the large body size was unwieldy, and the right-hand technique was more difficult than it might appear. On top of that, the price – it was Gibson's most expensive model – made it a luxury item for most musicians.

Gibson offered Style U in catalogs into the late 1930s, but few if any were made after the mid 1920s. A handful of guitarists still play harp guitars today, but most prefer the traditional flat-top style over Gibson's carved-top design.

MODEL
Gibson Style U harp guitar

YEAR
1912

PRODUCTION
1902-38

Orville Gibson invented the carved-top or archtop guitar in the 1890s, and the company was founded in 1902 to exploit that concept. Gibson enjoyed complete domination of the market until 1931, when Epiphone introduced not just one but six new archtops.

Gibson fired back in 1934 with a new model intended to blow the competition out of the water. At a time when the standard archtop body size had just been increased from 16 to 17 inches, this new guitar was 18 inches wide. It was heavily ornamented and came in a leather-covered case with its own protective case cover. The price was $400 and it was included in the model name: Super 400

The Super 400 inaugurated a new era of large-body archtops and set a standard not only for Epiphone but for such renowned individual makers as D'Angelico and Stromberg. A cutaway version was added in 1939 and it lasted into the 1980s. Gibson's Custom, Art & Historic division revived the Super 400C (cutaway version) in 1993.

MODEL
Gibson Super 400

YEAR
1935

PRODUCTION
1934 to 1981, 1993 to current

39

GIBSON

In 1931, Gibson's position as a leading maker of acoustic guitars was assaulted on two fronts, with a barrage of new archtops from Epiphone and two new large-bodied "dreadnought" flat-tops from Martin. Gibson had already used a dreadnought shape on an obscure Hawaiian model in the late 1920s, and a mahogany-body version appeared as a standard guitar under the model name Jumbo in 1934. In the meantime Gibson increased or 'advanced' the body sizes of their archtops to keep up with Epiphone.

In 1936, still without a rosewood-body flat-top to compete with Martin's D-28, Gibson appropriated the catchword *advanced* and combined it with Jumbo to create the Advanced Jumbo (although it was no larger than the Jumbo).

The Advanced Jumbo was a fine guitar that could stand toe-to-toe with a Martin, but the model was soon overshadowed in the Gibson line by the larger, non-dreadnought Super Jumbo, soon to be called SJ-200. The AJ was rediscovered by bluegrass players in the late 1980s, and Gibson made sporadic runs of reissues through most of the 1990s.

MODEL
Gibson Advanced Jumbo

YEAR
1938

PRODUCTION
1936 to 1939, 1990 to 1998

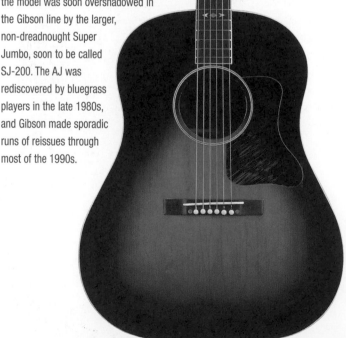

In the 1930s, a new wave of guitar stars emerged: the singing cowboys in western movies. To complement their fancy fringed outfits, they needed a highly ornamented guitar, and Gibson obliged Ray Whitley, Gene Autry and Tex Ritter, among others, by creating a new, 17-inch flat-top.

The new body shape, with a circular lower bout, was inspired by Gibson's L-5 archtop (early examples were labeled *L-5 Spec.*) and was unrelated to the thick-waisted, flat-bottom dreadnought shape of Gibson's Jumbo model. Nevertheless, *Jumbo* was already a familiar term to guitarists, as was *Super* from Gibson's recent archtop success, the Super 400. Gibson called the model the Super Jumbo and, after initially offering it by custom order only, added the $200 price to the model name to create the SJ-200.

The first SJ-200s shipped in 1938, and the model soon became a badge of identification for country artists ranging from Eddy Arnold to Emmylou Harris. Gibson touts it as "The King of the Flat-tops" and it remains the flagship of Gibson's acoustic line today.

41

MODEL
Gibson SJ-200

YEAR
1954

PRODUCTION
1938 to current

GIBSON

Since World War II, the most popular and versatile guitars have been basic mahogany-body dreadnoughts, and in the Gibson line, that model is the J-45.

Gibson had made dreadnoughts with the "round-shouldered" or "slope-shouldered" design since 1934 and, just as America entered the war, the company replaced the J-35 – the prewar favorite – with a more heavily built model and raised the model name by 10 'points' to J-45. Due to materials shortages, some wartime examples had a maple body or a mahogany top or no truss-rod. Nevertheless, the J-45 offered the perfect combination of price and performance, and it became known as the 'workhorse' model of Gibson's acoustic line.

Gibson could not resist "improving" the J-45 with a tone-killing height-adjustable bridge (optional from 1956 and standard through the 1960s), and the model suffered the indignity of a "square-shouldered" body shape from 1969 to 1982, when production was briefly halted. It came back in 1984 with sloped shoulders and continues today as the leading model of Gibson's dreadnought line.

MODEL
Gibson J-45

YEAR
Circa 1947

PRODUCTION
1942 to current

With Gibson's purchase of Epiphone in 1957, Gibson gained the opportunity to try out new models under the Epiphone brand that, if they failed or proved controversial, would not diminish the prestige of the Gibson name. Gibson president Ted McCarty created a new acoustic model for the 1958 Epi line that was built on Martin's "square-shouldered" dreadnought shape rather than Gibson's traditional "round-shouldered" design.

The Epiphone Frontier, which featured maple and sides, was successful enough that McCarty quickly introduced the same body shape, but with mahogany back and sides, under the Gibson brand in 1960. The new model broke with Gibson's traditional model numbering system with a descriptive model name: the Hummingbird. It drew attention to itself with a cherry sunburst finish – a first for a Gibson acoustic guitar – and it was further ornamented with the engraved image of a hummingbird and flower blossoms on the pickguard.

The Hummingbird led the way for the Dove, a fancier, "square-shouldered", maple-body model introduced in 1962. Both bird models continue today as the standard-bearers of the square-shoulder shape in Gibson's acoustic lineup.

43

MODEL
Gibson Hummingbird

YEAR
1966

PRODUCTION
1960 to current

GIBSON

Don and Phil Everly were among the most successful rock'n'roll artists in the late 1950s with such hits as 'Bye Bye Love' and 'Wake Up Little Susie,' and they were the only Gibson artists of the 1960s to have a signature flat-top model.

The brothers learned guitar from their father Ike Everly, who played a Gibson and, when they gained their first notoriety, they special-ordered a pair of J-200s. When Gibson made the relationship official with a signature model, they based it on the J-185, which had the J-200's circular lower bout but was slightly smaller. Its unique features had a purpose. The black finish matched the tuxedos that the Everlys wore onstage. The oversized double pickguards protected more of the top from pick scratches. And the pinless bridge (Ike Everly's design) allowed for quicker string changes.

The Everlys had their last Top 10 singles in 1962, just as the Gibson Everly Brothers model was introduced, but the model lasted through the 1960s. It was revived from 1986 to 2005 as the J-180.

MODEL
Gibson Everly Brothers

YEAR
1963

PRODUCTION
1962 to 1971

44

Sheryl Crow hit the pop charts in 1994 with 'All I Wanna Do,' which introduced her fresh new take on classic rock music. Five years and six Grammy Awards later, she became the first female artist to be given a Gibson signature model.

The Gibson Sheryl Crow has a familiar look because it is *not* a model with a unique combination of features specified by the artist. Rather, it is a replica of Crow's favorite songwriting and recording guitar, a 1962 Gibson Country-Western.

The Country-Western model name appeared in 1956, but it was simply the natural-finish version of the Southerner Jumbo, a "round-shouldered" dreadnought that Gibson introduced in 1944 as a fancier version of the J-45. Late in 1962 Gibson changed the body shape to "square-shouldered", possibly in an attempt to compete more directly with Martin's D-18. After a production hiatus in the 1980s, the model returned in its original "round-shouldered" form, but Crow's personal guitar was from the "square-shouldered" era, and so her signature model sported the same body style.

MODEL
Gibson Sheryl Crow

YEAR
2000

PRODUCTION
1999 to current

45

GRETSCH

The Gretsch company of New York introduced its first archtop guitars in 1933 but didn't hit its stride until 1939 with its large-body Synchromatic series, which were easily distinguishable from Gibsons, Epiphones and the guitars of every other archtop maker by their modernistic "cat's eye" soundholes.

At the top of the line, the Gretsch Synchromatic 400 sported the same model number as Gibson's Super 400, which had started the movement to 18-inch bodies in 1934. Like the Gibson and Epiphone's Emperor, the Synchromatic 400 was highly ornamented, with multiple layers of binding around the body, slashed "humptop" blocks on the fingerboard, and gold-plated hardware. The stairstep bridge extension, elongated pickguard and harp-shaped tailpiece added distinctive aesthetic touches.

The Synchromatics attracted their share of players, most notably Fred Green in Count Basie's band and noted teacher/performer Harry Volpe, but, despite their appearance, they were not as well-made as those of such contemporaries as Gibson, Epiphone, D'Angelico, or Stromberg. Surviving examples in good playing condition are quite rare.

46

MODEL
**Gretsch
Synchromatic 400**

YEAR
1945

PRODUCTION
1940 to 1955

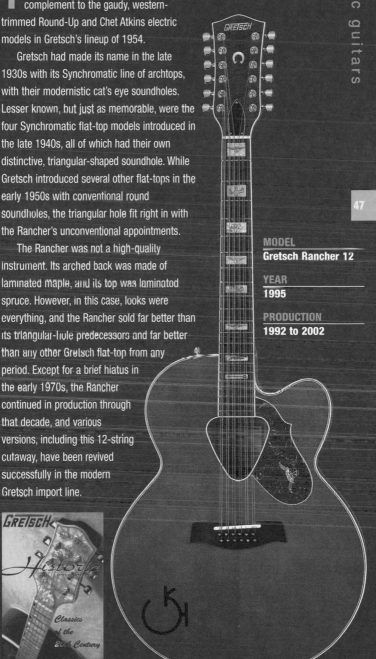

The original Rancher provided an acoustic complement to the gaudy, western-trimmed Round-Up and Chet Atkins electric models in Gretsch's lineup of 1954.

Gretsch had made its name in the late 1930s with its Synchromatic line of archtops, with their modernistic cat's eye soundholes. Lesser known, but just as memorable, were the four Synchromatic flat-top models introduced in the late 1940s, all of which had their own distinctive, triangular-shaped soundhole. While Gretsch introduced several other flat-tops in the early 1950s with conventional round soundholes, the triangular hole fit right in with the Rancher's unconventional appointments.

The Rancher was not a high-quality instrument. Its arched back was made of laminated maple, and its top was laminated spruce. However, in this case, looks were everything, and the Rancher sold far better than its triangular-hole predecessors and far better than any other Gretsch flat-top from any period. Except for a brief hiatus in the early 1970s, the Rancher continued in production through that decade, and various versions, including this 12-string cutaway, have been revived successfully in the modern Gretsch import line.

MODEL
Gretsch Rancher 12

YEAR
1995

PRODUCTION
1992 to 2002

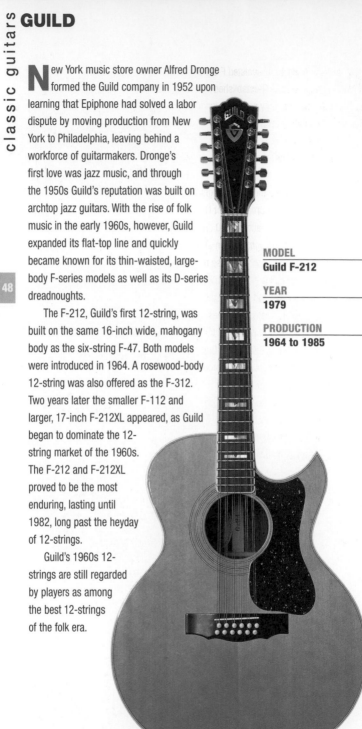

New York music store owner Alfred Dronge formed the Guild company in 1952 upon learning that Epiphone had solved a labor dispute by moving production from New York to Philadelphia, leaving behind a workforce of guitarmakers. Dronge's first love was jazz music, and through the 1950s Guild's reputation was built on archtop jazz guitars. With the rise of folk music in the early 1960s, however, Guild expanded its flat-top line and quickly became known for its thin-waisted, large-body F-series models as well as its D-series dreadnoughts.

The F-212, Guild's first 12-string, was built on the same 16-inch wide, mahogany body as the six-string F-47. Both models were introduced in 1964. A rosewood-body 12-string was also offered as the F-312. Two years later the smaller F-112 and larger, 17-inch F-212XL appeared, as Guild began to dominate the 12-string market of the 1960s. The F-212 and F-212XL proved to be the most enduring, lasting until 1982, long past the heyday of 12-strings.

Guild's 1960s 12-strings are still regarded by players as among the best 12-strings of the folk era.

MODEL
Guild F-212

YEAR
1979

PRODUCTION
1964 to 1985

48

Although Guild's thin-waisted F-style flat-top shape was well-established by the early 1960s, the company could not ignore the enormous influence of traditional bluegrass and blues music, where the thick-waisted dreadnoughts of Martin and Gibson ruled.

In 1963 Guild joined the dreadnought club with the mahogany Dreadnaught D-40 and the rosewood Dreadnaught D-50 (Guild typically spelled *dreadnaught* with an *a*). To underscore the market at which these models were aimed, Guild quickly renamed them Bluegrass Jubilee D-40 and Bluegrass Special D-50, respectively. Ironically, Guild was never able to crack the hold that Martin had on bluegrass players, but in folk music, Guild provided strong competition for the more established companies. Such popular performers as Tom Smothers and Richie Havens played Guilds, and one artist – Carolyn Hester – was better known for her Guild magazine ads than for her music.

When Richie Havens appeared in the 1970 film *Woodstock*, vigorously strumming his D-40 as the festival's opening act, Guild's dreadnaught replaced the F-style as the company's most identifiable acoustic model.

49

MODEL
Guild D-50

YEAR
1975

PRODUCTION
1963 to 1992

HARMONY

In the 1930s the Harmony company of Chicago cashed in on the popularity of singing cowboy entertainers by marketing cheap guitars with stenciled or decaled western scenes.

Gene Autry was the first and most successful of these guitar-playing cowboys. A Texas native and former telegraph operator, he was a member of the WLS *National Barn Dance* show in 1932 when he had his first big hit, 'That Silver-Haired Daddy of Mine.' Two years later he starred in his first film, *The Phantom Empire*, which combined western and science fiction themes.

The giant Sears Roebuck catalog company owned WLS – the call letters stood for World's Largest Store – as well as Harmony. The company created its first themed guitar in 1929 for hillbilly singer and WLS star Bradley Kinkaid. The Gene Autry Roundup, introduced in 1932, featured a generic lariat-swinging cowboy figure and a covered wagon. It opened the floodgates for numerous cowboy guitars, most of which were barely above toy quality. The Roundup lasted until 1938 when it was replaced with the Gene Autry Melody Ranch model.

50

MODEL
**Harmony/Supertone
Gene Autry Roundup**

YEAR
1938

PRODUCTION
1932 to 1938

As Harmony's flagship large-bodied flat-top model, the Sovereign reigned as one of the most popular budget-priced guitars of the folk music era.

Harmony was founded in Chicago in 1892 by German immigrant Wilhelm Schultz and was providing guitars for the Sears Roebuck mail-order company by 1897. Sears eventually gained ownership of the company. Harmony acquired the Sovereign name in 1938 with its purchase of the Oscar Schmidt company of Jersey City, New Jersey, which had had been using Sovereign as a brand name on a line of cheap guitars. Harmony's Sovereign dreadnought, with a body shape called "western jumbo," was introduced in 1958 and followed the Sovereign tradition with a price of only $69.50.

The Sovereign started as a plain model, but eventually gained the fancy moustache bridge and double pickguards of this 1971 example. The attention-grabbing appointments belied Harmony's faltering position in a market filled with even cheaper Japanese-made guitars. The brand was sold in 1976, and after that it appeared sporadically on import models.

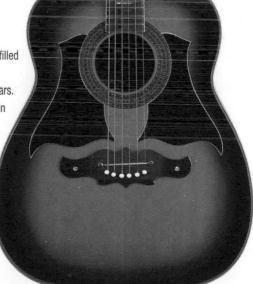

51

MODEL
Harmony Sovereign

YEAR
1971

PRODUCTION
1958 to 1972

In the late 1990s, the Artwood model helped re-establish Ibanez, whose reputation at that time rested primarily on electrics, as a maker of high-quality flat-top guitars.

The Ibanez name was already well-known in the U.S. as well as in Japan. The first Ibanez instruments were made by the Hoshino Gakki Ten company in Matsumoto, Japan, in the 1930s. Philadelphia music store owner Harry Rosenbloom, founder of the Elger brand, began importing them in the 1960s. Unlike many other Japanese-made guitars, Ibanezes were inspected at an Elger facility befor being distributed to dealers, and as a result, they immediately gained a reputation for better quality than their competition.

Ibanez's most successful models were copies of popular American guitars, electric as well as acoustic, but following Gibson's lawsuit against Elger in 1977, Ibanez began introducing more original designs. The original Artwoods featured solid spruce or cedar tops and bodies of such elite woods as quilted maple, flamed maple, bubinga and walnut. They spawned over 20 different Artwood models, identifiable today by *AW* on the peghead and in the model name.

MODEL
Ibanez Artwood

YEAR
2002

PRODUCTION
1996 to 2002

This memorable archtop model features the unique combination of traditional features and modern flair that characterized guitars made in the 1970s and '80s by Sam Koontz of Linden, New Jersey.

Koontz built his first guitar in 1959 and worked in the 1960s for Framus and Martin before being hired to design and produce guitars for Standel (best known as an amplifier maker) and Harptone. When those two companies faded in the early 1970s, he concentrated on making custom guitars under his own brand name.

The scrolled upper bass bout on this custom example from circa 1977 has been a signature feature of Gibson's "F-style" mandolins going back to Orville Gibson's designs in the late 1800s, but Gibson only used it on one guitar model (the Style O Artist). The scroll motif is repeated in the pickguard design. The ornamental headstock cutout, a familiar feature from the Koontz-designed Harptone flat-tops of the 1970s, was inspired by the "broken scroll pediment" of legendary archtop maker John D'Angelico.

MODEL
Koontz Custom

YEAR
Circa 1977

PRODUCTION
Circa 1977

LOWDEN

Based in Northern Ireland, George Lowden has had an off-and-on relationship with the instruments that bear his name, but he has nevertheless gained a reputation for handbuilt flat-tops that offer a viable alternative to traditional American designs.

Lowden built his first guitars in the town of Bangor in 1973. Within three years he had established a standardized line that included Style 25, exemplified by the rosewood body, cedar top and wood bindings of this S-25C from 2002 (*S* for Standard, *C* for cutaway).

Increasing sales prompted Lowden to contract production of some models to Japanese makers from 1981–84. He brought all production back to Northern Ireland in 1985, but the company went into receivership in 1989. Lowden consulted with the new owners but resumed making guitars as an individual luthier, relocating to France for a short time. By 1998 he was successful enough that he put together a group to buy controlling interest in his original business, but in 2003 he left the Lowden Guitar Co (it became Avalon) and established George Lowden Guitars Ltd in Downpatrick, Northern Ireland.

MODEL
Lowden S-25C

YEAR
2002

PRODUCTION
1976 to current

Although the brand name and Style O designation identify this guitar as a Lowden, its three-digit model number belies its relationship to Lowden's offshoot, Avalon guitars. George Lowden had a hand in the design of the original Avalon guitars, development of which began in 2000. The first models debuted in 2002, Lowden left at the end of 2003, and the Lowden company was reorganized under the Avalon name in 2005.

The Style O was so-named because it was one of Lowden's originals, although it is no longer used. The model-numbering system was devised specifically for the Avalon guitars, and it does continue today. The first digit designates the ornamentation level; guitars in the 300s are part of Avalon's Legacy Premier series. The second digit is the body wood, which includes quilted maple, Australian blackwood, koa, cocobola and, designated by 2, Indian rosewood. The last digit denotes the top wood; 8 is for Engelmann spruce.

Today Avalon splits production between high-end guitars made in Northern Ireland with more affordable models made by the Furch company in the Czech Republic.

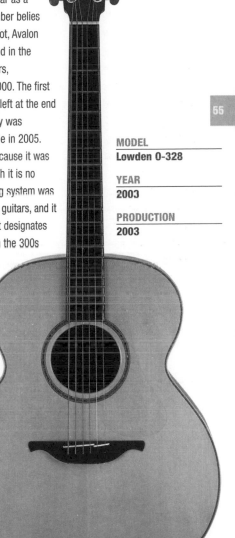

MODEL
Lowden O-328

YEAR
2003

PRODUCTION
2003

55

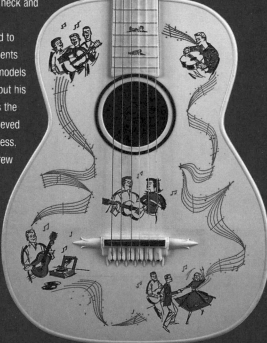

MACCAFERRI

Contrary to appearances, this plastic guitar is not a toy but a fully functioning instrument, designed by one of the most famous names in guitar history, Mario Maccaferri.

The Italian-born guitarist is best-known for designing a line of flat-top acoustic guitars for Selmer, the French band instrument company, that were played by gypsy jazz great, Django Reinhardt. Maccaferri's interest in developing a more reliable saxophone reed led him to plastics and, after relocating to New York at the beginning of World War II, he invented a plastic clothespin. After the war he turned his attention back to guitars and worked with the Dow chemical company to come up with the best type of plastic. He introduced his first models in 1953.

The New Romancer's corny artwork belied a surprisingly decent sound, the result of a sheathed wood neck and wood body bracing. Maccaferri continued to build plastic instruments and introduce new models through the 1960s, but his Islander ukulele was the only model that achieved even moderate success, and he finally withdrew the line in 1969.

MODEL
Maccaferri New Romancer

YEAR
1960

PRODUCTION
1957 to 1969

The mid-sized Magpie was among the more popular standard models offered by Andy Manson, one of England's best-known individual luthiers. Based in Devon, Manson began making guitars in the late 1960s. In addition to his regular models, he became known for multi-neck acoustics, the most of famous of which were triple-necks made for Led Zeppelin bassist John Paul Jones and guitarist Jimmy Page.

As his production increased, Manson brought on two assistants, Simon Smidmore and Andy Petherick, in 1993. Within three years they established their own shop – they actually took over Manson's workshop – where they made their own Brook brand instruments and also made Manson guitars under license.

Manson eventually settled in a shop called The Ark in Crediton, Devon, and began making custom instruments exclusively. His works have ranged from conventional instruments for such artists as Dave Matthews, Sarah McQuaid, and John Paul Jones, to a combination guitar and sculpture called the Mermaid, and he has offered intimate insight into his guitar-making philosophy through a published diary called *Talking Woods*.

57

MODEL
Manson Magpie Custom

YEAR
1990

PRODUCTION
1970s to current

Christian Friedrich Martin worked in his early years as a foreman for Johann Stauffer of Vienna, Austria, one of the most important figures in the development of the guitar in the first half of the 19th century. After a guild dispute in Martin's home town of Mark Neukirchen, Saxony (in eastern Germany), he emigrated to New York in 1833.

Not surprisingly, Martin's earliest guitars looked very much like Stauffers. The large upper bout, giving the body an almost-symmetrical hourglass shape, was typical of Stauffer's instruments, as was the scrolled peghead shape with all the tuners on the bass side. The ornamentation was nothing short of opulent – and quite a contrast to the reserved elegance that became a hallmark of Martins from the 1850s to today. The fingerboard, peghead veneer, bridge, and even the bridge pins are all made of elephant ivory. The top is bordered with alternating green and white pearl.

After six years in New York, C.F. Martin relocated in 1839 to Nazareth, Pennsylvania, leaving the retail music business and Germanic guitar influences behind him.

MODEL

Martin Stauffer style

YEAR

1830s

PRODUCTION

1830s

Even before C.F. Martin had left New York for the countryside of Pennsylvania in 1839, dealers were asking for less expensive guitars, and in the 1840s he abandoned his native Germanic designs to develop a simpler, distinctively American guitar.

By 1852 Martin had standardized his body sizes and ornamentation styles. Size 1 was 12¾ inches wide, which would be called a parlour guitar today but was Martin's largest size at the time. Style 40, with a top border and soundhole ring of abalone pearl, was relatively plain for a guitar of any era, but it was Martin's fanciest style at the time. Model names, then as now, simply combined the body size and style number, so that model 1-40 is a size 1 with style 40 trim.

Despite Martin's move to Nazareth, Pennsylvania, where the company is still located, Martin guitars continued to be sold through a New York distributor. Consequently, the guitars were branded "New York" until the distribution agreement was dissolved in 1898.

MODEL
Martin 1-40

YEAR
Circa 1874

PRODUCTION
1860s to 1870s

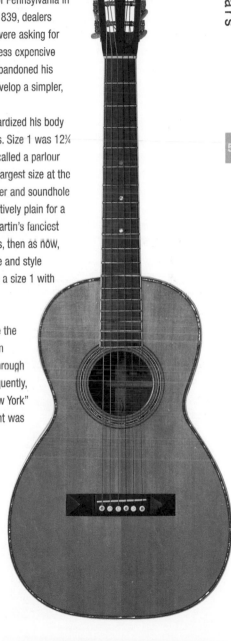

MARTIN

In response to demands for louder guitars, Martin introduced ever larger body sizes, although the size numbers decreased from the original Style 1. The 13½-inch Size 0 appeared in 1854, followed in 1877 by the 14⅛-inch model Size 00.

When it came to ornamentation, however, Martin remained content almost to the end of the 19th century with the abalone pearl border of Style 40 as its fanciest offering. In 1898 the pearl trim was extended around the end of the fingerboard to create Style 42. At the same time Martin added pearl-inlaid markers to the fingerboard, which previously had had no inlays at all.

"Pearl fever" then took hold of the usually slow-moving Martin company. In 1902 a special-order 00-42 featured pearl borders on the back and rims as well as the top. The peghead, until that time devoid of even the Martin logo, sported an elaborate pearl inlay that came to be known as the "torch" pattern. Martin made it official in 1904, calling it Style 45.

MODEL
Martin 00-45

YEAR
1914

PRODUCTION
1904 to 1938, 1970 to current

60

Martin's 000-45 would be considered a mid-sized model, with a body width of 15 inches. And its abalone pearl borders and delicate snowflake-pattern fingerboard inlays qualify it as only a moderately fancy instrument. But from 1904 to the introduction of dreadnought bodies in 1931, the 000-45 was the biggest and fanciest model available from the C.F. Martin company.

Martin introduced Size 000 in 1902, the same year the first Style 45 guitars were made (although they were initially called special-order Style 42s). The new size was almost a full inch wider than Size 00. It provided added power that guitar players needed, yet in an era dominated by mandolins, and later by tenor banjos, it was not an immediate success. It wasn't until the late 1920s that players discovered the Martin 000-size guitars.

Although most makers today offer left-handed guitars, they were quite rare in the first part of the 20th century, and this 000-45 is one of, if not the only guitar from that period that came from the factory as a lefty.

MODEL
Martin 000-45

YEAR
1931

61

PRODUCTION
1904 to 1942, 1970 to 1985

MARTIN

The standard guitar neck of the 1800s and early 1900s had one octave, or 12 frets, clear of the body, and that is still the standard for classical guitars. However, in the late 1920s, when banjoists began moving to the guitar, the 12-fret neck seemed limiting compared to a banjo, which had all the frets clear of the body.

Perry Bechtel, a banjoist who also used a Gibson L-5 archtop with a 14-fret neck, wanted to expand his arsenal to include a 14-fret flat-top. Martin built him one in 1929, taking its largest body size, the 000, and shortening it to leave 14 frets clear. Martin dubbed it OM for Orchestra Model. At the same time, Martin began offering a sunburst finish, sported by this OM-18 from 1932.

The OMs only lasted a short time – ironically, because the 14-fret neck was so well-received that Martin implemented it across the line, making the 000 essentially the same as the OM. The OM was revived in 1990s; its 25.4-inch scale delineates it from the modern 000, which has 24.9-inch scale.

MODEL
Martin OM-18

YEAR
1932

PRODUCTION
1929 to 1933

The word "herringbone" or even just "bone" is enough to evoke thoughts in a guitar player's mind of an instrument with the richest tone and most powerful sound of any flat-top guitar ever made – Martin's legendary pre-World War II D-28.

Martin had made the thick-waisted body style under contract for the Ditson company since 1916, and in 1931 the company introduced it under the Martin brand. Rather than extending the nomenclature system from 000 to 0000, Martin named it *dreadnought* after the British ship HMS Dreadnought, which was, in its day, the largest class of battleship. Style 28 featured rosewood back and sides with a top border of herringbone purfling.

The combination of Brazilian rosewood, Adirondack red spruce top and Martin's X-pattern bracing resulted in an instrument that blew its competition out of the water. By 1947 Martin had made changes to the bracing and eliminated the herringbone, leaving the original prewar D-28s as the standard to which all makers – including Martin – still aspire to reach.

63

MODEL
Martin D-28

YEAR
1941

PRODUCTION
1931 to current

MARTIN

artin's prewar dreadnought-size guitars are considered by many players to be the pinnacle of guitar design, and the fanciest model available from Martin during that period, the D-45, has become the Holy Grail of the vintage guitar world.

Martin initially offered only Styles 18 and 28 in the dreadnought size, but cowboy singing star Gene Autry was so impressed with their performance that he special-ordered one in 1933 in the abalone-trimmed Style 45, with the added feature of his name inlaid in the fingerboard. The production version that followed initially had the snowflake fingerboard inlays that were standard on Style 45 guitars in smaller sizes, but Martin quickly changed to the larger hexagonal inlays that had just been introduced on its high-end archtops.

Martin made only 91 D-45s before discontinuing the model as America entered World War II, and it wasn't reintroduced until 1968. Although the company has since offered more highly ornamented models in limited editions and has also given some models higher style numbers, Style 45 remains the fanciest standard ornamentation of any regular-production Martin model.

MODEL
Martin D-45

YEAR
1938

PRODUCTION
1933 to 1942

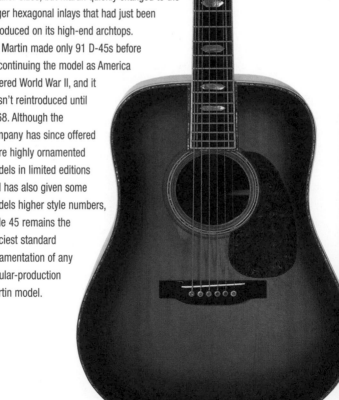

Martin moved with uncharacteristic speed in recognizing the growing popularity of archtop guitars at the beginning of the 1930s. The first Martin archtops appeared in 1931, the same year Epiphone mounted the first serious attack on Gibson's domination of the archtop market. The Martin line quickly grew to include three different sizes, the largest of which was the 16-inch F-series, with the F-7 second from the top.

Martin's archtops did not appear to have been fully developed. The bodies were the same as those of Martin's flat-tops and were made of mahogany or rosewood rather than maple. They had their own unique sound, but it was not what players were looking for.

A bigger problem was the neck. Martin seems to have been unwilling to redesign its neck joint for the arched top, so the neck angled off awkwardly behind the player. The archtops did introduce the vertically oriented, all-caps peghead logo, as well as a 16-inch body that would later be appropriated for Martin's M-size flat-tops, but none of the models lasted past 1942.

65

MODEL
Martin F-7

YEAR
1938

PRODUCTION
1935 to 1941

MARTIN

Martin's D-35 simply should not have worked. Its three-piece back was designed *not* for any musical purpose but for a pragmatic business reason, as a solution to the dwindling availability of large pieces of Brazilian rosewood.

The suggestion came from Bob Johnson, Martin's computer engineer, a man with no background in guitar design or production. Against all odds, the guitar with the three-piece back sounded good – not as boomy as Martin's D-28 but still with the resonance that players would expect from a rosewood-body guitar.

With the extra labor required to join three pieces rather than two, the D-35 was more expensive to make than the D-28, and Martin gave it a bound fingerboard so that it would look more expensive, too (although it did not get the abalone soundhole ring that earlier 30-series Martins had). The D-35 debuted in 1965, and by 1970 it was selling as well as the venerable D-28. Although the three-piece back concept has not successfully migrated to other body sizes, the D-35 remains a mainstay of Martin's current dreadnought line.

MODEL
Martin D-35

YEAR
1969

PRODUCTION
1965 to current

This pearl-laden, custom-ordered Martin was inspired by the OM-45 Deluxe of 1930, Martin's most highly ornamented catalog model.

The first OMs (for Orchestra Model), introduced in 1929, were offered in Styles 18 and 28, but the new 14-fret necks were well-enough received for Martin to add the fancy Style 45 to the offering. Even though it was the beginning of The Great Depression in 1930, it was also the tail end of the Jazz Age, a period of highly ornamented banjos. The demand for opulence apparently carried over to the guitar, and in 1930 Martin made 14 OM-45 Deluxe models, featuring the typical Style 45 pearl borders with additional inlays in the pickguard and on the ends of the bridge.

Martin brought back the OM-45 Deluxe in limited production in 1977, and one customer took it to the next level by ordering an elaborate fingerboard inlay pattern. By the end of the 1900s, the demand for fancy guitars like this one led Martin to create more fancy custom and limited edition models.

MODEL
Martin OM-45 Custom

YEAR
1983

PRODUCTION
1983

The cutaway, the oval soundhole, and the large body of Martin's JC-40 signaled a subtle expansion from tradition under the leadership of C.F. (Chris) Martin IV, great-great-great-great grandson of the founder.

Although Martin's legendary dreadnoughts had long been the largest guitars in the line, the 1930s archtop line had featured a larger body shape, with the thin-waist of the 000 rather than the thick waist of the dreadnoughts. In the 1960s, some luthiers had successfully converted old archtops to flat-tops, and Martin appropriated the concept for its M-series in 1977. Cutaway M-series models were added in 1981.

Although Size M, at 16 inches wide, was ⅜-inch wider than a dreadnought, it had the same depth as the smaller 000 size. Chris Martin, then working in sales, thought a deeper body would compete better with Gibson's J-200, and the result was the J-40. Introduced in 1985, a year before C. F. Martin III died and Chris became CEO, the J-40 was an immediate success, and the model quickly grew into an entire series of Martin J models.

MODEL
Martin JC-40

YEAR
1994

PRODUCTION
1987 to 1996

Vintage Martin aficionados consider the late 1920s through the 1930s to be the company's Golden Era. It was a period that saw the introduction of heavier bracing for steel strings, the short-lived but highly influential OM models, and the dreadnoughts that came to dominate the acoustic guitar world. All of the elements of materials and design converged in the 1930s, and Martins from that period are more highly prized than those of any other era.

The term Golden Era became so widely used that, in 1999, Martin appropriated it for a D-18GE that featured such 1934 specifications as an Adirondack red spruce top (Martin had changed to Sitka in 1946) and a wide, V-shaped neck.

The Golden Era concept was so well-received that Martin extended it to higher models, such as this OM-45GE. Like the originals, its back and sides are of Brazilian rosewood, an endangered species that Martin stopped using in regular production in 1969. Consequently, Golden Era versions of Martins above Style 18 are only made in limited numbers.

MODEL
Martin OM-45GE "1933"

YEAR
2001

PRODUCTION
2001

MONTELEONE

John Monteleone's combination of artistic imagination and traditional design, exemplified by his Radio Flyer model, brought him to prominence as one of the leading lights of the new wave of archtop guitar builders in the 1990s.

Based now in Islip on New York's Long Island, Monteleone was initially known for his mandolins. After starting with copies of Gibson's F-5 in 1974, he quickly developed a more modern adaptation of that traditional style, which he called the Grand Artist.

Monteleone made his first guitars in the late 1970s, and the large, elliptical soundholes of his flat-top Hexaphone and archtop Eclipse models were a sign of more non-traditional designs to come. When he turned his full attention to archtop guitars in the early 1990s, he introduced the elegant Radio Flyer, the mandolin-inspired scroll-body Grand Artist and the Art Deco-influenced Radio City. These three, along with the Eclipse, set the industry standard for sophisticated, unified aesthetics, and they make up Monteleone's current lineup of standard models.

MODEL
Monteleone Radio Flyer

YEAR
1993

PRODUCTION
1992 to current

At the height of the Jazz Age, guitarists had a pressing need for an instrument that could match the volume of a tenor banjo. To that end, Los Angeles instrument maker John Dopyera and vaudeville guitarist George Beauchamp teamed up to invent the resonator guitar. Introduced under the National brand in 1927, these new instruments featured a metal body with three thin cones of spun aluminum that functioned much like the cone of a loudspeaker.

The original "tri-cone" models (single-cone models were also available) featured nickel-alloy bodies, ornamented with floral-pattern engraving. In 1936 a pair of less expensive tri-cones debuted with nickel-plated brass-bodies and flashier, airbrushed enamel artwork on the back. Model 35 sported a Renaissance musician, while Model 97 had a Hawaiian surf rider.

The resonator guitar accomplished its goal of providing guitarists with a louder instrument but, by the late 1930s, the electric guitar had eclipsed all acoustics in the quest for volume, and National abandoned its resonator guitars in 1942.

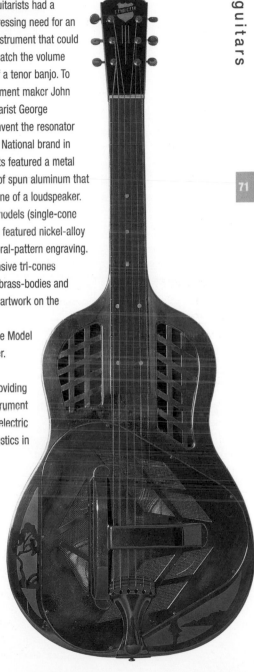

71

MODEL
National Model 35

YEAR
Circa 1937

PRODUCTION
1936 to 1941

OVATION

The Ovation Custom Legend is the fanciest of the traditional round-hole models made by the company whose calling card is a decidedly untraditional, molded fiberglass back.

Ovation was founded in 1965 by Charlie Kaman, whose Kaman Aircraft company had been a leading helicopter builder since 1945. Due to political changes in the early 1960s, Kaman saw a need to diversify and, being an accomplished guitar player, he chose to redesign the acoustic guitar with modern materials and scientific methodology, using oscilloscopes and the same vibration sensors he used in aircraft testing to quantify the sound of a great guitar.

Ovation's bowlback design gained a foothold in the guitar market, but the company hit its stride in the early 1970s with superior acoustic/electrics equipped with piezo pickups. Kaman Music strengthened its position by securing a distribution agreement with Takamine, which produced some of the best traditional-design amplified acoustics, and by acquiring several distribution companies. It was one of the largest entities in the instrument business when it was sold to Fender in December 2007 for $700 million.

MODEL
Ovation Custom Legend

YEAR
1976

PRODUCTION
1974 to current

Typical of instruments made by the Larson Brothers, this enormous 19-inch flat-top cutaway guitar does not bear the Larson name anywhere on the instrument. Less typical is the lack of a brand name – the letters *J* and *R* on the headstock are the initials of country performer Jay Rich, who commissioned the instrument – but shares many features with the Larsons' Prairie State models.

Based in Chicago, Carl and August Larson had been well-known in Midwest guitar circles since the early 1900s for guitars, harp guitars and mandolins made for Stahl, Dyer and Wack, as well as their own Maurer, Euphonon and Prairie State brands. In the 1930s their clientele included many performers on WLS radio's *National Barn Dance* and local star Rhubarb Red, who would later gain greater fame as Les Paul.

The cutaway on this guitar was quite a modern feature for 1939. Gibson introduced its first cutaway models that same year, but only on archtops. Martin, then as now the most leading maker of flat-top acoustics, wouldn't offer a flat-top cutaway for another 40 years.

MODEL
Prairie State Custom

YEAR
1939

PRODUCTION
1939

73

SANTA CRUZ

Tony Rice brought jazz influences into bluegrass music in the late 1970s and he brought a new level of prestige to the Santa Cruz Guitar Company with the Tony Rice signature model in 1981.

Santa Cruz started as a custom shop, founded in 1976 by luthier Richard Hoover and repairmen Bruce Ross and William Davis. Rice was one of most influential acoustic guitarists of the 1970s, thanks to his work with J.D. Crowe and the New South and then with David Grisman. His favorite guitar was a 1935 D-28 that had been owned by hot-picking country-rock pioneer Clarence White. It was in poor condition, with an enlarged soundhole, a replaced fingerboard made by Gretsch, and a bullet hole in the top. Santa Cruz reproduced the guitar, sans bullet hole, and Rice began using it onstage. Within two years, Rice had generated enough demand that Santa Cruz made it an official model.

Today, Santa Cruz still makes around half its guitars to custom specs, while the Tony Rice model remains the flagship of the regular production line.

MODEL
Santa Cruz Tony Rice

YEAR
1998

PRODUCTION
1981 to current

74

Through its 100-plus years of existence, the Paris-based Selmer company has been a prominent maker of reed instruments but, thanks to legendary gypsy jazz guitarist, Django Reinhardt, Selmer also holds an important place in guitar history. The Selmer guitars played by Reinhardt and the other guitarists in the Quintette du Hot Club were designed by Mario Maccaferri, an Italian-born guitarist who later gained notoriety for a line of plastic guitars. Maccaferri was living in England in 1931 when he presented his new idea to Ben Davis, head of Selmer's London branch, who passed it on to company founder Henri Selmer in Paris.

The Maccaferri-designed Selmer flat-tops, introduced in 1932, were easily recognizable by their large D-shaped soundhole and a cutaway that extended in a straight line at a right angle from the neck. The body of the Orchestre, typically a rosewood-mahogany-rosewood laminate, produced a crisp, compressed, cutting tone that proved perfect for Reinhardt's lightning fast runs.

Although Maccaferri split with Selmer in 1933, the company continued making his designs until the guitar operation was sold in 1952.

MODEL
Selmer Orchestre

YEAR
1938

PRODUCTION
1932 to 1952

TAKAMINE

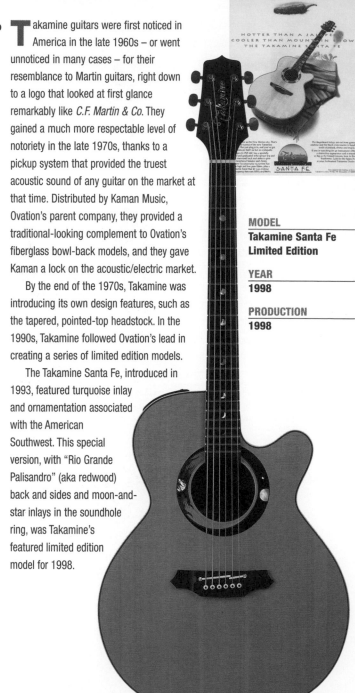

Takamine guitars were first noticed in America in the late 1960s – or went unnoticed in many cases – for their resemblance to Martin guitars, right down to a logo that looked at first glance remarkably like *C.F. Martin & Co.* They gained a much more respectable level of notoriety in the late 1970s, thanks to a pickup system that provided the truest acoustic sound of any guitar on the market at that time. Distributed by Kaman Music, Ovation's parent company, they provided a traditional-looking complement to Ovation's fiberglass bowl-back models, and they gave Kaman a lock on the acoustic/electric market.

By the end of the 1970s, Takamine was introducing its own design features, such as the tapered, pointed-top headstock. In the 1990s, Takamine followed Ovation's lead in creating a series of limited edition models.

The Takamine Santa Fe, introduced in 1993, featured turquoise inlay and ornamentation associated with the American Southwest. This special version, with "Rio Grande Palisandro" (aka redwood) back and sides and moon-and-star inlays in the soundhole ring, was Takamine's featured limited edition model for 1998.

MODEL
Takamine Santa Fe Limited Edition

YEAR
1998

PRODUCTION
1998

76

With his 1969 album *6- and 12-String Guitar*, Leo Kottke single-handedly revived and reinvented the acoustic 12-string guitar with a new level of sophistication and virtuosity. Through the 1970s and '80s, he established himself as one of the most popular and influential solo guitarists – on six-string as well as 12-string. In 1990, Kottke teamed up with Bob Taylor to design his own 12-string, becoming the second of only three signature artists in Taylor history (Dan Crary was the first, Doyle Dykes the most recent).

The Leo Kottke Signature Model used Taylor's largest body style, the jumbo, along with a custom bracing pattern to produce the robust tone that Kottke is known for. A cutaway provided additional access up the neck. In contrast to its sound, the LKSM's ornamentation is quite subdued; the body binding is rich Indian rosewood, and the ebony fingerboard looks like that of a classical guitar, with no pearl inlays.

The 12-string model was so successful that it spawned a six-string version, the LKSM-6 in 1997. Both models remain in production today.

MODEL
Taylor LKSM-6 Leo Kottke Signature Model

YEAR
1997

PRODUCTION
1997 to 2003, 2005 to current

TAYLOR

Taylor will probably go down in guitar-making history as the company that brought the precision of CNC (computer numerically controlled) routers to a business in which *handmade* had previously been the catchword for the finest instruments. However, guitar players will remember Taylor as the company that made acoustic guitars easier to play, thanks to a thin or "low-profile" neck that has become the industry standard.

Playing ease is particularly important with 12-strings, and when Taylor combined the thin neck with the options of a cutaway body and onboard electronics – designated by CE in Taylor's model names – Taylor's 12-strings easily dominated the market.

The *55* in the 455CE's model name is Taylor's designation for a 12-string built on its 16-inch Jumbo body. The first digit denotes the wood and trim package. For example, 300-series models, have sapele back and sides, the 500s are mahogany, and the 700s are fancier with Indian rosewood bodies. Like all the 400-series guitars, the Taylor 455 features a body of ovangkol, an attractively figured West African wood that produces a tone similar to Indian rosewood.

MODEL
Taylor 455CE

YEAR
2000

PRODUCTION
2000 to current

I n the mid 1990s, the Taylor company expanded in all directions, first with a new plant in El Cajon, California, then with a bass guitar, a grand auditorium body size and, on the smaller end, a new baby. Introduced in 1996, the Baby Taylor featured a ¾-size body. It also had a small price, thanks to its laminated sapele back and sides and lack of binding, although the solid spruce top maintained the Taylor sound.

The Baby was designed to be a travel guitar for musicians of all levels, and also to be a starter instrument that young players with small hands could handle. It succeeded on both fronts. As company founder Bob Taylor noted, "We've made gazillions of these things."

Inspired by the success of the Baby, Taylor created another addition to the family in 2000. The Big Baby Taylor was a no-frills, ¹⁵⁄₁₆ version of a full-size guitar that provided an intermediate step-up from the Baby to the standard Taylor models. Both Baby models are healthy members of the current Taylor line.

MODEL
Baby Taylor 305GB

YEAR
2002

PRODUCTION
1996 to Current

TAYLOR

Bob Taylor, Kurt Listug and Stever Schemmer, left the American Dream guitar repair shop in 1974 to found the Taylor company in Lemon Grove California. Three years later, the still-struggling company introduced the high-end 900-series, featuring bodies of birdseye maple. Although sales of expensive guitars were slow, a Taylor model line began taking shape as they filled in the 700- and 800-series in 1977 and the 500- and 600-series the next year.

By the time Taylor reached its 20th anniversary in 1994, Taylor was well-established not only for the quality of its instruments but as the company that brought modern production methods to the art of guitar making. To celebrate the occasion, the company introduced a new body size. Designated by *14* in a model number, the new Grand Auditorium was the first body shape to be designed from scratch by Bob Taylor.

Although Taylor's 900-series models got off to a slow start, they are still the company's top-of-the-line production models, featuring back and sides of the highest grade of Indian rosewood along with deluxe abalone pearl ornamentation.

MODEL
Taylor 914CE

YEAR
2003

PRODUCTION
1994 to current

The eye-catching gold paint on the Washburn's Style A of the mid-to-late 1920s was the last hurrah for a name that had once been the most prominent in the American guitar market.

The Washburn brand was originally owned by the Lyon & Healy company of Chicago, founded in 1864 by George Washburn Lyon and Patrick Healy. By the time they introduced guitars in the 1880s, they were the largest music company in the U.S., selling instruments as well as sheet music. Early Washburn catalogs showed highly ornamented guitars, mandolins, and zithers, but in the first decades of the 20th century, Lyon & Healy's focus began to shift toward budget brands, and the Washburn guitars became progressively plainer.

In 1928 Lyon & Healy sold its entire instrument-making business (except for harps) to the Tonk Bros distribution company, which proceeded to market ever-cheaper Washburns until they abandoned the brand at the beginning of World War II. Washburn was revived in 1974 on imported guitars, and it continues today under the ownership of Rudy Schlacher.

MODEL

**Washburn Style A
(Model 5203)**

YEAR

Circa 1928

PRODUCTION

1922 to circa 1935

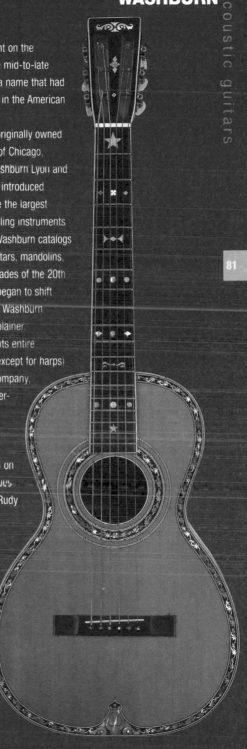

YAMAHA

Even without its motorcycles and consumer electronic products, Yamaha would still be the largest company in the musical instrument industry, thanks to its lines of keyboards, band instruments, and sound equipment, as well as guitars.

The Japanese conglomerate traces its roots to a pedal-driven reed organ invented by Torakusa Yamaha in 1887. The company he founded, Nippon Gakki, began making guitars in 1946. The first Yamaha guitars to arrive in America, in 1964, were classicals. Three years later the first steel-string flat-tops debuted. In a nod to the music of the times, the line was called *FG* for Folk Guitar. In the era of copy guitars, Yamahas were easily distinguishable by the subtle *V*-shape at the top of the headstock.

The first FG model numbers were in the 100s, and through the 1970s, the numbers got higher and higher as an apparent indication of Yamaha's success. The FG-612S was one of the top models of the early 1980s, featuring a solid top (designated by the *S* in the model name), along with a bound fingerboard and peghead.

MODEL
Yamaha FG-612S

YEAR
1983

PRODUCTION
1979 to 1980s

82

From the very beginning, Yamaha took an independent path into the U.S. musical instrument market. Rather than working through a distributor, the Japanese giant established its own subsidiary in the U.S. in 1960 to import pianos, then guitars. Even through the "copy era" of Japanese imports, Yamaha always had its own recognizable designs.

Yamaha's APX cutaway guitars, which were introduced in 1987 to showcase new electronics, soon became known for exotic woods and colorful finishes. In 1998, based on the success of the APX line – and possibly in response to Takamine's success with the Southwestern-themed Santa Fe guitars – Yamaha created an offshoot called the Compass series. Identified by a compass figure on the headstock, these CPX models typically sported nautical themes, represented by the blue sunburst finish on this CPX55-TMB from 2003.

The original CPX models faded out of production by 2005, but the prestige of the Compass designation was not forgotten, and Yamaha appropriated it in 2006 to give credence to a pair of models that introduced another new pickup system.

83

MODEL
Yamaha CPX55-TMB

YEAR
2003

PRODUCTION
2003 to 2005

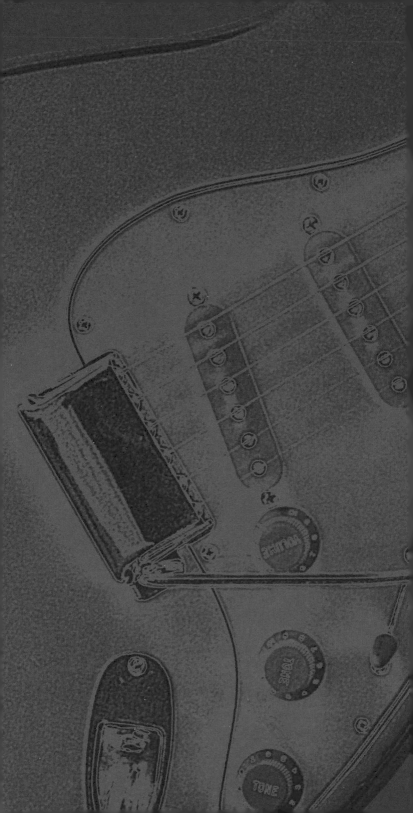

classic guitars
SOLIDBODY GUITARS

ELECTRIC
SOLIDBODY

Electric solidbody guitars have hardly been around long enough to be called classics – at least not in the sense that a Shakespeare play, a Renaissance cathedral, a Stradivari violin, or even a 19th-century "classical" guitar is a classic design. The "test of time" that traditionally defines a classic hasn't even started yet for the solidbody guitar, since many of the first generation of solidbody players are still alive today. But in a world where technological advances have accelerated the passing of one era into another, the "real time" of a single generation can correspond to centuries in earlier times. In that context, these solidbody designs have more than passed the "classic" standard, by their influence as well as their endurance.

It took the guitar world almost 20 years to accept the fact that an electric guitar did not have to look like a traditional guitar. While the solidbody seemed to do away with much of the traditional art and craft of making a fine guitar, it established new standards of quality based more on aesthetics and electronics. Still, the solid guitar might be a curiosity except for one property – the reduced tendency to "feed back" through an amplification system – that distinguished its performance from all other hollow electric and acoustic styles and made it the best design for an amplified world. That, even more than the aesthetic freedom it offered to guitar makers, propelled the electric solidbody guitar – and, of course, the music and musicians associated with it – into one of the strongest, most influential forces that popular music has ever experienced. These classic instruments are the tools with which those musicians changed our culture.

Alembic guitars are less frequently sighted than Alembic basses but, like the basses, they are easily identifiable by the "hippie sandwich" – the multi-piece neck-thru-body construction – along with the rich, handcrafted look of exotic wood and brass "fittings."

Alembic started as a consulting company with the task of making the Grateful Dead sound better. Founded in 1969 by Ron and Susan Wickersham, who were joined a year later by Rick Turner, Alembic put active pickups in the guitars of the Dead's Bob Weir and Jerry Garcia. It was Alembic's basses, however, that put them on the map as instrument makers. With brass bridges and nuts, neck-thru design and highly figured walnut, maple, and purple heart wood, Alembic basses led the way for many high-end bass makers.

Numerous influential bassists, ranging from Jack Casady (who had #001) to Stanley Clarke, have played Alembics. While the company's guitars were never as pervasive, an elite group of guitarists, most notably blues legend Johnny Winter and David Bowie bandmembers Carlos Alomar and Adrien Belew, have played Alembics.

MODEL
Alembic Series I

YEAR
1978

PRODUCTION
1970s

87

The "see-through" Ampeg guitars of 1969–71 represented three legendary names in electric guitar history. Ampeg pioneered electric basses with an amplification device in the end peg – hence the name Ampeg. In 1968 the Linden, New Jersey-based company tapped New York luthier and session musician Dan Armstrong to develop a guitar made of transparent acrylic glass, known by such trade names as Lucite and Plexiglas. Armstrong in turn tapped Bill Lawrence, a German-born musician, to help design not just one but six easily interchangeable pickups, giving guitarists a bass or treble option for rock, country and jazz (Rock Treble, Country Bass, etc.).

Its unique look and tonal versatility, plus onstage use by Rolling Stone Keith Richards, should have put the "see-throughs" over the top, but they lasted only three years. Ampeg continued to make basses and bass amps, Armstrong developed a line of effects boxes, and Lawrence went on to design pickups for Fender, Gibson and Peavey. Thanks in part to Dave Grohl's (Foo Fighters) use of a Dan Armstrong, Ampeg launched a reissue in 1998.

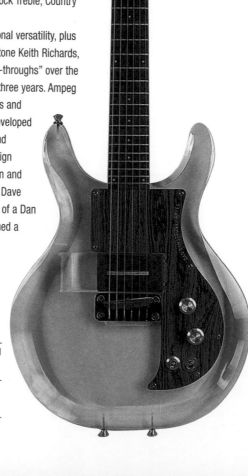

MODEL
Ampeg Dan Armstrong

YEAR
1969

PRODUCTION
1968 to 1971

This Diamond-brand 12-string from 1968 marked the end of an era for the Japanese-based Aria company, which was founded as an import company in 1956 by classical player Shiro Aria. In the 1960s, Aria gained a foothold in the U.S. market with cheap instruments that looked expensive.

The ADSG 12T took Fender's Jazzmaster body and gave it a sleeker look with more pointed horns and a more elongated shape. The pickups, pickguard, knobs and three-tone sunburst finish also had a Fenderish look, while the "tiger stripe" wood grain of the top evoked memories of Gibson's sunburst Les Paul Standards of 1958–60 – a look that Gibson abandoned in the 1960s – and the pearl dot fingerboard inlays were no doubt inspired by Gretsch's edge-hugging "thumbprint" inlays.

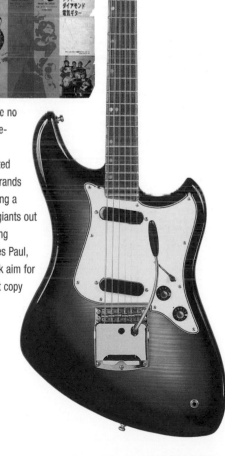

Through 1968, Arias competed directly with American budget brands such as Harmony and Kay, playing a major role in driving those two giants out of business. A year later, following Gibson's reintroduction of the Les Paul, Aria changed directions and took aim for the major makers with their first copy of Gibson's Les Paul.

MODEL
Aria ADSG 12T

YEAR
Circa 1968

PRODUCTION
1960s

89

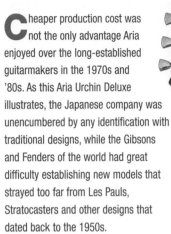

Cheaper production cost was not the only advantage Aria enjoyed over the long-established guitarmakers in the 1970s and '80s. As this Aria Urchin Deluxe illustrates, the Japanese company was unencumbered by any identification with traditional designs, while the Gibsons and Fenders of the world had great difficulty establishing new models that strayed too far from Les Pauls, Stratocasters and other designs that dated back to the 1950s.

By the early 1980s, the angular bodies and sharply pointed horns of Bernie Rico's guitars, marketed under his B.C. Rich brand, were capturing the attention of guitar buyers, and Aria jumped on the bandwagon from with a series of Urchin guitars, produced from 1982–84, that clearly drew their inspiration from B.C. Rich.

Ironically – or appropriately, many of Aria's "victims" from the 1960s and '70s might say – Aria's success was eventually undermined by cheap imports, and by the end of the 1980s Aria had moved most of its production to Korea.

MODEL
Aria Urchin Deluxe

YEAR
Circa 1983

PRODUCTION
1982 to 1984

90

BALDWIN electric solidbody

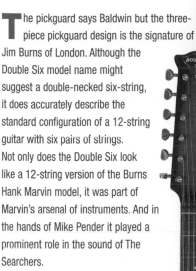

The pickguard says Baldwin but the three-piece pickguard design is the signature of Jim Burns of London. Although the Double Six model name might suggest a double-necked six-string, it does accurately describe the standard configuration of a 12-string guitar with six pairs of strings. Not only does the Double Six look like a 12-string version of the Burns Hank Marvin model, it was part of Marvin's arsenal of instruments. And in the hands of Mike Pender it played a prominent role in the sound of The Searchers.

Baldwin was founded as a piano retailer in Cincinnati, Ohio, in 1857 and became one of America's leading piano makers by the turn of the 20th century. In the 1960s Baldwin branched out into guitars, but after making little headway into the market with its own designs, the company bought Burns of London in 1965 and then Gretsch in 1967. As the Double Six illustrates, the Burns connection provided some of the more memorable, if least successful, instruments from the two acquisitions, and Baldwin stopped making Burns guitars in 1970.

MODEL
Baldwin Double Six

YEAR
Circa 1967

PRODUCTION
1965 to 1970

Paul Bigsby's most successful invention was his vibrola tailpiece, but the Downey, California, inventor's most important contribution to the world of musical instruments may well be this soldibody electric guitar that he made for singer-songwriter Merle Travis in 1948.

Though not the very first solidbody electric, it predated Leo Fender's Broadcaster by two years. It featured neck-thru-body construction, a style that would distinguish some of the early Rickenbacker solidbodies and would be appear in the 1960s on Gibson's Firebirds. Its most obvious influence on future guitars was its headstock, which Travis reportedly drew up on a napkin for Bigsby. The six-on-a-side tuner configuration not only became a standard feature on Bigsby's instruments, it appeared in a very similar form on the Fender Stratocaster in 1954.

Bigsby continued to make electric guitars in the 1960s, including a doubleneck for Nashville legend Grady Martin and the pedal steel guitar that Bud Isaacs played on the 1954 hit "Slowly," ushering in the modern era of pedal steel, but he never expanded production custom orders for individuals.

MODEL
Bigsby Custom guitar for Merle Travis

YEAR
1948

PRODUCTION
1948

ORMSTON
BURNS

THE FINEST IN MUSICAL ENGINE

Sharply pointed horns highlighted the new fashion looks of 1961 in the solidbody guitar world. In America, Gibson overhauled its Les Pauls with the new body style, while in England, Burns of London put pointed horns on its new Bison model. The Bison trumped Gibson's top model, the three-pickup Custom, with four low-impedance pickups, a better vibrato system, a flashier pickguard, and a sleek tuner-post cover. Even the name Bison – aka the American buffalo – was better than Gibson's, which soon became the unimaginative SG (for Solid Guitar).

After the first 50 Bisons, Burns backed it down to three pickups, a bolt-on neck, and a simpler vibrato. While it was never the company's best seller, it provided the most memorable image of Jim Burns's innovative ideas. It survived the acquisition of Burns by Baldwin in 1965, but disappeared with the entire Burns line in 1970. A new Burns London, founded in 1992, revived it as the Bison 64, and it can be sighted today in the hands of band members of Dead Poets Society.

MODEL
Burns Bison (four pickups)

YEAR
1961

PRODUCTION
1961

BURNS

As lead guitarist with the Shadows, who had dual fame as an instrumental group and as pop star Cliff Richard's band, Hank Marvin was England's most influential rock guitarist in the late 1950s and early '60s. In 1964, the leading player teamed up with the leading British guitarmaker, Jim Burns, to create the Burns Hank Marvin model.

Prior to his association with Burns, Marvin was "joined at the hip" with his 1959 Fender Stratocaster with Fiesta Red finish – believed to have been the first Stratocaster in England – and it became the starting point for Marvin's signature model. The double-cutaway body and three single-coil pickups are basic Strat features, but the double-bar handrest, the three-piece pickguard, and the peghead scroll are distinctive Burns touches.

Only a year after Burns London introduced the Hank Marvin model, Burns sold his company to the Baldwin Piano & Organ Co. As Marvin was still virtually unknown in the U.S., Baldwin did not continue the model. A new Burns London company brought the Marvin model back in limited production in 2004.

MODEL
Burns Hank Marvin

YEAR
1964

PRODUCTION
1964 to 1965

The Stratocaster-inspired body of this 1989 Contemporary Spectrum reflects the origin of the Charvel company as a parts house specialising in such items as Stratocaster-style bodies, while the pointed headstock angling off to the bass side – the opposite direction from a conventional Fender – and the "dive-bomb" vibrato exemplify the innovative ideas that gave rise to new guitar companies in the 1970s, as Gibson and Fender began to show their age.

Ironically, the Charvel designs did not come from Wayne Charvel, who founded the business in 1974 in Los Angeles and went on to design guitars for several major guitar makers. They came from Grover Jackson, a Charvel employee who bought the company in 1977 and began marketing guitars under his own name as well as Charvel.

By the late 1980s, Charvels were among the most respected of high-end Japanese-made guitars, and production was expanded to Korea (Charvotto by Charvel) and back to the U.S. in the 1990s. The run ended for Charvel when Aria bought the company in 1997.

MODEL
Charvel
Contemporary Spectrum

YEAR
1989

PRODUCTION
1989 to 1991

DANELECTRO

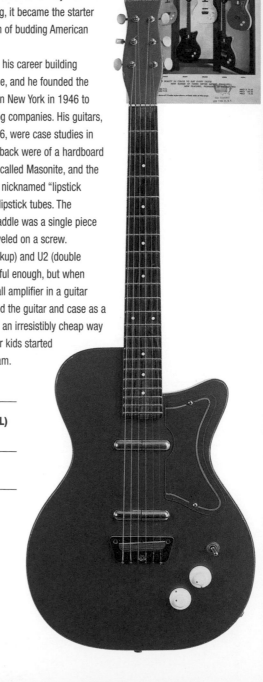

The Danelectro U2 offered 1950s guitarists an electric guitar in its simplest, most basic form and, when it found its way into the Sears Roebuck catalog, it became the starter guitar for a generation of budding American rock'n'rollers.

Nat Daniel started his career building amplifiers for Epiphone, and he founded the Danelectro company in New York in 1946 to supply amps to catalog companies. His guitars, which debuted in 1956, were case studies in frugality. The top and back were of a hardboard construction material called Masonite, and the pickups were not just nicknamed "lipstick tube," they used real lipstick tubes. The "adjustable" bridge saddle was a single piece of rosewood that swiveled on a screw.

The U1 (single pickup) and U2 (double pickup) were successful enough, but when Daniel installed a small amplifier in a guitar case and Sears offered the guitar and case as a set, they proved to be an irresistibly cheap way for parents to get their kids started on the rock'n'roll dream.

MODEL
**Danelectro U2
(Silvertone G01301L)**

YEAR
Circa 1958

PRODUCTION
**1956 to 1958
(Danelectro),
1958 to 1959
(Silvertone)**

96

The Epiphone Crestwood of 1958 was the first solidbody offered under the venerable Epiphone name and, moreover, it served notice that the Epiphone was alive and well under its new owners – the Gibson company. Epiphone had been one of Gibson's most formidable competitors in the tenor banjo market of the 1920s and the archtop guitar market of the 1930s, but when Epiphone faltered after World War II, Chicago Musical Instrument Co. (Gibson's parent company) bought its former foe.

Although Gibson introduced such innovative designs as the solid Flying V and Explorer, and the semi-solid ES-335 in 1958, the new Epiphone Crestwood featured a more derivative, proven body shape, which was essentially a Fender Telecaster with a mirror-image double-cutaway.

Epiphones were made in Gibson's Kalamazoo, Michigan, factory but were priced slightly below comparable Gibsons and consequently were quite successful. The Crestwood received a body makeover and an upgrade in name to Crestwood Custom in 1963 and continued to lead the Epiphone solid line until Gibson moved Epi production overseas in 1970.

MODEL
Epiphone Crestwood (first version)

YEAR
1959

PRODUCTION
1958 to 1962

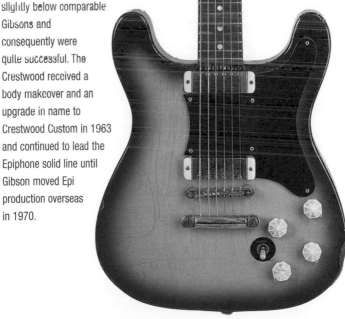

Except for the name on the peghead, the Fender Broadcaster is familiar throughout the guitar world as the Telecaster – the instrument that revolutioned the music world as the first commercially successful solidbody electric.

The Broadcaster debuted in October 1950 as a two-pickup version of Fender's first model, the Esquire. The Gretsch company, a prominent guitar maker and instrument distributor since the turn of the 20th century, had marketed a Broadkaster drum model, and Gretsch asked Leo Fender to find another name. Fender complied immediately by clipping the "Broadcaster" part off the logo decal (examples of which are known today as "No-casters"). Early in 1951 the model was rechristened Telecaster.

The Broadcaster/Telecaster established the solidbody electric guitar – as well as the Fender company – as a force to be reckoned with. It was overshadowed by the three-pickup, contoured-body Stratocaster in 1954, but the Telecaster was the guitar of choice for such influential players as Buck Owens, James Burton, Albert Lee and Danny Gatton and it continues to play a vital role in Fender's success today.

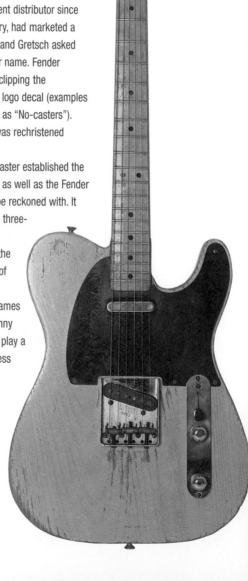

MODEL
Fender Broadcaster

YEAR
1950

PRODUCTION
1950 to early 1951

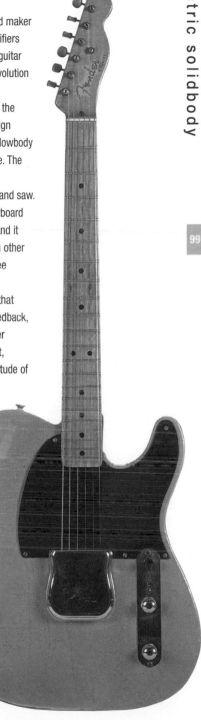

I n June 1950, a small California-based maker of electric Hawaiian guitars and amplifiers debuted a solidbody "electric Spanish" guitar called the Esquire. And thus began a revolution in the guitar world.

Like Leo Fender's Hawaiian models, the Esquire had a simple, almost crude design compared to the elegant carved-top hollowbody models of Gibson, Gretsch and Epiphone. The Esquire's "slab" body could have been fashioned by anyone with access to a band saw. The neck did not have a separate fingerboard and was simply bolted on to the body. And it only had a single pickup at a time when other makers were offering two and even three pickups.

The Esquire offered one advantage that hollow guitars did not have: reduced feedback, which meant it could be played at higher volume than conventional electrics. That, coupled with the restless, rebellious attitude of post-World World War II America, made the plebeian Esquire an attractive alternative to traditional guitars. The double-pickup Broadcaster (soon to be renamed Telecaster), introduced three months later, would put Fender over the top.

MODEL
**Fender Esquire
(black pickguard)**

YEAR
1952

PRODUCTION
1950 to 1954

FENDER

The black pickguard identifies the first version of the Telecaster, which began in 1950 as the Broadcaster, then became the "No-caster" in 1951 (with no model name on the peghead) before Fender finally came up with the Telecaster name. The classic "black guard Tele" look features the wide, grayish wood grain of an ash body showing through the slightly translucent "blonde" finish, which often ages to a butterscotch hue.

Among the first prominent Telecaster players were musicians from Fender's home area in southern California. Bill Carson, playing a black-guard Tele in Hank Thompson's Brazos Valley Boys, demonstrated the solidbody guitar's capability of being turned up loud enough to be heard in a Western swing band without feeding back. The Tele's bright tone and clean attack enhanced the lightning-fast licks of Jimmy Bryant, famed for his duet work with steel guitarist Speedy West, as he became the archetype for the hot-picking country guitarist.

The black guard Tele established not just Fender, but the electric solidbody guitar, as a viable new force in the guitar world.

MODEL
Fender Telecaster
(black pickguard)

YEAR
1953

PRODUCTION
1952 to 1954

A white pickguard appeared on the Fender Telecaster in 1955, presumably because it would not show wear like the earlier Bakelite black guard, but the model was otherwise unchanged. With the white guard, the "butterscotch" look of the early Teles changed to a more opaque finish that aged to a rich ivory color.

Although Fender introduced a "new and improved" solidbody, the Stratocaster, in 1954, it would be several years before the Strat overtook the Tele in sales. In the meantime, the Telecaster continued to gain a foothold in Los Angeles recording studios.

James Burton's string-bending work on Ricky Nelson's hits, beginning in 1958, helped establish the "twangy" sound that would forever associate the Telecaster with the rockabilly element of country music. Buck Owens, prior to his emergence as a country superstar, brought his Telecaster to numerous L.A. sessions in the late 1950s. California's top studio guitarists, including Barney Kessel, Tommy Tedesco and Howard Roberts even bought Telecasters along to sessions to keep up with the new sounds in popular music.

MODEL
**Fender Telecaster
(white pickguard)**

YEAR
1957

PRODUCTION
1955 to 1981

FENDER

The familiar, distinguishing look of Fender's one-piece maple neck changed in the late 1950s when the company adopted a more durable rosewood fingerboard. At the same time, Fender standardized a palette of custom finish colors that offered guitarists a range of individual expression from bright Fiesta Red to shining Gold metallic to basic Black.

The most famous custom color Tele from that era is the red guitar played by blues legend Muddy Waters. Not surprisingly, a red Tele also appeared in the hands of one of Muddy's disciples in England, Eric Clapton of The Yardbirds.

Although Fender's more expensive models, the Stratocaster and Jazzmaster, had become more popular with California surf bands, the Tele thrived in blues-based music of the early 1960s. Chicago guitarist Mike Bloomfield used a blonde-finish rosewood-fingerboard Tele as he began laying the groundwork for the guitar styles that would dominate rock music in the late 1960s, and Memphis session man Steve Cropper used a Tele for the memorable, minimalist licks that provided musical hooks on the instrumental hits of Booker T. and the MGs.

MODEL
Telecaster
(Fiesta Red finish)

YEAR
1960

PRODUCTION
1958 to 1969

Although the Stratocaster had overtaken the Telecaster in popularity as the 1950s came to a close, Fender maintained faith in the company's original model, as shown by a series of upscale Tele variations that began with the Telecaster Custom in 1959.

The "slab" body style of the Telecaster offered one aesthetic opportunity that the rounded edges of the more expensive Stratocaster, Jazzmaster and Jaguar could not accommodate, and that was body binding. Fender introduced this enhanced Telecaster (and Esquire) in mid 1959 as the Telecaster Custom. Along with the body binding, the Telecaster Custom was further delineated from the regular Telecaster by its sunburst finish.

Fender literature promoted the Telecaster Custom as a "startling new look," although vintage guitar aficionados would consider it more beautiful than startling. The startling look came in 1965, when Fender offered the Custom in a traditional "Tele blonde" finish that was enhanced by contrasting black body binding. The Telecaster Custom would never rival the standard Tele in popularity, but it remains a favorite of collectors today.

MODEL
Telecaster Custom

YEAR
1963

PRODUCTION
1959 to 1972

FENDER

Brazilian rosewood has been the preferred wood for acoustic guitar bodies since the mid 1800s, appreciated for its bold grain patterns as well as its rich tonal qualities. Curiously, it was late in 1968 before Fender became the first company to exploit the aesthetic appeal of rosewood on a solidbody guitar.

Fender gave the prototype of the Rosewood Telecaster to The Beatles' George Harrison, who used it on the album *Let It Be* and in the accompanying movie. Fender couldn't have asked for a better endorsement for a new model, but the company's timing proved to be horrible. Brazil put an embargo on the export of uncut rosewood logs in 1969, thereby forcing most guitarmakers to switch to the less dramatically figured Indian rosewood.

Fender made the Rosewood Telecaster through 1972, but the importation problems with Brazilian rosewood, coupled with the heavy weight of a solid rosewood guitar, doomed it to very limited production. A Japanese-made reissue revived interest in the model but it, too, was only made in limited numbers, from 1989 to the mid 1990s.

MODEL
Fender Rosewood Telecaster

YEAR
1968

PRODUCTION
1968 to 1972

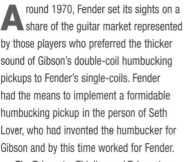

A round 1970, Fender set its sights on a share of the guitar market represented by those players who preferred the thicker sound of Gibson's double-coil humbucking pickups to Fender's single-coils. Fender had the means to implement a formidable humbucking pickup in the person of Seth Lover, who had invented the humbucker for Gibson and by this time worked for Fender.

The Telecaster Thinline and Telecaster Deluxe had a pair of humbuckers, but that was not what players wanted. The "model" they wanted was already in use by such influential guitarists as Mike Bloomfield, Albert Lee, and Keith Richards, all of whom were playing Telecasters that had been customized with a humbucking pickup in the neck position.

In 1972, Fender offered that single-coil and humbucker configuration but gave it the confusing name of Custom Telecaster. It did not have the bound body of the earlier Telecaster Custom, and Fender further confused the two models by referring to the new model in literature as the Telecaster Custom. Although it seemed to be the perfect combination of Fender and Gibson sounds, it never caught on with players and was discontinued in 1980.

105

MODEL
Fender Custom Telecaster

YEAR
1977

PRODUCTION
1972 to 1979

The Telecaster was pushed down near the bottom of Fender's model line in the 1960s by such flashy new models as the Jazzmaster and Jaguar, but by the early 1980s, the stars of the '60s had fallen and disappeared from the line, and the Telecaster and Stratocaster reemerged as the company's most popular models. Not only had they maintained a loyal following among guitarists, they were now beginning to attain iconic status.

Bill Schultz, who became Fender president in 1981 and would lead the employee group that bought Fender in 1985, recognized the Telecaster's fan base and began offering fancier versions of the basic model, exemplified by the Gold Elite Telecaster of 1983.

The Elite's upgrades included active electronics with a pair of white-covered poleless pickups, a bound top and a tremolo bridge with six individual saddles and drop-in string loading. For the elite of the Elite, Fender added gold-plated hardware and pearloid tuner buttons to create the Gold Elite. A Walnut Elite with black walnut body and neck completed the Elite family.

MODEL

**Fender Telecaster
Gold Elite**

YEAR

1983

PRODUCTION

1983 to 1985

It was officially called the Marble Telecaster, but the swirling, multi-color finish that appeared on Fenders in 1984 quickly earned them the nickname Bowling Ball Telecaster.

Designer Darren Johansen developed the finish technique and brought it to Fender in 1984. Fender committed to 300 instruments, 50 of which were Telecasters and 250 of which were Stratocasters. Most have a red-black-white or blue-black-yellow color scheme while a few (45 total) have a gold-silver-yellow finish. The base model was the short-lived (1982–84) and ironically named Standard Telecaster, which featured a non-standard six-saddle bridge, with strings anchored at the bridge rather than through the body.

By 1985, when the Marble Teles and Marble Strats were shipped to dealers, the attention of Fender's owners had been distracted from model design and refocused on selling the struggling company to a group of employees (the sale was finalized in March 1985), and a followup order for marble-finish guitars was never placed. Johansen applied his technique to clothing and went on to greater success as a clothing designer.

MODEL

Fender Marble Telecaster

YEAR

1984

PRODUCTION

1984

FENDER

One of the "battlefronts" in the long-running war between Fender and Gibson has been the neck joint. Fenders have a bolt-on neck, designed by Leo Fender himself so that a player could perform a do-it-yourself neck replacement if his fingerboard wore out. Gibsons have a "set" neck that is glued into the body. Neither side was been able to venture into the other's territory with much success until the 1990s.

Fender's Set Neck Telecaster of 1990 spearheaded the attack. The model name only began to describe its Gibson-esque design. It had a mahogany body (routed to reduce the weight) with a curly maple top cap, just like Gibson's Les Paul Standard but without the top carving. The neck, too, was mahogany, like a standard Gibson neck. It came with various optional pickup and tremolo configurations: two humbuckers, two humbuckers and Strat-style tremolo, two humbuckers and single-coil, plus a Custom Shop version with a coil-tapped neck-position humbucker.

Fender pushed Set Neck Telecasters (and Stratocasters) through the 1990s but ultimately retreated to the safety of its bolt-neck design in 2000.

MODEL
Fender Telecaster Set Neck

YEAR
1992

PRODUCTION
1990 to 1999

Fender introduced the American Deluxe series in 1998 to offer just what the name suggests: upscale, American-made versions of its standard Teles and Strats – in essence, custom guitars without the Custom Shop price – or exclusivity.

The regular Telecaster in the American Deluxe series featured a bound alder body, six-saddle bridge, pearloid pickguard, abalone fingerboard dots and "Noiseless" pickups. Otherwise the American Deluxe retained the same basic look – pickguard shape, control plate, pickup configuration etc. – as a traditional Telecaster.

Not so with the QMT and FMT that Fender introduced in 2004. To show off the Quilted Maple Top and Flamed Maple Top, Fender did away with the pickguard and mounted the controls directly into the top. Although most of the models in the series featured new Samarium Cobalt Noiseless pickups, designed by Bill Lawrence (the man responsible for many of Gibson's 1970s pickup designs), the Telecaster QMT and FMT opted for the extra power of a pair of "Enforcer" humbucking pickups. Transparent stained finishes, in amber, sunburst cherry or blue, enhanced the figuration of the maple top.

109

MODEL
Fender American Deluxe Telecaster QMT

YEAR
2004

PRODUCTION
2004 to current

FENDER

As successful as Fender's Telecaster was, it soon became apparent that the design left plenty of room for improvement. With input from musician Bill Carson and several Fender employees, Leo Fender went back to the drawing board.

Fender abandoned the Telecaster's "slab" body design for a sleek, double-cutaway shape with contours to fit the player's body. He added a third pickup. He upgraded the Tele's three-piece adjustable saddle system to six pieces – one for each string. He introduced a new vibrato – which Fender erroneously called "tremolo" – that offered players a truer return to pitch than the Bigsby design that had been the industry standard. And he upgraded the blonde, whitewashed finish of the Tele with a two-tone sunburst finish. Don Randall, Leo Fender's partner in Fender's sales and marketing division, named the new model Stratocaster.

Starting with Buddy Holly's first hits in 1957, the Strat became a vital element of rock'n'roll, and it gained iconic status in the hands of such artists as Jimi Hendrix and Eric Clapton. It remains today the foundation of Fender's continuing success.

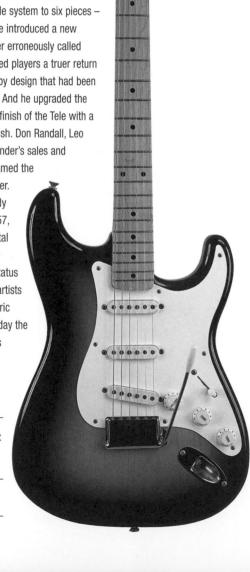

MODEL
**Stratocaster
(two-tone sunburst
finish)**

YEAR
1957

PRODUCTION
1954 to 1959

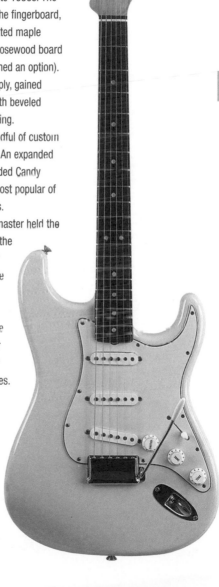

The Stratocaster of the early 1960s had the same basic design as the original, but several details changed in the late 1950s. The most obvious new feature was the fingerboard, which switched from the integrated maple neck/fingerboard to a separate rosewood board (although the maple neck remained an option). The pickguard, originally single-ply, gained several laminate layers along with beveled edges to simulate multi-ply binding.

Fender had introduced a handful of custom color options in 1958 and 1959. An expanded selection of colors in 1963 included Candy Apple Red, which became the most popular of the custom finishes in the 1960s.

In the early 1960s, the Jazzmaster held the top place in the Fender line, but the Strat remained the most popular model. Today, Stratocasters made prior to CBS's acquisition of Fender in 1965 are among the most prized guitars in the vintage guitar market, with custom-color models bringing a premium over standard sunburst-finish examples.

MODEL
Stratocaster (Sonic Blue finish with rosewood fingerboard, small headstock)

YEAR
1964

PRODUCTION
1958 to 1965

FENDER

By the mid 1960s, Leo Fender was tiring of the electric guitar business, and in January 1965, he sold Fender to the CBS broadcasting conglomerate for $13 million. At that point, Fender quality – design quality as well as production quality – began to decline.

The first design change on the Strat initiated by the CBS ownership group was a simple, seemingly innocent one: They made the headstock of the Stratocaster larger. Today, the large headstock, which appeared near the end of 1965, is considered by the vintage guitar world as the mark of the true end of Leo Fender's guitars and the beginning of the CBS era.

Despite the damage that CBS would do to the Stratocaster in its 20 years of Fender ownership, the Strat began to reemerge in the late 1960s. George Harrison gave his 1966 Strat important exposure in 1967 on The Beatles' *Magical Mystery Tour* performances. That same year, Jimi Henrix's album *Are You Experienced* took rock guitar to a new plane as Hendrix brought the Strat back into the spotlight, making it once again Fender's premier model.

112

MODEL
Stratocaster (Lake Placid Blue finish, large headstock)

YEAR
1966

PRODUCTION
1965 to 1985

Fender began referring to its basic Stratocaster as the Standard Stratocaster in the 1980s to distinguish it from such offshoot models as the Anniversary and the '57 Reissue, but in 1983, shortly after the introduction of the first reissue Stratocaster, the standard-production version received a makeover that seemed to gut the Strat's identity and tradition.

The new version had only two knobs – the input jack took over the third knob position – and the traditional tremolo bridge, which required the strings to load from the back of the guitar, was simplified into a top-loading design.

Among the first moves from the new ownership group, which purchased Fender from CBS in 1985, was to fix the Strat, to right the "wrongs" that had been committed with the 1983 Standard. In late 1986, the Standard was overhauled with a new tremolo system, a new truss-rod design, and a selection of new colors. To reassure guitarists that this new Strat was made in the U.S.A., Fender named it the American Standard. It remains, as its name suggests, the standard, basic, production-model Stratocaster in Fender's line today.

MODEL
**Fender Stratocaster
25th Annivesary**

YEAR
1979

PRODUCTION
1979

By the early 1980s, the Stratocaster had emerged as the only model that could carry Fender into the future. While the struggling company was starting to produce some models overseas, a dressed-up, high-end, made-in-U.S.A. Stratocaster helped divert attention from growing financial problems.

Fender had offered cosmetic upgrades in the form of the Walnut Strat and Gold Strat (with black walnut body and gold-plated hardware, respectively) in 1981, but the Elite Stratocaster of 1983 introduced upgraded performance as well. The poleless, white-covered pickups were part of an active electronics system, and the traditional pickup selector switch was replaced by three on-off pushbuttons. The tremolo bridge unit offered drop-in string loading (rather than through-the-back) along with a snap-on whammy bar. And the jack was moved out of the way of the player's right hand, to the rim of the guitar.

In the end, even Walnut Elite and Gold Elite options could not save the Elite Stratocaster, and when the employee group led by Bill Schultz bought Fender from CBS in early 1985, the Elite disappeared.

MODEL
Fender Elite Stratocaster

YEAR
1983

PRODUCTION
1983 to 1984

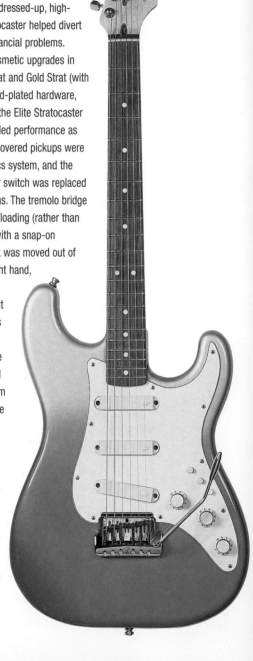

Prior to 1987, Fender's single-coil pickups were based on Leo Fender's designs, while the company's humbuckers were designed in-house by former Gibson employee Seth Lover. With the Strat Plus of 1987, Fender went outside of the company for the first time and made the new Lace Sensor pickup standard equipment on this model.

Lace Sensors were designed by Don Lace, who had consulted with Fender on speaker designs and pickups as early as 1967 and founded his own electronics company, Actodyne General, Inc., in 1979. In the 1980s, to help Fender alleviate a high rejection rate during the production of its pickups, Lace began developing a single-coil pickup with higher fidelity and more resistance to interference.

The Strat Plus introduced Fender-Lace pickups, along with such "plusses" as locking tuners, a roller bridge, and a pearloid pickguard. Higher-grade models, such as the Deluxe Plus and Ultra Deluxe Plus piled on the extras, including an ash veneer or figured maple veneer. Lace Sensor pickups became established on the Eric Clapton models, but the Plus did not last past 1997.

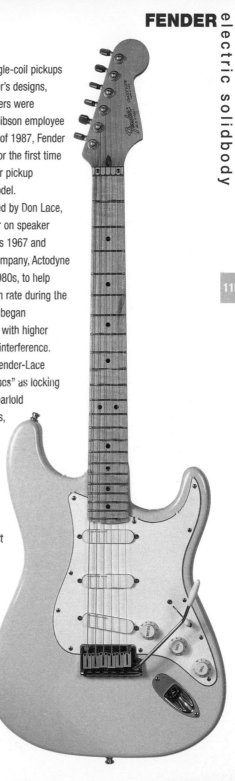

115

MODEL
Fender Strat Plus

YEAR
1990

PRODUCTION
1987 to 1997

FENDER

Although Eric Clapton gained his fame in the 1960s playing Gibson guitars as a member of Cream, he had started out on a Fender – a Telecaster – with the Yardbirds. In 1970, on a visit to Nashville to perform on the Johnny Cash TV show, he purchased a handful of used Stratocasters from Gruhn Guitars (then called GTR) and Sho-Bud Music.

When Clapton's new band, Derek and the Dominos, debuted later in 1970, their hit "Layla" featured Clapton with one of those Strats, nicknamed "Brownie." Another Strat that he pieced together from his Nashville purchases, nicknamed "Blackie," became his most famous instrument.

Fender's Eric Clapton signature model, introduced in 1988, was essentially a 1957 reissue with a blocked tremolo like Blackie's, but it was no Blackie replica (that would come later). The 1988 Clapton sported the new Fender-Lace Sensor pickups, which not only looked different, with their pole-less design, but also produced a "quieter" (not to be confused with softer) signal. The Clapton Strat also came in a lot more colors than the basic black, including Olympic White, Candy Green and Torino Red.

MODEL

Fender Eric Clapton Stratocaster

YEAR

1990

PRODUCTION

1988 to current

Jeff Beck never attained the commercial success of the guitarists who preceded him and followed him in the Yardbirds – Eric Clapton and Jimmy Page, respectively – but among rock'n'roll guitarists, Beck is as revered and influential as his fellow Yardbirds alumni.

Fender had wooed Beck in the late 1980s, but Beck demurred, and the model originally developed for him was introduced in 1987 as the Strat Plus. It featured the quiet Lace Sensor pickups, as did the Clapton model that followed it a year later, and as did the Jeff Beck Stratocaster when it finally debuted in 1991.

Like Clapton, Beck had started out with Fenders but developed his signature sound on a humbucker-equipped Gibson. Appropriately, his Fender model featured two adjacent single-coil pickups – in essence a humbucker – in the bridge position. This "fat Strat" configuration was perfect for the thick, distorted tone that Beck was known for, and by the end of the decade, the HSS (humbucker-single-single) had become an established option in the Strat lineup.

MODEL
Fender Jeff Beck Stratocaster

YEAR
1991

PRODUCTION
1991 to current

In 1956, only two years after Fender introduced the model that is still considered a pinnacle of electric solidbody guitar design – the Stratocaster – Fender swung its focus in the opposite direction.

The Duo Sonic offered guitarists – especially beginning players or players on a budget – a genuine, two-pickup Fender at an affordable price. Its body was sleeker and thinner than the Stratocaster, though not quite as aesthetically developed, and it had a double-cutaway design, which seemed to make it more attractive than the Telecaster.

The main drawback to the Duo Sonic was its shorter, 22.5-inch scale, which limited its appeal to younger players. That feature was "corrected" in 1964 with an optional 24-inch scale (still shorter than Fender's standard of 25.5 inches). At the same time, the Duo Sonic's body was upgraded to the more contemporary shape of the Mustang. As the Stratocaster began to emerge as the dominant Fender model in the 1969, the Duo Sonic fell by the wayside in 1969.

MODEL
Fender Duo Sonic

YEAR
1959

PRODUCTION
1956 to 1968,
1994 to 1997

From the very beginning, going back to the K&F lap steel guitars made by Leo Fender and Doc Kauffman in 1945, Fender instruments had been designed simply, for efficient production and low cost to the end user. The Esquire of 1950 would seem to have been the most basic, elemental, electric solidbody guitar possible but, in 1956, inspired perhaps by the success Gibson was enjoying with its Les Paul Junior (a simplified, single-pickup version of its Les Paul Model), Fender introduced the Musicmaster.

Although the Musicmaster's double-cutaway body shape was more modern than the Esquire's, it was thinner and lighter in weight so that it did not feel as substantive to a player. Its single pickup did not have the separate polepieces of the Esquire's pickup. And its short scale length of 22.5 inches limited its appeal to beginning players.

Despite its place at the low end of the Fender line, early Musicmasters were outfitted with the gold-colored metal pickguard (made of anodized aluminum) that would appear on Fender's high-end Jazzmaster in 1958.

MODEL
Fender Musicmaster

YEAR
1957

PRODUCTION
1956 to 1980

FENDER

Although Fender's Stratocaster of 1954 remains, in the opinion of generations of players, the pinnacle of the electric solidbody, Leo Fender continued to refine his designs. They came together in what Fender described as "America's finest electric guitar" in 1958 – the Jazzmaster.

The Jazzmaster took the Strat's modern, curvy body to the next level, with offset "waists" to make it more comfortable for a player who was sitting down. A more refined control system added roller knobs for neck pickup control, plus on/off switches for each pickup. The saddles featured ridges to keep strings from moving, and the tremolo was a new design. In the larger picture of Fender history, the most important feature was the rosewood fingerboard, which would soon be implemented across the line.

The Jazzmaster's pickups gave it a warmer sound than the Strat, a sound that was aimed at jazz players, who never embraced it. Ironically, just as the model was being discontinued in 1980, it found a home in anti-elite music, starting with angry-young-man Elvis Costello and extending into grunge rock bands of the 1980s.

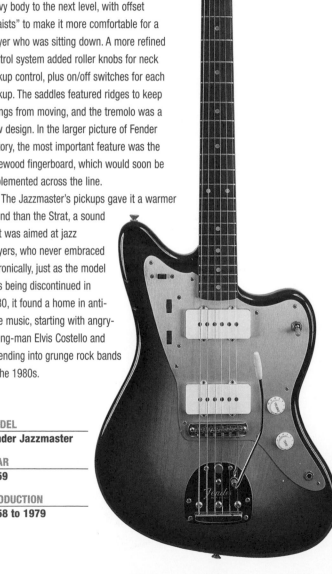

MODEL
Fender Jazzmaster

YEAR
1959

PRODUCTION
1958 to 1979

Its 30-inch scale made it a bass (albeit a short-scale bass), but the tremolo on Fender's Bass VI, along with its guitar-style string spacing, revealed its true identity as a low-tuned guitar.

The Bass VI's body and tremolo came from the Jazzmaster, and the three pickups were Stratocaster-style. Its simple, sensible electronics system consisted of individual on/off switches for each pickup, controlled by a master tone and volume. It was tuned an octave below the guitar, so that it reached the same low range as an electric bass, but its high strings extended well into the mid-range of a guitar.

Fender introduced this hybrid in 1961, inspired possibly by the moderate success of Danelectro's inexpensive six-string bass, but without a clear market demand for such a model. Although it had a unique sound – either a thin, high bass or a low, thick guitar sound, depending on the perspective – that appeared occasionally in a variety of musical settings (Jack Bruce played one on *Fresh Cream*), few bands used the Bass VI on a regular basis, and Fender last made it in 1975.

MODEL
Fender Bass VI

YEAR
1962

PRODUCTION
1961 to 1974

FENDER

Four years after the Jazzmaster, Fender introduced another model aimed at jazz players, and the result would be much the same: The Jaguar of 1962 sold moderately well to everyone *but* jazz guitarists.

The new model had the basic look of the Jazzmaster, including the same body and tremolo. Upgrades included pickup shielding – which look like teeth protecting the sides of the pickups – and even more switches than the Jazzmaster. The main difference was the Jaguar's shorter scale length, prompted, perhaps, by Gibson's Byrdland model (with 23.5 inch scale) and intended to accommodate greater finger stretches for modern jazz chord voicings. Fender settled on a 24-inch scale, an inch-and-a-half shorter than standard.

Fender's best intentions were thwarted when Carl Wilson of The Beach Boys began playing a white Jaguar, and the model was forevermore associated with surf music. Like the Jazzmaster, the Jaguar later found a home in grunge music, thanks in part to a customized Mustang/Jaguar used by Kurt Cobain of Nirvana. Also like the Jazzmaster, the Jaguar has been revived successfully in recent years.

MODEL
Fender Jaguar

YEAR
1964

PRODUCTION
1962 to 1975

Despite Fender's expectations, the company's elite, expensive models – the Jazzmaster and Jaguar – failed to inspire jazz players, but they did appeal to younger rock'n'roll guitarists. To capitalize on that demand, Fender crossed the Jaguar with the low-end Duo Sonic model in 1964 and, in keeping with the animal theme, named it the Mustang.

The Mustang featured the Jaguar's offset waists and 24-inch scale (the shorter 22.5-inch scale of the Duo Sonic and Musicmaster was available as an option), but it had the poleless pickups of the lower models.

Fortuitously, the Ford Motor Company introduced its Mustang car that same year, and it immediately captured the youth market before going on to become a collectible classic in the automotive world. Fender's Mustang did not fare quite so well, but with an upgrade in 1969 that featured an automotive racing stripe and an auto-related name – Competition Mustang – it lasted until 1982. Like the Jazzmaster and Jaguar, it then became a favorite of cult bands.

MODEL
Fender Mustang

YEAR
1971

PRODUCTION
1964 to 1982

123

Fender's timing for the introduction of the Electric XII could not have been better. It appeared in mid 1965, just after The Byrds brought folk and rock music together with the hit single "Mr. Tambourine Man," which featured a memorable opening guitar lick on an electric 12-string. Unfortunately, the guitar on The Byrds' records was a Rickenbacker 12-string, and Fender was unable to ride on the coattails of Rickenbacker's success.

124

Shortly after the Electric XII appeared, Fender upgraded it along the same lines as its other top models of the period, the Jazzmaster and the Jazz Bass, changing the fingerboard inlays from dots to blocks and adding binding to the fingerboard.

Although 12-string guitars did find a place in rock music in the late 1960s, it was the same place the acoustic 12-strings had held in folk music, providing tonal enhancement or a change of sonic scenery, but never as an instrument that was a vital element of the genre. Fender last made the Electric XII in 1969.

MODEL
Fender Electric XII

YEAR
1966

PRODUCTION
1965 to 1969

The Fender Bronco, as the name suggests, was a member of the same family as the Mustang. Introduced in 1967, it offered players a less-expensive, single-pickup version of the Mustang. Or, from the opposite perspective, it was an upgraded version of Fender's simplest guitar, the Musicmaster.

The Bronco had a more Fenderlike sound than the Musicmaster, thanks to its pickup placement near the bridge (the Musicmaster's was in the neck position). A pearloid pickguard gave it a classier look than the Musicmaster. And its tremolo was all its own, found on no other Fender.

The Bronco's shorter, 24-inch scale, and its single pickup limited its appeal to beginners or players with small hands. Fender offered it into 1980, but it was never a popular model. It made sporadic appearances in videos as "window dressing" in the hands of such guitarists as Mick Taylor of The Rolling Stones and Billy Corgan of Smashing Pumpkins, but unlike its fellow short-scale models, the Mustang and Jaguar, it was never revived.

MODEL
Fender Bronco

YEAR
circa 1972

PRODUCTION
1967 to 1980

125

FENDER

Kurt Cobain, left-handed guitar-playing leader of the Seattle band Nirvana, brought "grunge" rock to the forefront of popular culture with a custom Fender that combined his modified Mustang with favorite Jaguar neck. He called it a Jag-stang, and so did Fender when they offered it as a regular production model.

The Jag-Stang's neck copied Cobain's, with the shorter, 24-inch scale that the Jaguar and Mustang shared, and the Jag-Stang had a Mustang tremolo, but the body was different, and the pickups were from neither of the vintage models. Cobain used a humbucker in the bridge position and a vintage-style Stratocaster pickup in the lead position.

As influential as Cobain was, he became even more famous after he committed suicide in April 1994, and it was late 1995 – a year-and-a-half after his death – before Fender put the Jag-Stang into production. As Cobain's notoriety faded, so did the Jag-Stang. It lasted in the line for five years and made a short comeback from 2003–05.

MODEL
Fender Jag-stang

YEAR
1997

PRODUCTION
1995 to 2000,
2003 to 2005

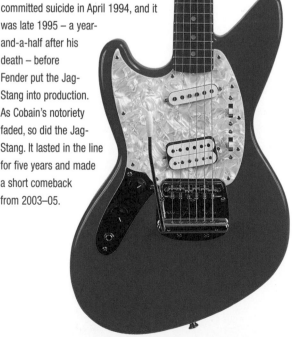

From the wave of publicity that surrounded the 1994 suicide of Nirvana leader Kurt Cobain, Cobain's wife Courtney Love emerged as a star in her own right, as an actress (starring in *The People versus Larry Flynt*) as well as the leader of the band Hole.

In 1997, shortly after Fender introduced the Jag-Stang as a Cobain signature model, the Venus Vista debuted under the Squier brand (in six-string and 12-string versions) as Love's signature model. Its design seemed to show good intentions – a double-cutaway body, a humbucker in the bridge position and single-coil pickup in the neck position, strings anchoring through the body, and a bound fingerboard. But the body shape looked like a squat Stratocaster, the pickguard had the shape of a blob, and the angles of the pickups, bridge and string holes appeared to be at odds with the body and pickguard. The controls were oversimplified, with a three-way switch, one tone, and one volume.

Fender only offered the Squier Venus for two years, but it coincided with the high point of Love's career.

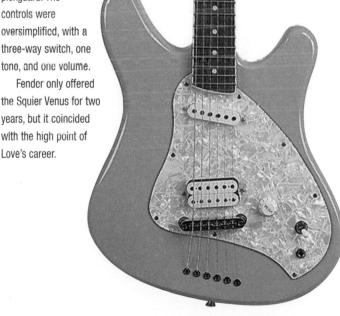

MODEL
Fender Squier Venus

YEAR
Circa 1997

PRODUCTION
1997 to 1998

127

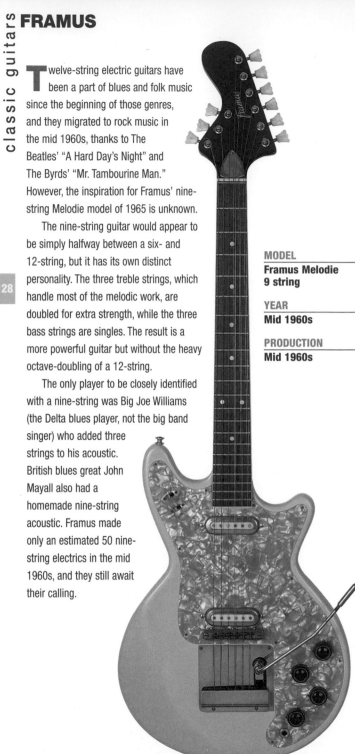

Twelve-string electric guitars have been a part of blues and folk music since the beginning of those genres, and they migrated to rock music in the mid 1960s, thanks to The Beatles' "A Hard Day's Night" and The Byrds' "Mr. Tambourine Man." However, the inspiration for Framus' nine-string Melodie model of 1965 is unknown.

The nine-string guitar would appear to be simply halfway between a six- and 12-string, but it has its own distinct personality. The three treble strings, which handle most of the melodic work, are doubled for extra strength, while the three bass strings are singles. The result is a more powerful guitar but without the heavy octave-doubling of a 12-string.

The only player to be closely identified with a nine-string was Big Joe Williams (the Delta blues player, not the big band singer) who added three strings to his acoustic. British blues great John Mayall also had a homemade nine-string acoustic. Framus made only an estimated 50 nine-string electrics in the mid 1960s, and they still await their calling.

MODEL
**Framus Melodie
9 string**

YEAR
Mid 1960s

PRODUCTION
Mid 1960s

128

Framus used the Strato name on numerous models, and the Strato Deluxe (model 5/168) did have three single-coil pickups like a Fender Stratocaster, but most of the Strato Deluxe's features came from a different Fender model: the Jazzmaster. The body is almost an exact copy, and with circuitry overload from five knobs and six switches, plus a mute, a vibrato, and six-on-a-side tuner configuration, the Jazzmaster influence is unmistakable.

This Strato Deluxe from 1965 goes a step beyond the Jazzmaster, and all other guitars of the major manufacturers in the mid 1960s, with its onboard Organtone effect. The player could hook his pinkie finger into the curved switch handle and engage a spring-loaded volume control to create an effect similar to that of the rotating horn of a Leslie organ amplifier.

The Organtone was available on various Framus models, but guitarists quickly showed their reluctance to sound like an organ, and the Strato Deluxe did not make it into the 1970s, much less into the revived Framus line of 1995.

MODEL
Framus Strato Deluxe

YEAR
1965

PRODUCTION
1960s

G&L

Leo Fender, worrying about his health and his ability to continue running a guitar company, sold Fender to CBS in 1965 and then proceeded to advance and refine electric solidbody guitar designs for another 26 years – longer than his tenure as head of the Fender company. After nine years of designing and producing instruments for the Music Man company, he partnered with former Fender employee George Fullerton to organize G&L in 1979.

G&L's best-known model appeared in 1985, and it looked a lot like Fender's legendary Telecaster (nee Broadcaster), with its single-cutaway, slab-style body, angled bridge pickup, oblong control plate and six-on-a-side tuner configuration. Leo even tried to name it Broadcaster, but the Fender company objected. Fender historian Richard Smith suggested ASAT, which was military jargon for an anti-satellite missile (it was not short-hand for After Strat, After Tele).

Leo Fender died in 1991, but the new owners, BBE Sound of Huntington Beach, California, continued the ASAT, and it is offered today in over a dozen variations.

MODEL
G&L ASAT

YEAR
1989

PRODUCTION
1985 to current

Gibson employees initially derided Leo Fender's Broadcaster/Telecaster as a crude design that resembled a toilet seat, but by 1952 Gibson could ignore the solidbody electric no longer. Gibson began working on a more elegant design with a carved top that not only identified it with Gibson's tradition as the company that invented the carved-top guitar but also would be difficult for Fender to copy without considerable new tooling.

To ensure maximum publicity and support for the new model, Gibson enlisted the most popular guitarist of the era, Les Paul, who had been an ardent proponent of the solidbody electric guitar for over a decade. Paul contributed his own patented bridge/tailpiece design and suggested a metallic gold top finish to further distinguish the Gibson from a Fender.

The Les Paul Model debuted in 1952, on the heels of Les Paul and Mary Ford's #1 hit "How High The Moon." With Les and Mary both playing Gibson "goldtops," Gibson was instantly established in the solidbody market.

MODEL
Gibson Les Paul Model (trapeze tailpiece, left-handed)

YEAR
1952

PRODUCTION
1952 to 1953

Gibson's Les Paul Model, as the "goldtop" was officially called, had one shortcoming, and that was its bridge. Due to a shallow neck-set angle, the combination bridge/tailpiece was too high, requiring the strings to wrap underneath the crossbar. It felt awkward to guitarists, and Gibson fixed the problem in late 1953 by increasing the neck angle and introducing a new bridge/tailpiece.

The "wraparound" bridge, as it has come to be known, took the strings over the top of the bar, and it was anchored more securely than the Les Paul-designed trapeze, by means of two "studs" screwed into the top of the guitar.

In the meantime Les Paul and Mary Ford dominated the radio with hit after hit – including a run of five Top 10 records between August 1952 and March 1953. Despite the Les Paul Model's bridge problem, sales rose in 1953, establishing a strong foundation in the new solidbody market from which Gibson would quickly expand the Les Paul line in both directions.

MODEL
Gibson Les Paul Model (wraparound bridge)

YEAR
1954

PRODUCTION
1953 to 1954

In 1954, two years after the introduction of the goldtop Les Paul Model, Gibson offered a fancier version called the Les Paul Custom. Personal design input from Les Paul included the black finish – the color of a tuxedo – and low frets to facilitate the speedy runs that Paul was known for. Both features inspired nicknames for the new model: Black Beauty and Fretless Wonder.

The Custom also introduced two Gibson innovations. The neck-position pickup featured height-adjustable Alnico V magnets rather than screws for polepieces, although it was still essentially the same single-coil design as Gibson's standard P-90 pickup. The bridge, however, was a significant improvement over the goldtop's wraparound. Designed by Gibson president Ted McCarty, the "tune-o-matic" offered individually adjustable saddles and overall height adjustment.

Though not quite as versatile as the saddles on Fender's Stratocaster, which was also introduced in 1954, Gibson's tune-o-matic proved more than adequate, and it continues today as the standard Gibson bridge for almost all electric models.

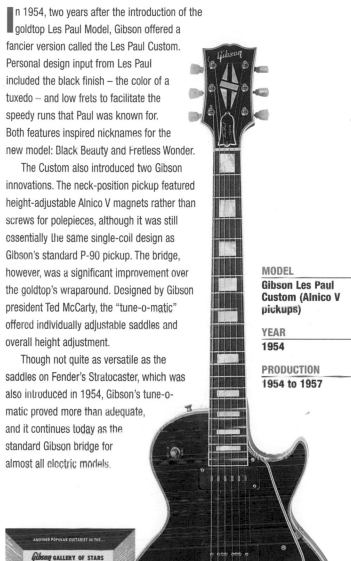

133

MODEL

Gibson Les Paul Custom (Alnico V pickups)

YEAR

1954

PRODUCTION

1954 to 1957

GIBSON

Midway through 1957, Gibson gave the Les Paul Custom a major upgrade, adding a third pickup and, more important, replacing the single-coil pickups with the new double-coil "humbuckers." The gold-plated metal pickup covers added a new dimension of elegance to the Custom's look, and the powerful pickups opened up a new world of sound for guitarists.

It was not the perfect guitar, however. For most players, three pickups was overkill, and the Custom's switching system limited the choices of pickup combinations to neck pickup alone, middle and bridge pickups together, or bridge pickup alone, making it actually less versatile than a two-pickup Gibson. Consequently, the Custom wasn't as popular as the Standard, but it still held a considerable level of status as Gibson's top solidbody.

Despite its shortcomings, the Custom worked quite well for such players as Robert Fripp (in the early days of King Crimson) and 1970s rocker Peter Frampton, who ended up with a Gibson signature model based on his Les Paul Custom.

MODEL
Gibson Les Paul Custom (humbucking pickups)

YEAR
1957

PRODUCTION
1957 to 1960, 1968 to current

The most important improvement to the Les Paul Model, aka goldtop, on its way to becoming a legendary model, came in mid 1957 with the introduction of Gibson's innovative double-coil "humbucking" pickups.

"Hum" – electrical interference from outside sources such as rheostats (light faders) or fluorescent lights – had been a problem for electric guitar players since the invention of the instrument. Electrical engineers had long known that two coils of wire wound in the opposite directions would have a hum-canceling effect on each other, and by 1955, Gibson engineer Seth Lover had applied the concept to guitar pickups, but Gibson did not push the pickups into production until word spread through the industry that Gretsch had developed a very similar unit.

Humbuckers provided a level of power that single-coils simply didn't have, and blues artists were among the first to take advantage. Blues great Freddie King's humbucker-equipped goldtop had a profound influence on the future of rock'n'roll; it was a photo of King that inspired Eric Clapton to buy his first Les Paul.

MODEL

Gibson Les Paul Model (goldtop, humbuckers)

YEAR

1957

PRODUCTION

1957 to 1958, 1983 to current

GIBSON

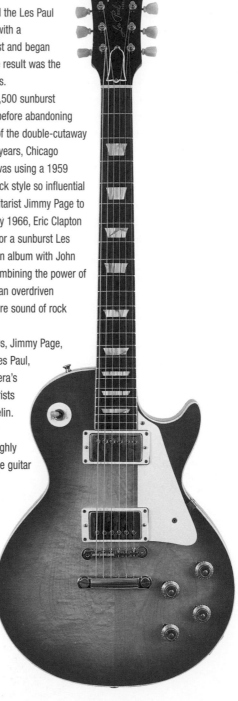

I n 1958, Gibson replaced the Les Paul Model's gold top finish with a transparent cherry sunburst and began calling it the Standard. The result was the Holy Grail of electric guitars.

Gibson produced around 1,500 sunburst Standards from 1958–60 before abandoning the entire design in favor of the double-cutaway SG style. But within a few years, Chicago guitarist Mike Bloomfield was using a 1959 model to create a blues-rock style so influential that it prompted British guitarist Jimmy Page to buy a sunburst Les Paul. By 1966, Eric Clapton had set aside his goldtop for a sunburst Les Paul. When he used it on an album with John Mayall's Bluesbreakers, combining the power of humbucking pickups with an overdriven Marshall amplifier, the future sound of rock guitar was set.

By the end of the 1960s, Jimmy Page, armed with his sunburst Les Paul, would become one of the era's most influential rock guitarists as a member of Led Zeppelin. And the sunburst Les Paul would become the most highly sought model in the vintage guitar world.

MODEL

Gibson Les Paul Standard

YEAR

1958

PRODUCTION

**1958 to 1960,
1968 to 1969,
1976 to current**

The non-sunburst cherry finish on this 1959 Les Paul Standard is also found on two examples that predate the familiar "cherry sunburst" finish. Presumably, Gibson felt in 1958 that red should be the new color of the model, but exactly what shade and pattern of red was not exactly determined.

This rich cherry shade came straight out of Gibson tradition, from guitars and mandolins of the late 1910s and 1920s. While it was certainly an attractive finish, it had two drawbacks. In 1958, the prevailing philosophy at Gibson was to break with tradition (this was the year Gibson would introduce the Flying V and Explorer), so reviving a 40-year-old finish style would be moving in the opposite direction. Additionally, the two earlier examples had a "shaded" effect on the back of the body and neck as well as on the top, which required more time to apply.

In 1958, Gibson settled on what is considered today to be the classic look – a cherry border on the top and a uniform cherry stain on the back and neck.

MODEL

Gibson Les Paul Standard (cherry finish)

YEAR
1959

PRODUCTION
1958 to 1959

GIBSON

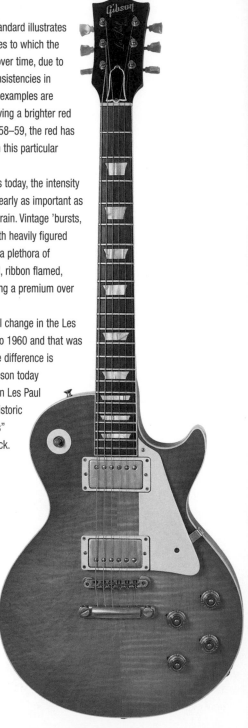

This 1960 Les Paul Standard illustrates the wide range of hues to which the cherry sunburst can fade over time, due to exposure to light and inconsistencies in paint batches. While 1960 examples are generally thought of as having a brighter red border than those from 1958–59, the red has completely disappeared on this particular model.

To Les Paul enthusiasts today, the intensity of the cherry stain is not nearly as important as the intensity of the wood grain. Vintage 'bursts, as they are nicknamed, with heavily figured "curly" tops have inspired a plethora of descriptives – tiger-striped, ribbon flamed, quilted, etc. – and they bring a premium over those with plainer tops.

Gibson made one small change in the Les Paul Standard from 1959 to 1960 and that was to slim down the neck. The difference is significant enough that Gibson today offers its regular-production Les Paul Standards, as well as its historic reissues, with a "fat 1950s" neck or a "slim 1960s" neck.

MODEL

Gibson Les Paul Standard

YEAR

1960

PRODUCTION

1958 to 1960, 1968 to 1969, 1976 to current

Ironically, Les Paul had very little personal input into the design of the classic 1950s Gibsons that bore his name. That changed in 1969 with the Les Paul Personal.

Paul's first stint with Gibson had ended in 1963, but when Gibson revived the Standard and Custom in 1968, Paul returned. This time Gibson gave him free rein to design a guitar that truly represented his personal preferences, and he came up with two models. Both had the body lines of the earlier models but were larger – a full inch wider. The Personal was just that, with one of the most personalized features ever to appear on a production guitar – a microphone jack on the bass-side rim allowing the player to attach a mic to the guitar, just as Paul did in his live performances. The second model, the Professional, had more universally appealing features, such as an in-phase/out-of-phase switch and an extra tone control.

Both models featured low-impedance pickups, which Paul preferred because they were better suited for a recording studio, and, two years after they were introduced, Gibson combined the electronics of the Professional with the ornamentation of the Personal to create the Les Paul Recording.

139

MODEL
Gibson Les Paul Personal

YEAR
1969

PRODUCTION
1969 to 1970

I n Gibson's 1970s nomenclature system, "Deluxe" was applied ironically to the lowest of three model levels (the other two designations were Custom for midline and Artist for high-end models). Consequently, despite such features as a custom blue sparkle finish (available from 1975–77), the Les Paul Deluxe was *not* a deluxe Les Paul. It was a Standard with smaller, mini-humbucking pickups.

The Deluxe began as a model of convenience, the result of Gibson's decision in 1969 to send production of its second-tier brand, Epiphone, to Japan. That left Gibson with a surplus of mini-humbucking pickups (previously used only on Epis). Gibson had just revived the Les Paul Standard with the original-style "soapbar" pickups, and the minis fit perfectly in the pickup routings. Voila! The Les Paul Deluxe.

In response to players' demands, a Standard with full-size humbuckers soon returned, but some players preferred the Deluxe. The Who's Pete Townshend had several Deluxes with various modifications that he numbered. The model lasted until 1985 and has since been reissued, with standard specs as well as three Townshend signature versions.

MODEL

Gibson Les Paul Deluxe

YEAR

Circa 1975

PRODUCTION

1969 to 84, 1992, 2001

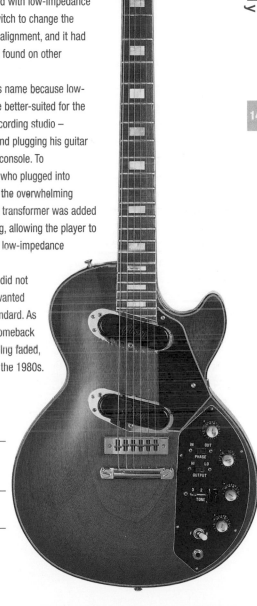

Upon Les Paul's return to Gibson in 1968, he designed two models that featured his personal preferences. In 1971, Gibson combined the Les Paul Personal and Professional into one model – the Les Paul Recording. Like the Personal and Professional, the Recording was spec'd with low-impedance pickups, along with a switch to change the pickups to out-of-phase alignment, and it had an extra tone control not found on other Gibsons.

The Recording got its name because low-impedance pickups were better-suited for the way Paul worked in a recording studio – bypassing an amplifier and plugging his guitar directly into a recording console. To accommodate guitarists who plugged into amplifiers – which were the overwhelming majority of guitarists – a transformer was added to the Les Paul Recording, allowing the player to switch between high- or low-impedance output.

Ultimately, guitarists did not want Les's guitar; they wanted the original Les Paul Standard. As the Standard made its comeback in the 1970s, the Recording faded, and it did not make it to the 1980s.

MODEL
Gibson Les Paul Recording

YEAR
Circa 1972

PRODUCTION
1971 to 1979

With renewed interest in Les Pauls in the 1970s, Gibson expanded on the original four models, exemplified by the Les Paul Artisan of 1976. The Artisan had the gold-plated hardware and multi-layer binding of the Custom, but with floral inlays on the fingerboard and peghead. This example has two additional Gibson upgrades from 1976 and 1977, respectively: the "wide-travel" or "Nashville" tune-o-matic bridge, which provided extended intonation adjustment, and the TP-6 fine-tune tailpiece. The model was also offered with three humbuckers.

The inlay pattern, including the prewar-style peghead logo, was familiar to a world of musicians as far away from Les Pauls as one can get – bluegrass banjo players. "Hearts and Flowers" had been a standard inlay pattern on Gibson's pre-World War II banjos but had only been used briefly in the postwar years on the expensive Style 800 banjo.

The upgraded inlays and hardware of the Artisan carried the Les Paul line into a higher range of ornamentation and performance, and it lasted in the line until 1981.

MODEL

Gibson Les Paul Artisan

YEAR

1981

PRODUCTION

1976 to 1981

By the mid 1970s, a tiger-striped maple top had become a coveted feature on vintage Les Paul Standards from 1958–60, and in 1976 Gibson used spectacularly figured maple as a starting point from which to build the ultimate Les Paul. It was called simply The Les Paul.

The plastic parts on a standard model were replaced with rosewood on The Les Paul, including the knobs, the pickguard, the pickup mounting rings, the selector switch cap, the washer surrounding the selector switch, and the control cavity covers on the back. Rosewood was even used for the outer layer of binding (the inner layers were colored wood) and as the center portion of the ebony-rosewood-ebony fingerboard. The fingerboard inlays were of figured abalone pearl, and the metal parts were, of course, gold plated.

Gibson produced the model in limited numbers (less than 100 total) for only three years, but The Les Paul remains the most luxuriously appointed model of any catalog solidbody ever offered by Gibson.

MODEL
Gibson The Les Paul

YEAR
1978

PRODUCTION
1976 to 1979

GIBSON

Gibson's 1952 goldtop Les Paul Model priced at $210 (without case) competed effectively with Fender's $189.50 Telecaster, but Fender also offered the single-pickup Esquire at a significantly lower price of $149.50. In 1954, Gibson came after the Esquire with its own single-pickup model – the Les Paul Junior.

Gibson knew from experience that the least expensive models would always outsell the fancier models, as long as the essential elements were present. The Les Paul Junior did not have the Les Paul Model's goldtop finish or even its maple top cap, and the Junior had no binding, but it had the same body shape, the same neck, and the same pickup. At $99.50 it was the best value on the solidbody market.

The Les Paul Junior, especially when sold with a companion amplifier, became the "starter guitar" for thousands of young guitarists in the 1950s. And as Leslie West proved when he used his Junior to create the memorable lead part on Mountain's 1970 recording "Mississippi Queen," some guitarists never saw a need to put their Junior down.

MODEL

Gibson Les Paul Junior (single cutaway)

YEAR

1956

PRODUCTION

1954 to 1958, 1986 to 1992, 1998 to current

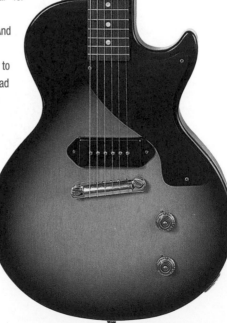

The Special was the last of Gibson's four original Les Paul models. The wide gap between the entry-level Junior, with its single pickup and flat "slab" body, and the original goldtop Les Paul Model, with its two pickups and carved, contoured top, begged to be filled, and Gibson did just that in 1955 with the Les Paul Special.

The Special offered the same performance as the goldtop, with a pair of P-90 pickups, but it had the cheaper-to-produce slab body design of the Junior. Gibson appropriated the newly introduced "TV yellow" finish – soon to be known as "Limed Mahogany" – from the Les Paul TV model and made it the standard finish on the Special.

Sales of the Les Paul Special were as expected for its place in the Les Paul line – fewer than the less-expensive Junior and more than the higher-priced Model/Standard. Possibly the most famous of the single-cutaway versions is an early 1970s Special that was the main guitar of reggae legend Bob Marley.

MODEL

Gibson Les Paul Special (single cutaway)

YEAR

1955

PRODUCTION

1955 to 1959

GIBSON

Sales figures for every Les Paul model fell in 1958 and, towards the end of that year, Gibson modernized the Junior with a double-cutaway body and a cherry red finish. Sales picked up immediately and, not surprisingly, the Special received the same makeover in 1959 (cherry finish was optional on the Special). The results were similar, with Les Paul Special sales almost doubling from 1958 to '59.

Curiously, by the end of 1959, Gibson began calling it the SG Special (SG for Solid Guitar). This seemed to anticipate the 1961 changeover to what would become known as the SG body shape, with pointed horns, but how Gibson could drop the Les Paul designation with Les Paul still under contract, and why the company would do it on just one model, has never been explained.

Gibson revived the double-cutaway (non-SG) Special in the mid 1970s as a separate model from the single-cutaway version, and the basic model remains in production, although sometimes under the confusing name of Junior Special.

MODEL
Gibson Les Paul Special (double cutaway)

YEAR
1959

PRODUCTION
1959

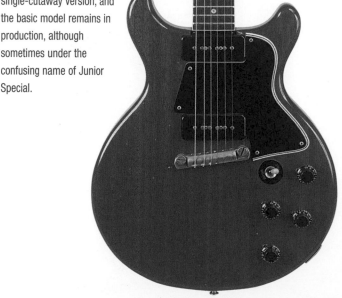

The Les Paul Junior was already a double-cutaway model when Gibson overhauled the entire Les Paul line in 1961 with a sleeker body and bold, pointed horns. Technically, the models were still Les Pauls until Paul's contract ran out in late 1963. Then they officially became SG models.

The Junior maintained the same position as an SG that it had held in the 1950s as a Les Paul – an entry level guitar and the best-selling model of the four. With Gibson's acquisition by the Norlin company in 1970, however, the entire SG line underwent a series of design changes (none for the better) and, despite the Junior's status as the least expensive, good-quality Gibson solidbody, it was absent from the new SG line of 1971.

While the original Les Paul Junior enjoyed a comeback, the SG version of the Junior made only brief appearances, in 1991–93 and 2000–02. Even when Gibson equipped it with a humbucker and renamed it the All American I (1995–97) or SG-X (1998–2000), the single-pickup SG guitar was short-lived.

MODEL
Gibson SG Junior

YEAR
1961

PRODUCTION
1961 to 1970,
1991 to 1993

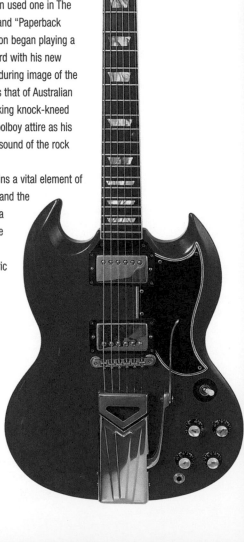

GIBSON

When sales of Gibson's Les Paul Standard, with its recently introduced cherry sunburst finish, flattened out in 1960, Gibson changed the entire line to a new body style. Although they weren't officially called SG models until late 1953, the effect on sales was dramatic. With the more modern look and lighter weight of the SG body, Standard sales jumped from 635 in 1960 to 1,662 in 1961.

The SG Standard gained some notoriety in 1966 when George Harrison used one in The Beatles' videos for "Rain" and "Paperback Writer." In 1967, Eric Clapton began playing a custom-painted SG Standard with his new group Cream. The most enduring image of the SG Standard, however, was that of Australian guitarist Angus Young, walking knock-kneed about the stage in his schoolboy attire as his SG provided the signature sound of the rock band AC/DC.

The SG Standard remains a vital element of Gibson's solidbody legacy, and the company currently makes a Standard and a '61 Reissue as regular-production models, as well as a Historic Collection version and an Angus Young signature edition.

MODEL
Gibson SG Standard

YEAR
1961

PRODUCTION
1961 to 1970,
1972 to 1980,
1983 to 1986,
1988 to current

The SG model name inexplicably debuted on what had been the Les Paul Special in late 1959, over a year before it received the SG body and more than three years before Les Paul's contract with Gibson ended.

Otherwise, though, Gibson maintained its identifying features – two single-coil pickups and bound fingerboard with dot inlays – through the changeover. The "TV" finish of the 1950s gave way to a more opaque cream or white finish, or else a cherry stain finish, or in rare cases such as this 1966 example, a Pelham Blue finish (aged to a dark green).

As it had in the 1950s, the Special occupied an awkward spot between the cheaper single-pickup Junior and the humbucker-equipped Standard. It gained its moment in the spotlight in the late 1960s when Carlos Santana appeared onstage at Woodstock with an SG Special and Pete Townshend of The Who made it his main guitar. Various versions (typically with humbucking pickups) have been in production since 1985, and Gibson replicated Townshend's guitar in a limited edition in 2000.

MODEL
Gibson SG Special (SG body shape)

YEAR
1966

PRODUCTION
1961 to 1970

GIBSON

The Les Paul Custom switched to the SG body at the beginning of 1961 and, until late 1963, it retained the Les Paul name on a small plate at the end of the neck. Only at that point did it officially become the SG Custom.

The Custom's ebony fingerboard, large pearl block inlays, five-piece peghead inlay, and gold-plated hardware carried over from the single-cutaway, carved-top model. However, the black finish that had identified the Custom as the Black Beauty since its inception in 1954 did not survive the change, and the new SG style sported a creamy white finish. Another change was the addition of a vibrato as standard equipment. Typically a large coverplate extended from the vibrato base to the end of the guitar; the ebony block with three pearl inlays on this example is purely ornamental.

More expensive and less popular than the Standard, the Custom survived virtually intact until 1980, after which it went in and out of production several times. The Les Paul/SG Custom lives on today in Gibson's Custom, Art & Historic division.

MODEL
Gibson SG Custom

YEAR
1962

PRODUCTION
1961 to 1979,

Gibson started making doubleneck Hawaiian guitars in 1937, within two years of the company's first electric model, but the concept did not take hold on conventional "Spanish" style guitarists until the 1950s. Gibson tested the doubleneck waters in 1958 with several custom-order models. Any conceivable combination of guitar necks and banjo necks was possible, but the six- and 12-string EDS-1275 (EDS for Electric Double Spanish) emerged as the most popular.

The first version was an unusual design, with hollowbody and carved spruce top with no soundholes, but Gibson changed it to the more practical SG design around 1962 and put it into regular production. Doublenecks did not sell well, however, and Gibson discontinued them in 1968.

As rock'n'roll players discovered doublenecks, demand grew and Gibson revived the EDS-1275 in 1977. Thanks to regular use by such guitarists as Alex Lifeson of Rush, Charlie Whitney of Family, Steve Howe of Yes, and Jimmy Page of Led Zeppelin, the EDS-1275 remains in production today.

151

MODEL
**Gibson EDS-1275
(SG body shape)**

YEAR
1966

PRODUCTION
**Circa 1962 to 1967,
1977 to current**

GIBSON

Gibson was well-established by the mid 1950s as Fender's top competitor, but while Fender pushed solidbody guitar design to a new level with the Stratocaster, Gibson was coming up with little more than cosmetic changes. Leo Fender allegedly made remarks about Gibson being a stodgy old company, and Gibson president Ted McCarty responded in 1958 with not one but three angular solidbody shapes – the Flying V, Explorer, and Moderne – that threw traditional designs out the window.

The Flying V was the most successful (the Moderne was not produced at all), and such influential players as bluesman Albert King and early rocker Lonnie Mack became closely identified with their original Flying Vs. However, most Vs ended up as unsold attention-grabbers in dealers' windows. After shipping only 98 instruments, Gibson gave up.

The V turned out to be only a few years ahead of its time, as Gibson found out when they reintroduced it in late 1965. Within two years, Jimi Hendrix began playing Flying Vs, and the model found a permanent home on the cutting edge of rock'n'roll.

MODEL
Gibson Flying V

YEAR
1959

PRODUCTION
1958 to 1959

GIBSON electric solidbody

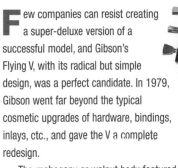

Few companies can resist creating a super-deluxe version of a successful model, and Gibson's Flying V, with its radical but simple design, was a perfect candidate. In 1979, Gibson went far beyond the typical cosmetic upgrades of hardware, bindings, inlays, etc., and gave the V a complete redesign.

The mahogany or walnut body featured a contrasting layer of maple that, when the edges were beveled, created a sort of accent stripe that added curves within the straight lines of body outline. Reinforcing the V-shape were a pair of pickups whose coils had been split and angled to form a V; they were quickly nicknamed "boomerang" pickups.

Gibson introduced the new model as the Flying V II (or V2, as the truss-rod cover says) in 1979, but as it turned out, the basic model needed only a boost, not a make-over. Gibson changed the body of the standard model from mahogany to alder, put hotter pickups in it, and renamed it the Flying V I in 1981; the V II was gone within a year.

MODEL
Gibson Flying V II

YEAR
1981

PRODUCTION
1979 to 1982

153

The Explorer was the second of Gibson president Ted McCarty's three Modernistic designs. Gibson debuted the Explorer with the Flying V in 1958, but the V made the 1958 catalog while the Explorer did not, and the Explorer lagged well behind the V in production as well as sales.

The earliest version of the Explorer featured a "split" V-shaped headstock, which was the way McCarty drew it in his patent for the model. The design required the longer strings to bend around the tuner posts, however, and the split headstock was quickly replaced by a more practical and functional "scimitar" shape with six-on-a-side tuner configuration.

The Explorer's body was essentially a distorted and angled version of a standard guitar, complete with upper and lower bouts and body waists, and in that respect it was less radical than the Flying V's, but the Explorer's huge "tail fin" made it feel heavy and unwieldy compared to the lighter Flying V, and when the Flying V failed to generate sales, the Explorer never had a chance.

MODEL
Gibson Explorer (split headstock)

YEAR
1958

PRODUCTION
1958

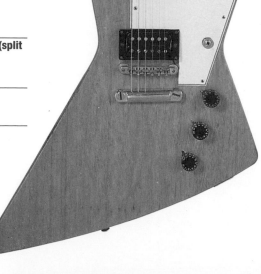

Gibson's quick redesign of the Explorer's headstock from the split-V to the curved "scimitar" shape could not save the model. Gibson shipping records do not list the Explorer specifically in 1958 and '59, only "Korina (Mod. Gtr)," and the total for those two years is a meager 22 instruments.

Unlike the Flying V, which Gibson successfully reintroduced in the 1960s, the Explorer remained out of production until the mid 1970s, when guitarists intent on pushing rock'n'roll to new limits began looking for an untraditional guitar to identify their music. In 1975, prompted by Hamer's introduction of a similar model and by Eric Clapton's appearance in a Music Man amplifier ad playing an original Explorer, Gibson brought back the Explorer.

James Hetfield of Metallica and Mathias Jabs of the Scorpions established the Explorer as an identification badge for heavy metal guitarists. Dave Grohl of the Foo Fighters and The Edge of U2 have also wielded Explorers. And the model received immortality of a sort when played by the character portrayed by Nigel Tufnel in the film *This Is Spinal Tap.*

MODEL
**Gibson Explorer
(curved headstock)**

YEAR
**Early 1960s (from
leftover parts)**

PRODUCTION
1958 to 1959

155

GIBSON

Ray Dietrich was an automotive designer, famous for his work with Chrysler, Packard and Lincoln, who by the early 1960s was retired and living in Kalamazoo, Michigan, home of Gibson guitars. Gibson president Ted McCarty invited Dietrich to design a guitar, and the result was the Firebird series of 1963.

The original version of the Firebird is known as "reverse body," and that is exactly what Dietrich did. He reversed the conventional solidbody shape, making the upper treble horn longer than the bass horn and extending the lower bass bout. (McCarty had gone in the same direction, but to an extreme, with his Explorer of 1958.) The peghead, too, was reversed, with all the tuners on the treble side. To make this configuration workable, Gibson used banjo-style tuners rather than the standard right-angle design.

The heart of Dietrich's design was a nine-ply neck that continued through the body. This "neck-thru" design eliminated the neck joint and provided a strong, unbroken connection between neck and body – a critical element in solidbody performance. Gibson introduced four Firebirds in 1963, with the single-pickup Firebird I as the basic model.

MODEL
**Gibson Firebird I
(reverse body)**

YEAR
1964

PRODUCTION
1963 to 1965

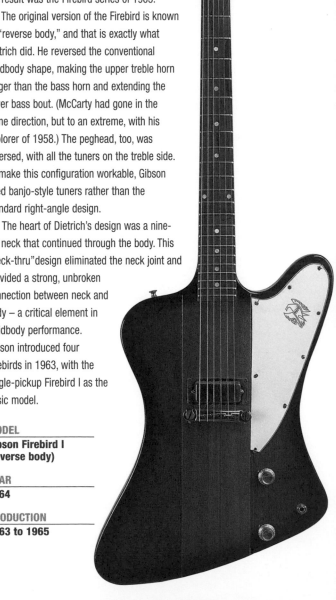

156

The Firebird V was the equivalent to Gibson's Les Paul Standard or SG Standard, identifiable by its trapezoidal fingerboard inlays. Gibson stopped making the original reverse-body style in 1965, but this version appeared in the hands of up-and-coming bluesman Johnny Winter when he made his major-label debut in 1969, and to this day, Winter has been the most visible and consistent proponent of the Firebird V.

Part of the Firebird's appeal was its smaller double-coil "mini-humbucking" pickups, which produced a more cutting tone than the thick-sounding, full-size humbuckers that Gibson had invented and introduced in 1957. Not only was it perfect for the blues that Johnny Winter played, it provided an alternative sound in the arsenal of numerous players, including Eric Clapton, Allen Collins of Lynyrd Skynyrd, Noel Gallahger of Oasis, Dave Grohl of Foo Fighters, Paul Stanley of KISS and Rolling Stones Brian Jones, Keith Richards and Mick Taylor.

When Gibson began reissuing the Firebird in 1972, the Firebird V was the base model, and it returned permanently to regular production in 1990.

MODEL
Gibson Firebird V (reverse body)

YEAR
1965

PRODUCTION
1963 to 1965

GIBSON

In the 1950s, Gibson had successfully split the original Les Paul design into four distinct models, delineated by pickups and ornamentation, and Gibson continued the pattern with the SG-shaped Les Pauls in 1961 and the Firebirds of 1963.

The Firebird I corresponded to the Les Paul Junior, with a single pickup, unbound fingerboard and dot inlays. The Firebird III had the same features as the Special. The Firebird V was the Standard. And at the top of the line, the Firebird VII was the equivalent of the Les Paul Custom, with three pickups, ebony fingerboard, pearl block inlays and gold-plated hardware.

Although the Firebird V, like the Les Paul Standard, has been the mainstay of the line, the Firebird VII has had its share of devotees. Phil Manzanera of Roxy Music was one of the earliest, using his VII onstage and in the studio in the early 1970s. More recent Firebird VII players include Gem Archer with Oasis, Kenny Olson with Kid Rock, Andy Abad with Marc Antony, and Peter Stroud with Sheryl Crow.

MODEL

**Gibson Firebird VII
(reverse body)**

YEAR

1964

PRODUCTION

1963 to 1965

Prior to Ted McCarty's patents on the Flying V, Explorer and Moderne, few guitar bodies varied far enough from tradition to warrant patent protection. Fender had not tried to patent the Telecaster or Stratocaster but, possibly as a result of McCarty's action, Leo Fender obtained a patent on the Jazzmaster body that Fender introduced in 1958.

Fender's patent covered one of the Jazzmaster's least noticeable features – offset waists. The typical guitar body (even Gibson's radical Explorer) curved inward at the same point on both sides, but the Jazzmaster's waists were offset to provide a more comfortable playing position for a seated guitarist. Gibson's Firebirds had slightly offset waists, and Fender complained.

Gibson used the complaint as an excuse to make the Firebird more conventional, reversing the body, giving rise to the term "non-reverse" for those models, and shortening the horns. At the same time, Gibson made the Firebird easier to produce by discarding the neck-thru-body design for a traditional set (glued-in) neck. The makeover, implemented in 1965, effectively clipped the Firebirds' wings, and they faded out of production in 1969.

159

MODEL
**Gibson Firebird I
(non-reverse body)**

YEAR
1965

PRODUCTION
1965 to 1969

With the Firebird's changeover from the original "reverse" body to the squatter "non-reverse" style of 1965, Gibson seemed to lose more than the innovative ideas of Firebird designer Ray Dietrich. The company lost a sense of model identification that it had established ten years earlier in the Les Paul line.

The lowest model in the Les Paul, SG, and Firebird lines had always had a single pickup. Now the non-reverse Firebird I had two pickups. The highest model had been the only one with three pickups, but now the Firebird III had three pickups as well. The Firebird V and VII did have humbuckers while the Firebird I and III had single-coils – a difference that was shared with the Les Paul and SG lines – but all four models had the lowest of Gibson's fingerboard ornamentation: pearl dot inlays and no binding.

The Firebirds simply lost their identity, along with their flair, and they were gone within five years. Gibson's Custom Shop offered a modernized reissue in 2002, but it fared even worse, lasting only two years.

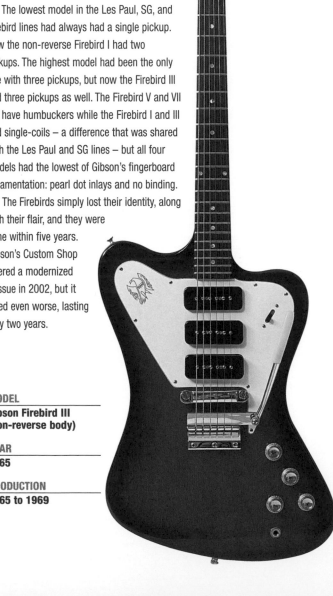

MODEL
Gibson Firebird III
(non-reverse body)

YEAR
1965

PRODUCTION
1965 to 1969

In an effort to bring the electric guitar into the modern world of solid-state electronics, Gibson created a model series in the late 1970s with "active" electronics, including expansion and compression controls, powered by an onboard nine-volt battery. Gibson developed the circuitry in conjunction with the Moog synthesizer company, which Norlin, Gibson's parent company, had acquired in 1973.

To reflect the high-tech creative atmosphere, Gibson named them RD, the commonplace techno-scientific abbreviation for Research & Development. The RD Artist, introduced in 1979, was the most expensive of the three models (the lowest version did not have active electronics), and the Artist designation branched out to include traditional models that were fitted with active circuitry, e.g., ES-Artist, L.P. Artist and SG Artist.

While the RD models did have an intriguing body shape that looked like a softer, curvier version of the original reverse-body Firebirds, and while high-fidelity electronics seemed like a good idea on paper, guitarists ultimately wanted a Gibson simply to sound like Gibsons had sounded since the late 1950s, and the RD models were gone by 1972.

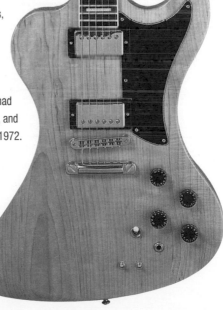

161

MODEL
Gibson RD Artist

YEAR
1979

PRODUCTION
1978 to 1981

GRETSCH

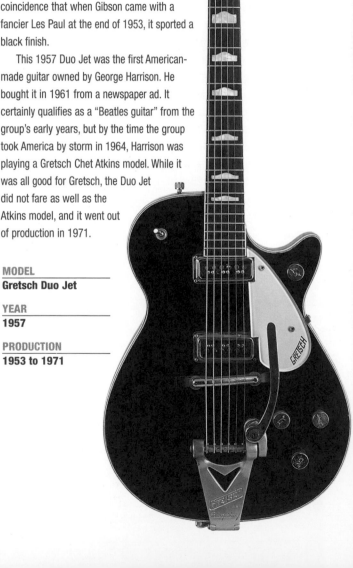

Gretsch initially ignored Leo Fender's solid guitars of 1950, but when Gibson jumped into the market with the Les Paul Model in 1952, Gretsch followed quickly with its first solidbody.

The Duo Jet of 1953 had a similar body to the Gibson, but its extra layers of body binding and its bound peghead gave it an extra level of ornamentation, and the black finish added a degree of elegance. It was probably no coincidence that when Gibson came with a fancier Les Paul at the end of 1953, it sported a black finish.

This 1957 Duo Jet was the first American-made guitar owned by George Harrison. He bought it in 1961 from a newspaper ad. It certainly qualifies as a "Beatles guitar" from the group's early years, but by the time the group took America by storm in 1964, Harrison was playing a Gretsch Chet Atkins model. While it was all good for Gretsch, the Duo Jet did not fare as well as the Atkins model, and it went out of production in 1971.

MODEL
Gretsch Duo Jet

YEAR
1957

PRODUCTION
1953 to 1971

Gretsch's 1955 catalog had the company's calling card right on the cover, with its high-end hollowbody electrics shown in yellow, green, and white finishes in addition to a traditional sunburst. In the solidbody line, the Gretsch Silver Jet took finish colors to the next level with a gleaming silver sparkle finish that was a step beyond the capabilities of its competitors.

In the middle years of the 20th century, Gretsch was as successful a drum maker as it was a guitar company. So when it came to creating an eye-catching guitar finish, rather than spraying lacquer with metallic particles – as Gibson did on its "goldtop" Les Paul Model – Gretsch simply "finished" its guitars with silver-sparkle drum coverings, giving them a more dramatic sparkle effect than any metallic paint.

As a company, Gretsch was even older than Gibson, but while Gibson fought its image as a stodgy traditional company, the Silver Jet had a flair that permeated the entire Gretsch line and underscored Gretsch's claim on its 1955 catalog – Guitars for Moderns.

MODEL
Gretsch Silver Jet
(single cutaway)

YEAR
1955

PRODUCTION
1955 to 1960

GRETSCH

Gretsch not only followed Gibson into the solidbody market in the early 1950s, Gretsch also followed Gibson's lead in enlisting a famous guitarist to promote its solidbodies. Chet Atkins was by no means as famous as Les Paul – no guitarist was – in late 1954, but he was on the verge of his first pop success ("Mr. Sandman" in 1955), and he would go on to be far more influential than Paul.

Gretsch gave Atkins his own semi-hollow and solidbody models, and Atkins's only requests were a vibrato and, for more sustain, a metal nut. Gretsch's Jimmie Webster had just created the Gretsch Round-Up in 1954 with full western ornamentation, which seemed to be appropriate for a country artist. (Record companies treated "country & western" as a single genre at the time.) With the substitution of the metal nut and the vibrato, the Chet Atkins Solid Bbody was created.

Atkins never cared for the western features, and his later models were not western-themed, but his signature Solid Body retained the same western look until it was discontinued in 1963.

MODEL
Gretsch Chet Atkins Solid Body

YEAR
1956

PRODUCTION
1955 to 1962

Gretsch had battled with Gibson and Epiphone in the pre-World War II acoustic arena with such flashy features as cat's eye soundholes on archtops and a triangular soundhole on flat-tops. In the postwar years, Gretsch continued to attract attention with aesthetic touches, especially finish colors, illustrated by a Duo Jet style solidbody with a bright red top. Gretsch introduced it in 1955 as the Jet Fire Bird.

The red-topped Gretsch did not affect Gretsch's sales as much as it did competitors' guitars. Within three years, Gibson changed the finish on the Les Paul Junior from sunburst to a red stain, and the Les Paul Standard changed from gold to a red sunburst. At the same time, Fender added a red layer to its regular sunburst and introduced a standard palette of custom finish colors.

Unlike Gibson and Fender, however, Gretsch heightened the impact of its color options by treating each as a different model. The Jet Fire Bird, though it followed all the spec changes of the black Duo Jet, kept its own identity through to its ultimate demise in 1971.

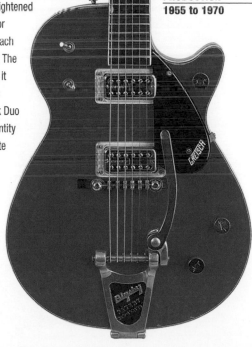

MODEL
Gretsch Jet Fire Bird

YEAR
1960

PRODUCTION
1955 to 1970

165

GRETSCH

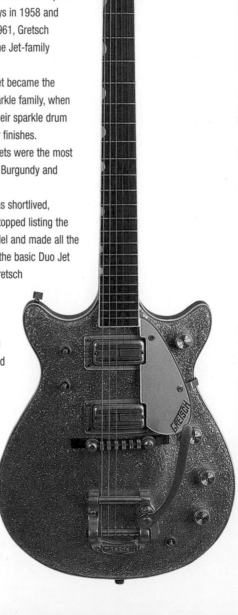

For all of Gretsch's flash and fanfare, when it came down to basics, Gretsch followed Gibson – in entering the solidbody market, enlisting a famous endorser, implementing humbucking pickups, and finally, adopting a double-cutaway body shape. Gibson had given its lower Les Paul Junior and Special a boost with double-cutaways in 1958 and 1959, respectively and, in 1961, Gretsch followed suit, changing all the Jet-family models to double-cutaway.

A year later, the Silver Jet became the patriarch of an unofficial sparkle family, when Gretsch officially made all their sparkle drum coverings available as guitar finishes. Champagne Jets and Gold Jets were the most popular choices after Silver; Burgundy and Tangerine were also listed.

The flash of notoriety was shortlived, however. In 1963, Gretsch stopped listing the Silver Jet as a separate model and made all the sparkle finishes optional on the basic Duo Jet models. Three years later, Gretsch stopped offering sparkle finishes officially, but this 1969 example shows that sparkles were available until the Duo Jet was discontinued in 1971.

MODEL
**Gretsch Silver Jet
(double cutaway)**

YEAR
1969

PRODUCTION
1961 to 1969

Gretsch's Astro Jet appeared in 1965 with a unique design that today looks like an early casualty of the drug culture that would permeate rock music by the end of the decade.

The double-cutaway body had elongated bouts on the upper bass and lower treble side, but they bulged awkwardly where the guitars of other makers had sleek, angular lines. The peghead appeared to have been left out in the sun too long, to the point that only two tuners would fit on the treble side.

Unfortunately for Gretsch, the Astro Jet was not just an aberration in an otherwise successful history of solidbody design. Instead, it was the model that, for all practical purposes, signaled the end of Gretsch's prominence in the solidbody market. Two years later, the Baldwin piano company acquired Gretsch and wisely deleted the Astro Jet, but aside from a pair of Chet Atkins solidbodies in the mid-1970s, none of Gretsch's subsequent owners ever came up with another respectable solidbody model.

MODEL
Gretsch Astro Jet

YEAR
1966

PRODUCTION
1965 to 1967

GUILD

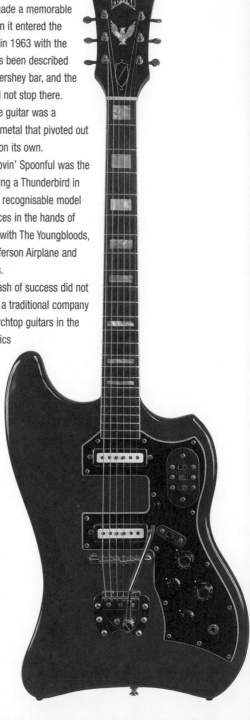

The Guild company made a memorable first impression when it entered the solidbody electric market in 1963 with the Thunderbird. The body has been described as resembling a melted Hershey bar, and the unconventional design did not stop there. Installed in the back of the guitar was a "kickstand" – a length of metal that pivoted out so the guitar could stand on its own.

Zal Yanovsky of The Lovin' Spoonful was the most visible guitarist playing a Thunderbird in the mid 1960s. The easily recognisable model also made spot appearances in the hands of Banana (Lowell Levinger) with The Youngbloods, Jorma Kaukonen with Jefferson Airplane and blues great Muddy Waters.

The Thunderbird's splash of success did not change Guild's identity as a traditional company – a respected maker of archtop guitars in the 1950s and flat-top acoustics in the 1960s. Guild replaced the Thunderbird in 1970 with the S-100 line, which was more conventional – similar to a Gibson SG – and more successful than the Thunderbird.

MODEL
Guild Thunderbird

YEAR
1966

PRODUCTION
1963 to 1968

After languishing through the 1970s with unremarkable solidbody guitars, Guild surprised the guitar world with an eye-catching "flying star" model in 1981. The X-79 Skyhawk was one of four Guild models with the stretched, four-point body shape. It was soon joined by the X-80 Skylark (soon to be renamed Swan), the X-82 Nova (soon to be Starfighter), and the X-88 Motley Crue model, plus three more variations with bolt-on necks.

Guild equipped the X-79 with all the right features, including humbucking pickups (two or three), a coil tap or phase control, an optional Kahler vibrato, and an array of finishes ranging from traditional sunburst to black sparkle to purple.

As Guild had discovered with the Thunderbird-style solidbodies of the1960s, guitar buyers thought of tradition rather than innovation when they thought of Guild guitars. By the time a new ownership group acquired Guild in 1986, the flying stars had proven to be shooting stars, and they had all fizzled out.

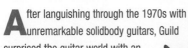

169

MODEL
Guild X-79

YEAR
1984

PRODUCTION
1981 to 1985

HAGSTROM

Hagstrom's greatest international
success came in the late 1960s,
when the brand became synonymous
with fast, thin necks. But, as this 1959
model P46 Deluxe shows, Hagstrom
guitars had been attracting attention with
innovative designs as well as flashy looks
since the Swedish company entered the
guitar market in 1958.

The sparkle finish and pearloid
fingerboard of the P46 were standard
ornamentation elements found on accordions,
and Hagstrom had, in fact, started out as an
accordion company, founded in 1921 in
Älvdalen, Sweden, by Albin Hagstrom. The
pushbutton controls of the P46 were also
inspired by accordion designs, and they
activated different electronic circuits as well
as pickup combinations. With the use of roller
controls for tone and volume, Hagstrom
eliminated standard control knobs
altogether from the P46.

The Les Paul-inspired
single-cutaway body gave
way in the 1960s to
Hagstroms (marketed in
the U.K. under the Futurama
brand) with a Stratocaster
body shape and a unique,
vinyl-covered back. The
company fell victim to
inexpensive Asian
imports in the
1980s.

MODEL
Hagstrom P46

YEAR
1959

PRODUCTION
**Late 1950s to early
1960s**

Hamer, based in the Chicago area, made its name in the late 1970s on the strength of Gibson-inspired models, such as the Standard (based on the Explorer) and the Sunburst (based on the double-cutaway Les Paul Special), but as soon as the company established a solid following among guitarists, Hamer began introducing its own original designs.

The Phantom A5 of 1984 – like its 1981 predecessor, the Prototype – had a fairly conventional body design that was basically a longhorn Stratocaster. "Fat Strats," with a humbucker in the bridge position, were becoming a popular modification to give Fenders a more powerful sound, and Hamer appeared to take the concept to the extreme with a triple-coil bridge pickup. A pair of switches offered conventional switching (bridge, neck or both), but the second switch allowed only a humbucker-or-single option for the triple-coil, making it effectively only a Fat Strat with a relocated middle pickup.

Andy Summers of The Police had a Phantom in his arsenal of Hamers, but it remained an obscure model and did not survive Hamer's acquisition by Kaman Music (Ovation's parent company) in 1988.

171

MODEL
Hamer Phantom A5

YEAR
1984

PRODUCTION
1984 to 1988

HOFNER

Hofner was founded in Germany in the 1880s by Karl Höfner, a maker of bowed instruments. The company was able to rebound after World War II and, thanks in part to the absence of American-made guitars in Britain, to establish a strong market there with electric and acoustic guitars that had the appearance, at least, of high-quality instruments.

When restrictions on American imports were lifted in 1959, Hofner enjoyed continued success in the 1960s by basing its solidbodies on the most popular American models. The body of this Galaxie from 1965 is a Fender Jazzmaster from the waist down, combined with the upper horns of a Fender Stratocaster.

When it came to ornamentation and electronics, however, Hofner did have its own style. The most obvious Hofner "signature" element on the Galaxie is found on the fingerboard in the horizontal bands that function as fret markers. And following the lead of Swedish-based Hagstrom, Hofner eliminated all conventional knobs, replacing them with an array of roller controls and switches.

172

MODEL
Hofner Galaxie

YEAR
Circa 1965

PRODUCTION
1960s

Perhaps in response to the Stratocaster-inspired, Swedish-made Hagstrom models that featured a vinyl covered back, the German-based Hofner company served up Model 175 in the late 1960s with a body completely covered in vinyl. But where the vinyl on the Hagstroms had the color-coordinated look of upscale automotive upholstery, the vinyl on the Hofner looked as if it might have been taken from a kitchen floor.

Aside from the vinyl covering, Model 175 was very similar to the Hofner Galaxie, with three pickups, numerous roller controls, a distinctive vibrato, a string mute, and Hofner's signature full-width fingerboard markers.

Hofner achieved considerable notoriety in the 1960s – not as a result of the 175 but on the strength of a violin-style hollow bass used by The Beatles' Paul McCartney. The company went through a series of ownership changes beginning in 1994, and although vintage-style Hofner instruments (primarily acoustics, hollow electrics, and basses) are still produced and distributed worldwide, the vinyl-covered 175 is mercifully not included in the current offering.

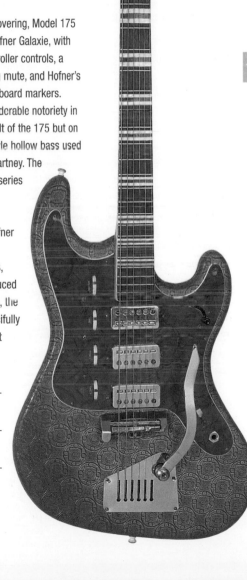

MODEL
Hofner 175

YEAR
Circa 1968

PRODUCTION
Late 1960s

173

Ibanez is the best known brand of Hoshino Gakki Ten, a Japanese company that started in the guitar business in the 1920s as an importer. In 1962, the company broke into the U.S. market the easy way, by forming a business partnership with American dealer Harry Rosenbloom of Ardmore, Pennsylvania, who was selling guitars under the Elger brand.

Model 882 was one of the earliest Ibanez-brand solidbodies. Ironically, Ibanez was still only producing acoustic guitars at the time, so the 882 was out-sourced to other Japanese makers. It was obviously based on Fender's Jazzmaster but, with its rocker-button controls and its simple, Bigsby-like vibrato, it was not an outright copy.

Through the 1960s, Ibanez maintained its own identity with models largely inspired by Burns of London, but they fell by the wayside in the 1970s when Japanese companies began unashamedly copying classic Gibsons and Fenders. The "copy era" ended when Gibson's filed a patent infringement suit against Elger in 1977, after which Ibanez went on to become one of the most respected of Japanese makers.

MODEL
Ibanez 882

YEAR
Circa 1963

PRODUCTION
Early 1960s

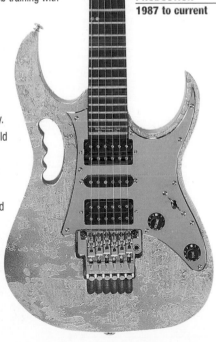

One of Ibanez's most successful signature models does not bear the artist's name, but any guitarist familiar with the Ibanez JEM knows it was designed by Steve Vai.

In the mid 1980s, Ibanez was scrambling to compete with Kramer and Jackson's "Super Strat" designs – basically a Stratocaster with a bridge-position humbucker and a "dive bomb" vibrato. At the same time, Vai was emerging as one of the most gifted guitarists in rock'n'roll, with hotshot technique from the Berklee School of Music and eclectic on-the-job training with Frank Zappa.

Vai and Ibanez created a personalized model featuring Dimarzio pickups (including humbuckers in the neck and bridge positions) and the "monkey grip" hole in the body. However, he felt his name would not sell enough guitars, so he suggested JEM, the name of a company owned by Joe Despagni, Vai's childhood friend and longtime guitar tech. Vai introduced the JEM playing on David Lee Roth's 1988 album *Skyscraper*, and the JEM's monkey grip remains a familiar sight in Ibanez's solidbody line.

MODEL
Ibanez JEM

YEAR
1989

PRODUCTION
1987 to current

Joe "Satch" Satriani was one of the most prominent rock guitar teachers when he introduced his virtuoso style to the masses with his 1986 solo album *Not of This Earth*. Within a year he was featured in Ibanez ads, and a year later he was an official endorser, playing Ibanez guitars onstage as the lead guitarist behind Rolling Stones singer Mick Jagger on Jagger's solo tour.

In 1990, Ibanez advertised a new JS signature model sporting a gleaming chrome finish, but when it appeared in stores, the JS1 had a standard paint finish. Like Ibanez's JEM guitars, which were designed by one of Satriani's former students, Steve Vai, the JS models featured Satriani's preferred setup – Dimarzio pickups in a humbucker-single-humbucker configuration.

In 1998, a decade after Satriani's official association with Ibanez, the company honored him with the JS 10th Anniversary. Nicknamed "Chrome Boy," the limited-edition model featured a pair of humbuckers rather than JS's typical HSH arrangement, and the twin humbuckers continue today as the standard offering on Ibanez's JS models.

176

MODEL
Ibanez JS 10th Anniversary

YEAR
1988

PRODUCTION
1988

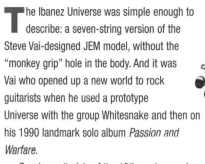

The Ibanez Universe was simple enough to describe: a seven-string version of the Steve Vai-designed JEM model, without the "monkey grip" hole in the body. And it was Vai who opened up a new world to rock guitarists when he used a prototype Universe with the group Whitesnake and then on his 1990 landmark solo album *Passion and Warfare*.

Russian guitarists of the 19th century and American jazz guitarists of the 20th century made use of the extra low string to provide additional harmonic possibilities, but they could not have dreamed of the power that Vai coaxed from the lower strings.

Introduced in three different versions in 1990, several of which sported green highlights, the Universe appeared to be a flash in the pan, and Ibanez actually discontinued it in 1995, just as the group Korn was using a Universe to create the monster low-end rhythm that would help define the alternative metal and nu-metal movements. Ibanez successfully reintroduced the Universe in 1996 and has since added less-expensive seven-strings in its RG line.

MODEL
Ibanez Universe

YEAR
1990

PRODUCTION
1990 to 1994,
1996 to current

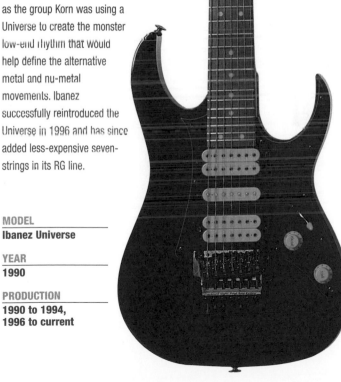

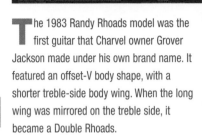

The 1983 Randy Rhoads model was the first guitar that Charvel owner Grover Jackson made under his own brand name. It featured an offset-V body shape, with a shorter treble-side body wing. When the long wing was mirrored on the treble side, it became a Double Rhoads.

Dave Linsk, who would become best known as the guitarist for the thrash band Overkill, had this Double Rhoads custom built for him in 1984. Robbin Crosby of RATT got his own Double Rhoads, which Jackson renamed the King V. After Dave Mustaine of Megadeth custom-ordered a King V in 1985, Jackson created a signature production model for Mustaine.

Randy Rhoads, who had gained fame in 1979 in the band of former Black Sabbath singer Ozzy Osbourne, was killed in a plane crash in 1982 at age 25, but he continues to be a strong influence on heavy metal guitarists, and his offset-V signature model remains one of the representative models of the innovative Charvel/Jackson company.

MODEL
Jackson Double Rhoads

YEAR
1984

PRODUCTION
1984

Grover Jackson merged his namesake company with International Music Corporation, a Texas-based importer, in 1986 and then left the business in 1989. IMC continued to introduce new designs, including the Stealth series in 1991.

IMC aimed at affluent buyers with the American-made Custom Shop series and a U.S. Series featuring airbrushed finishes, but the Stealth models kept Jackson's within the reach of the majority of players. They featured bodies of ash or basswood with the typical Jackson pickup and vibrato options. This Stealth TH2 from 1996 shows that IMC was not afraid of trading off one of Jackson's most identifiable elements, the angular pointed headstock, in exchange for a new headstock shape that provided straight string pull (a trademark feature of 1985 upstart Paul Reed Smith).

The Stealth Series last only until 1996, and IMC lasted only until 1997, when it sold Jackson/Charvel to the Japanese-based Akai company. Five years later Akai sold the brand to Fender, where such classic Jacksons as the Soloist, Rhoads and King V live on today.

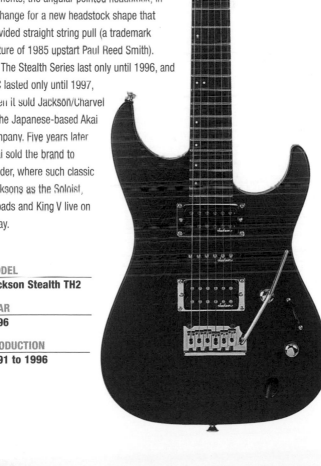

MODEL
Jackson Stealth TH2

YEAR
1996

PRODUCTION
1991 to 1996

KRAMER

While the early metal-neck Kramers attracted a lot of attention, they did not attract buyers, and management of the struggling company was taken over for a brief period (around 1980–81) by Guitar Center, the Los Angeles-based retail chain. During that time Kramer switched to more-conventional wood necks.

The elongated, four-point star shape of this Voyager Imperial, introduced in 1981, shows that not every element of Kramer's new designs was conventional. The single humbucking pickup was also unconventional, but it reflected the personal preference of the hottest guitarist of 1981, Eddie Van Halen.

The key element on this model was the Floyd Rose vibrato, which allowed extreme pitch changes while remaining in tune and consequently was becoming essential equipment for rock guitarists. In 1982, Kramer became the exclusive distributor for Floyd Rose, and that relationship helped seal the deal on an endorsement from Eddie Van Halen. Van Halen's two-handed fingerboard tapping and "dive bomb" vibrato techniques had made him the most influential guitarist of the era, and Kramer became one of the most visible guitar brands of the decade.

MODEL
Kramer Voyager Imperial (rounded tips)

YEAR
1982

PRODUCTION
1981 to 1984

KRAMER lectric solidbody

Kramer's American Sustainer of 1989 featured a Floyd Rose vibrato (as did most Kramers) along with a Floyd Rose-designed, distortion-generating humbucker in the bridge position. The Floyd Rose connection had been the foundation of Kramer's prosperity through the 1980s, but ironically, it was also the ultimate reason for Kramer's demise at end of the decade.

Kramer simply became a victim of its own success. As Kramer sold thousands of guitars with Floyd Rose's patented vibrato system, unpaid royalties piled up. Floyd Rose sued in 1990 to collect those royalties, and that was effectively the killing blow for Kramer.

The company's original financial backer, Henry Vaccarro, tried to revive Kramer in 1995, but after a handful of guitars were produced, the company was sold out of bankruptcy to Gibson in 1997. For the better part of a decade Gibson barely kept the brand alive as a cheap import line managed by its Epiphone division. In 2006, Epiphone pumped up the Kramer line with a new wave of imported reissues as well as several U.S.-made models.

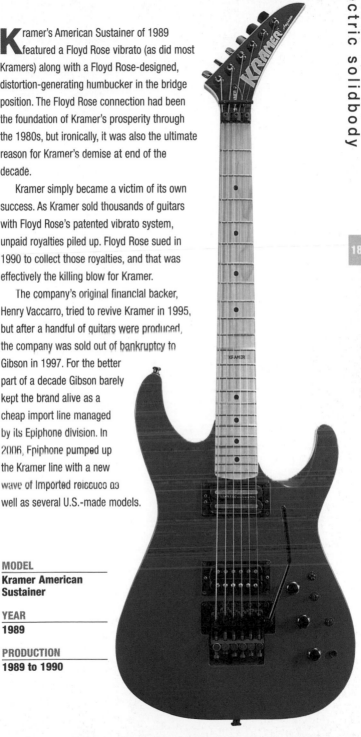

181

MODEL
Kramer American Sustainer

YEAR
1989

PRODUCTION
1989 to 1990

MELOBAR

Walt Smith of Sweet, Idaho, invented the Melobar in the 1960s so that steel guitarists – traditionally confined to a chair – could look as cool onstage as conventional guitarists. The Melobar gave them an instrument that was designed to be played standing up.

Smith took a steel guitar and rotated it 45 degrees along the axis of its strings, providing a more natural, comfortable playing position than that of a steel guitar played in the lap. The rest of the instrument's design was cosmetic but no less important. The steel guitar part was attached to a cool guitar body that ranged in shape from this generic double-cutaway Skreemr model to the angular lines of a Gibson Explorer.

Such prominent steel players as David Lindley with Jackson Browne, Rusty Young with Poco, and Cindy Cashdollar with Asleep at the Wheel have played them onstage occasionally, but Melobars never gained widespread acceptance. Walt Smith's son Ted carried on the company after Walt's death in 1990, but they were struggling to stay in business by the end of 2007.

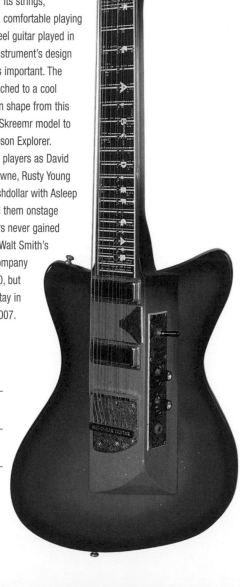

MODEL

Melobar Skreemr

YEAR

Circa 1973

PRODUCTION

1967 to current

The signature feature of Micro-Frets guitars was not in the fretwork, as the name would suggest, but in the nut – or to be technically correct, the six individually adjustable nuts that were intended to provide better intonation.

The segmented, adjustable nut was one of three innovative features developed by Ralph Jones of Frederick, Maryland, who founded the company with financial backer Marion Huggins in 1967. Early models featured a body with a routed top and routed back that were joined at the sides. Within a year he had introduced the Calibrato, a vibrato designed to provide better intonation by taking into account the differences in string gauges.

The bodies of Micro-Frets models typically had a modern element, like the pointed horns of this 1968 Signature, but with a body that looked a little overweight. And the micro-nut adjustment looked more useful than it actually was; it affected only the interval between the open string and the string played at the first fret. Jones died in 1973, and Micro-Frets guitars were gone within a year.

183

MODEL
Micro-Frets Signature

YEAR
Circa 1968

PRODUCTION
1967 to 1973

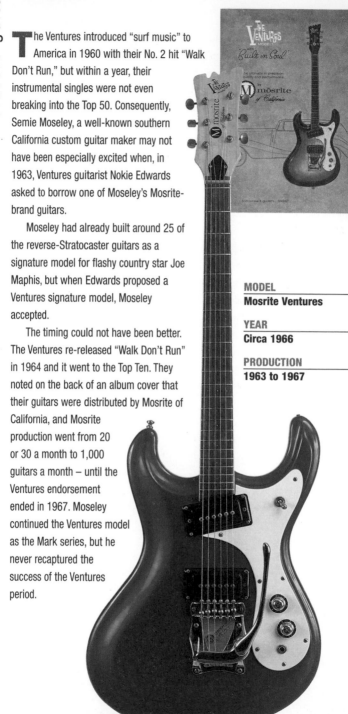

The Ventures introduced "surf music" to America in 1960 with their No. 2 hit "Walk Don't Run," but within a year, their instrumental singles were not even breaking into the Top 50. Consequently, Semie Moseley, a well-known southern California custom guitar maker may not have been especially excited when, in 1963, Ventures guitarist Nokie Edwards asked to borrow one of Moseley's Mosrite-brand guitars.

Moseley had already built around 25 of the reverse-Stratocaster guitars as a signature model for flashy country star Joe Maphis, but when Edwards proposed a Ventures signature model, Moseley accepted.

The timing could not have been better. The Ventures re-released "Walk Don't Run" in 1964 and it went to the Top Ten. They noted on the back of an album cover that their guitars were distributed by Mosrite of California, and Mosrite production went from 20 or 30 a month to 1,000 guitars a month – until the Ventures endorsement ended in 1967. Moseley continued the Ventures model as the Mark series, but he never recaptured the success of the Ventures period.

MODEL
Mosrite Ventures

YEAR
Circa 1966

PRODUCTION
1963 to 1967

It doesn't look much like a Ventures model, or any other Mosrite guitar, but the notches in the peghead forming the letter M clearly identify this oddball as one of Semie Moseley's creations.

Moseley used this skateboard-with-cutouts framework to create a green six-string, a red 12-string and a purple bass for the West Coast psychedelic band Strawberry Alarm Clark, a one-hit-wonder group who had a No. 1 record in 1967 with "Incense and Peppermints." Despite the odd, cumbersome-looking frame, the essentials were all there, including a pair of Mosrite pickups and (on the six-string) a Mosrite vibrato unit.

The finish work on the Strawberry Alarm Clock instruments was done by legendary hot-rod and motorcycle painter Von Dutch (the professional name of Kenny Howard), who was the first custom-builder to paint stripes and flames on motorcycles in the 1940s and '50s. Although Moseley fell on hard times shortly thereafter, the oddball guitars did not hurt Von Dutch's career, and his legacy continues today as Von Dutch Kustom Motorcycles.

MODEL
Mosrite Custom for Strawberry Alarm Clock

YEAR
Circa 1967

PRODUCTION
Circa 1967

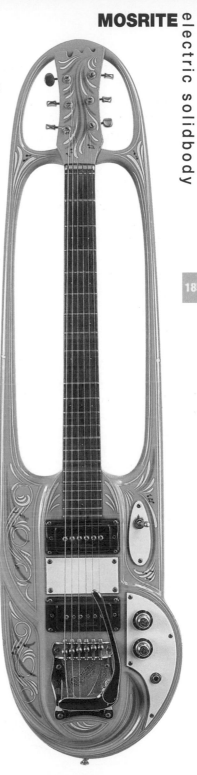

185

MOSRITE

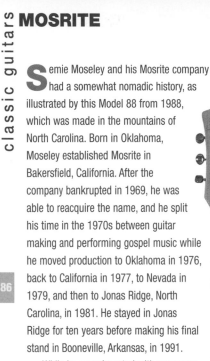

Semie Moseley and his Mosrite company had a somewhat nomadic history, as illustrated by this Model 88 from 1988, which was made in the mountains of North Carolina. Born in Oklahoma, Moseley established Mosrite in Bakersfield, California. After the company bankrupted in 1969, he was able to reacquire the name, and he split his time in the 1970s between guitar making and performing gospel music while he moved production to Oklahoma in 1976, back to California in 1977, to Nevada in 1979, and then to Jonas Ridge, North Carolina, in 1981. He stayed in Jonas Ridge for ten years before making his final stand in Booneville, Arkansas, in 1991.

While he experimented with numerous designs, Moseley's most popular were essentially Ventures reissues without the Ventures name. Model 88 had the familiar shape – which Moseley developed in the early 1960s by flipping over a Fender Stratocaster – but it lacked the pickguard and "German carve" (the elegant "lip" around the top edge) of the originals.

Semie Moseley died in 1992, and his widow Loretta continues the business today.

MODEL
Mosrite Model 88

YEAR
1988

PRODUCTION
1988

The Music-Man Stingray of 1976 marked the official return of Leo Fender to the guitar world after a ten year absence. Actually, he had been working with Music Man on amplifier designs for several years, but in secret, due to a non-compete clause in his 1965 agreement to sell the Fender company. The Stingray was his first post-Fender guitar.

Ex-Fender employees Forrest White and Tom Walker had formed their own company in 1971, calling it Tri-Sonic and Musitek before settling on Music Man in 1974. In 1975, they announced Leo Fender as president. A separate company owned by Fender, CLF Research, designed and built the instruments for Music Man.

The Stingray had an improved three-bolt neck system, but the rest of the design lacked the flair that players might have expected. The body was a little fatter than a Stratocaster and the headstock was smoother. Two humbucking pickups wore standard fare on Gibsons, but never on one of Leo's models. Business disagreements led to Leo's departure in 1978, and the Stingray guitar disappeared four years later.

MODEL
Music Man Stingray

YEAR
Circa 1978

PRODUCTION
1976 to 1982

MUSIC MAN

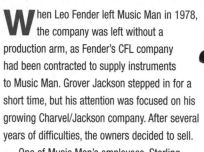

When Leo Fender left Music Man in 1978, the company was left without a production arm, as Fender's CFL company had been contracted to supply instruments to Music Man. Grover Jackson stepped in for a short time, but his attention was focused on his growing Charvel/Jackson company. After several years of difficulties, the owners decided to sell.

One of Music Man's employees, Sterling Ball, was the son of Ernie Ball, a musician, music store owner, string designer, and the maker of Earthwood acoustic basses in the early 1970s. In 1984 Ball became the new owner of Music Man, and he opened a new plant in San Luis Obispo, on the coast of California.

Ball was able to continue Music Man's success with the Sabre and Stingray basses, and in 1986 introduced his first new guitar, the Silhouette. Although it was basically a "Super Strat," it also featured such innovations as the four-and-two tuner arrangement, a Teflon-coated truss-rod for easier adjustment, and quick-change solderless pickup assemblies.

MODEL
Music Man Silhouette

YEAR
1988

PRODUCTION
1986 to current

Steve Lukather was already an in-demand session player when his melding of jazz and blues-rock influences gained national attention in 1978 as lead guitarist in the band Toto.

Through the 1980s, Lukather split his time between the group, session work, and a solo career, eventually participating in over 800 No. 1 albums as a guitarist, arranger or writer.

Lukather teamed up with Music Man in 1993 to create a signature model called the Luke. The body style was an elongated Stratocaster-inspired shape. The neck featured a deep-V profile, and the headstock sported the four-and-two tuner arrangement that had become a signature of Music Man's Ernie Ball era. The active pickups are in a humbucker-single single "Super Strat" configuration, and they are Lukather's design, too – a signature set made by EMG. The Floyd Rose vibrato completed the Super Strat features.

As Toto reached its 30th anniversary in 2008, Lukather was still the band's lead guitarist and the Music Man Luke was still in production.

MODEL
Music Man Luke

YEAR
1998

PRODUCTION
1993 to current

PARKER

The name Fly is a reference to boxing's lightest division, flyweight, but the Parker Fly represents a redesign of every element of the electric solidbody guitar.

Ken Parker began developing his ideas while repairing and customising instruments in a New York City guitar shop. His goal of minimising weight led not only to the minimalist shapes of his horns and headstocks but also to the use of carbon/glass fiber as a strengthening material. He also believed guitarists should be able to mix acoustic as well as traditional sounds, and to that end he partnered with acoustic pickup designer Larry Fishman. The Korg company (best known for synthesizers) financed the venture, and the Parker Fly debuted in 1992.

This Parker Nitefly from 1996 features three single-coil Dimarzio pickups in a traditional Stratocaster configuration, plus a Fishman piezo pickup in the bridge. The wood body – in this case maple – reflects Parker's belief that wood is as vital to the tone of an electric guitar as it is in an acoustic, and all Parker Fly models have a wood body.

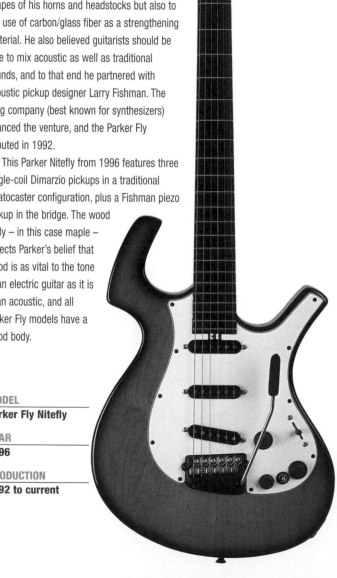

MODEL
Parker Fly Nitefly

YEAR
1996

PRODUCTION
1992 to current

AMIR DERAKH

The Parker Fly could not have been made without such modern materials as carbon fiber and epoxies, but Ken Parker felt that a wood-body was an integral part of a solidbody guitar's sound.

The Sitka spruce body of the Fly Artist model gave it the same tone-wood base as an acoustic guitar. An array of controls provided traditional volume and tone controls for the two humbuckers and the piezo. There was even a roller knob (below the bridge) for players to dial in their preferred tension on the vibrato unit.

The Fly shape debuted in 1992 and soon expanded to over three dozen models featuring every conceivable combination of pickups, woods, set or bolt-on neck, vibrato, or hardtail, etc. Although few guitarists embraced the Fly as their primary instrument, artists in virtually every style of music made good use of the Fly. Parker's endorsement list ranges from rockers Adrien Belew (David Bowie) and Joe Walsh (Eagles) to jazzers Phil Keaggy and Larry Coryell, and includes such diverse artists as bluesman Corey Harris, singer/songwriter Joni Mitchell, and country legend Merle Haggard.

MODEL
Parker Fly Artist

YEAR
1996

PRODUCTION
1996 to 2002

While dive-bomb vibrato units and dramatic body shapes carried a wave of upstart guitar companies through the 1980s, a new company called PRS introduced itself in 1985 with elegant refinements of traditional designs.

Paul Reed Smith, now based in Stevensville, Maryland, took his inspiration from the short-horn, asymmetrical double-cutaway shape of Gibson's low-end Les Paul Junior and Special of the late 1950s. His calling card was a contoured top of highly figured maple, the unbound edges of which gave his guitars the appearance of being bound with curly maple, but he redesigned almost every element of the traditional design. The result was a high-end instrument that appealed to guitar connoisseurs as well as to players.

Appropriate to Smith's ten-year background as a custom builder, he named the maple-top PRS model the Custom. He introduced his new guitar at the winter NAMM trade show in January 1985 and took orders. By the summer show his production team had made their first 20 instruments. Less than a year later, on June 16, 1987, the company celebrated its 1,000th guitar.

MODEL
Paul Reed Smith Custom

YEAR
1985

PRODUCTION
1985 to present

192

The PRS Standard, initially called simply the Paul Reed Smith Guitar, debuted along with the Custom in 1985. It had an all-mahogany body rather than the maple top of the Custom, but otherwise it sported all of the features that instantly identified a PRS guitar, including the "half-moon" figuration of the fingerboard inlays, the straight string-pull headstock shape, and a vibrato that stayed in tune.

The PRS pickup configuration was a standard two-humbucker setup, but the controls on the early models were anything but standard. The toggle switch, which, on most guitars of the day, would be a pickup selector, was actually a tone control – nicknamed the "sweet switch" – that rolled off high-end frequencies. One of the knobs was dedicated to a rotary pickup selector switch, and the other was a volume control; a tone control knob replaced the sweet switch in 1991.

MODEL
**Paul Reed Smith
Standard (24-frets)**

YEAR
1986

PRODUCTION
1985 to current

193

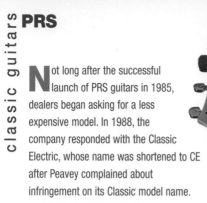

Not long after the successful launch of PRS guitars in 1985, dealers began asking for a less expensive model. In 1988, the company responded with the Classic Electric, whose name was shortened to CE after Peavey complained about infringement on its Classic model name.

The body of the CE had the same elegant shape of PRS's initial models, and the neck had the full 24-fret, two octave range. The cost-saving feature was a bolt-on neck. Because a bolt-on neck is a Fender feature, Paul Reed Smith made the CE more Fender-like with an alder body and a maple neck and fingerboard.

The Fender look did not fly, so a rosewood fingerboard, which had been an option, became standard in 1989, and the CE found a market. The other Fender-inspired feature, the alder body, lasted longer, but it was replaced by mahogany in 1995. A maple top option and 22-fret version secured the CE's position as a vital model of the PRS line.

194

MODEL
Paul Reed Smith CE (CE 24)

YEAR
1988

PRODUCTION
1988 to current

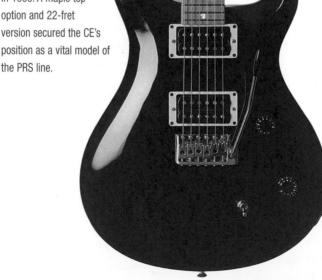

The expensive look of the original PRS models created a demand for even more expensive guitars and, within two years, Paul Reed Smith was making Signature models featuring the best woods available. He personally signed each one, but as the business grew he found himself traveling at times when guitars needed to be signed, so, in 1991, after 1,000 Signature models, he retired the Signature and replaced it with the Artist.

The Artist, standardized the Signature's high-end appointments. By this time, the optional "10-top" – a highly figured maple top cap – had become PRS's calling card, and the Artist went a step beyond, with a "10-plus" top. Bird inlays, another popular option, were standard on the Artist's Brazilian rosewood fingerboard. The only thing missing was Paul Reed Smith's personal signature, but he made up for it by inlaying the headstock signature with abalone pearl.

The Artist was not totally about cosmetics. The longer neck heel and the "wide fat" neck profile signaled Smith's dissatisfaction with his original design and were the first steps toward PRS's 22-fret models.

MODEL
**Paul Reed Smith
Artist I**

YEAR
1991

PRODUCTION
1991 to 1994

The PRS Dragon guitars were the realisation of a dream Paul Reed Smith had when he was 16. The first dragon model, introduced in 1992, was more than a showpiece, however. It featured several small but fundamental changes in the standard PRS design.

If anyone got past the dragon inlays on the neck, they would have noticed that it had only 22 frets, which was two less than all the other PRS guitars. It was one result of Smith's desire to improve on the 24-fret neck. The shorter neck (though not shorter scale length) made it stiffer, which provided a fatter sound and more sustain. A longer heel added support for the neck. A new Stop-Tail bridge/tailpiece provided further sustain. A "wide fat" neck (though not as fat as some vintage guitars) added even more.

PRS created a new dragon each year for three years. For 1994, the dragon had deep blue wings folded much more smoothly than previous creatures. The fourth dragon did not appear until 2000, at which time it took over the body of the guitar.

MODEL
Paul Reed Smith Dragon III

YEAR
1994

PRODUCTION
1994

The CE model of 1988 was created to offer guitarists a less expensive PRS, and to that end it featured a bolt-on maple neck and alder body. A year later, PRS made it more PRS-like with a maple top/mahogany back version, but the figuration of the CE tops would have been graded in the 5–6 range – less curly than the 7–8 top that was standard on the Custom, and much less dramatic than the optional "10 top" or the "10 plus" top of the Artist.

However, despite the company's best intentions, the bolt-neck CE gained a following in its own right – not as just a downgraded PRS Standard. It deserved, and received, a version with a 22-fret neck in 1994, and as this 1998 CE 22 Maple Top illustrates, a spectacular, quilted-maple top was *not* too good for a CE.

The CE Maple Top continues today as a mainstay of the PRS line, with 22 or 24 frets, a nicely figured maple top, and optional gold-plated hardware.

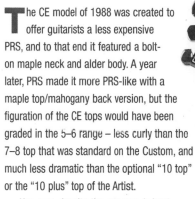

MODEL
Paul Reed Smith CE 22 Maple Top

YEAR
1998

PRODUCTION
1994 to current

The Gibson-like plastic toggle-switch cap identifies a PRS McCarty model. McCarty presided over Gibson from 1948–66, a golden era highlighted by the first Les Pauls and the invention of the humbucking pickup. McCarty was personally responsible for such influential designs as the semi-hollow ES-335 and the radical solidbody shapes of the Flying V and Explorer.

McCarty was in his 70s and semi-retired when, in 1986, Paul Reed Smith called him to ask about glues and pickups and other production issues. McCarty became not only a consultant but a friend and mentor to Smith, and Smith thanked him by creating the PRS McCarty model in 1994.

Like the PRS Custom (and the first Gibson solidbody, the Les Paul Model), the McCarty featured a carved maple top, but it was delineated from other PRS models by a mahogany back that was one-eighth-of-an-inch thicker than standard. A year later, the McCarty Standard joined the line, following the same progression as Gibson's Les Paul models (from Standard to Custom) with a solid mahogany body and no maple cap.

MODEL
Paul Reed Smith McCarty Standard

YEAR
1998

PRODUCTION
1995 to 2006

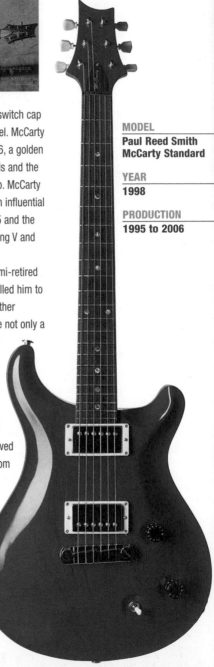

From the first PRS models of 1985, Paul Reed Smith's designs have been described as having evolved from the best features of traditional Gibsons and Fenders. The CE models of 1988, with bolt-on maple necks and alder bodies, strengthened the appeal to Fender fans. Finally, in 1996, PRS introduced a model with an unmistakably direct connection to classic Fender models.

The body shape of the new model was the tried-and-true PRS shape, but the wood was important enough to be incorporated into the model name – the Swamp Ash Special. Although the first PRS CEs had an alder body, which most Fender Stratocasters of the "pre-CBS" period (1965 and earlier) had, the earliest Stratocasters had an ash body and all of the blond-finish Broadcasters/Telecasters and Esquires had bodies of the wider and deeper-grained ash.

The maple neck/fingerboard added to the Fender look of the Swamp Ash Special, and a third pickup – a middle-position single-coil, controlled by a push-pull tone knob – sealed the deal on its Fender appeal.

199

MODEL
Paul Reed Smith Swamp Ash Special

YEAR
1997

PRODUCTION
1996 to current

In 1998, four years after PRS introduced the McCarty model, the company added two model variations with an obvious link back to the Ted McCarty era at Gibson – white "soapbar" pickup covers. The McCarty Soapbar featured two of the single-coil pickups (made by Seymour Duncan) and the Custom 22 Soapbar sported a trio.

As most guitarists with a sense of history knew, "soapbar P-90s" made their debut on Gibson's "goldtop" Les Paul Model – the company's first solidbody – and were used until the advent of metal-covered humbuckers in 1957. By the late 1990s, the P-90 was once again in demand.

The maple fingerboard – a Fender feature – on this Custom 22 Soapbar seems incongruous with the soapbars' strong identification with Gibson, and this version of the Custom 22 lasted only through 2001. The McCarty model, however, provided a fitting home for the pickups, and the McCarty Soapbar remains in production. By the time of McCarty's death in 2001, PRS had honored the legendary Gibson president with over a dozen model variations.

MODEL

Paul Reed Smith Custom 22 Soapbar

YEAR

1999

PRODUCTION

1998 to 2001

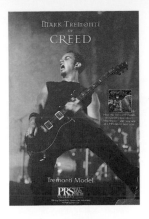

Mark Tremonti was the founder and lead guitarist of the mainstream rock group Creed, best known for their 1999 hit "Higher." While he did not have the influence of some of the "guitar gods" whose names were on signature models, he gave PRS guitars unique exposure due to the controversy among Christian music fans over whether or not Creed was a Christian rock band.

For his 2001 signature model, Tremonti chose PRS's Singlecut as a starting point. The Tremonti model featured the four-knob and three-way toggle switch controls that PRS had introduced on the Singlecut only a year earlier, but Tremonti went with a thicker mahogany back than the regular model. The pickups were wound to his personal specifications. Cosmetic touches included bird inlays on the fingerboard, a pearl-trimmed truss-rod cover, and Tremonti's signature inlaid at the 12th fret. pickups

Like the Singlecut model, Tremonti production was suspended while litigation between PRS and Gibson was settled. His signature model returned to production in 2005 and continues in PRS's signature line today.

MODEL
Paul Reed Smith
Mark Tremonti

YEAR
2001

PRODUCTION
2001 to current

"**S**ingle cutaway" would not seem to be a controversial issue. After all, guitarmakers have been "cutting away" or cutting into the upper treble bout to give players easier access up the neck for decades – long before anyone ever thought about an electric guitar. But in 2000, when Gibson pulled its dealership authorisation from the giant Guitar Center retail chain, PRS seized the opportunity to capture some of the Les Paul market with its own single-cutaway solidbody.

PRS already had a single-cutaway model in development but, unlike the prototype, which featured McCarty-style, two-knob electronic controls, the production model had a selector switch on the upper treble bout and four control knobs – the same general setup of Gibson's Les Paul Standard. Gibson thought the Singlecut looked too much like the Les Paul shape (which Gibson had patented), and Gibson sued.

In 2005, after a lengthy trial and appeal, during which Singlecut production was suspended, PRS was declared the winner. The basic Singlecut model was discontinued after 2006 but the Singlecut design continues in several standard and artist signature model.

MODEL

**Paul Reed Smith
Singlecut Trem Satin**

YEAR

2006

PRODUCTION

2002 to current

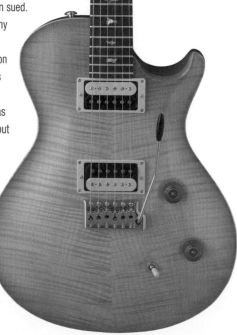

In the late 1990s, Paul Reed Smith began looking for a way to put the elegant design of a PRS guitar in the hands of beginning players and players on a budget. The answer lay in overseas production, and PRS created the SE (Student Electric) line for the import models.

The original EG series, introduced in 1990, had been an attempt to offer a U.S.-made PRS at an even lower price than the CE models. Like the CEs, the EGs had bolt-on necks, but their bodies were *not* the familiar PRS style. Instead, they had a shallower edge bevel that gave them a Stratocaster-inspired look. The connection was accentuated by a large, Strat-like pickguard and, on some models, Strat-like pickup configurations. The SE EG took the Strat look a step farther with a beveled lower bass bout.

While the original, U.S.-made EGs lasted only until 1995, the 20th-century versions, like most of the models in the SE import line, accomplished what the originals could not do – they brought PRS guitars to the masses.

MODEL
Paul Reed Smith SE EG

YEAR
2004

PRODUCTION
2003 to current

PRS made a limited run of 100 guitars in 1996 with a rosewood neck. That feature alone would have been intriguing enough to those guitarists – Paul Reed Smith, among them – who believe that wood is as important as electronics in shaping the sound of a solidbody electric. However, when PRS put a rosewood-neck model into regular production in 2004, the esoteric neck material turned out to be a relatively minor refinement compared to the electronic system introduced on this new model.

What appeared to be a humbucker-single-humbucker setup was really five single-coil pickups. The two blade-style selector switches created a total of 13 different pickup combinations. The system five-pickup, 13-selection system was sufficiently innovative for PRS to incorporate it into the model name of the 513 Rosewood. Newly designed bird inlays also received the designation "513 birds."

Introduced in 2004, the 513 Rosewood lasted only a few years, but the 513 electronics remained viable, and in 2007 PRS answered the increasing demand for this system with the more conventional mahogany-neck Model 513.

MODEL
Paul Reed Smith 513 Rosewood

YEAR
2004

PRODUCTION
2004 to 2006

PRS was a year short of its 20th anniversary when it introduced its first 12-string production model, but the company was hardly new to the neighborhood. Through their Custom Shop and their elite Private Stock models, PRS had made plenty of 12-strings through the years.

Consequently, the Custom 22/12 hit the market in 2004 as a fully developed model, with humbucking pickups designed specifically for a 12-string, a bridge with 12 individually adjustable saddles, and even a headstock with the straight string-pull that had been a hallmark of PRS guitars from the first models in 1985. The Custom 22 design provided the stiffer neck required to handle the extra string tension, along with the elegant aesthetic features of the Custom model.

The Custom 22/12 had an extra added attraction in the form of a single-coil middle pickup made by Lindy Fralin. With a coil-tap on the bridge pickup, the 22/12 had tonal capabilities unmatched by any of the classic 12-strings made by Fender, Gibson or Rickenbacker.

205

MODEL
Paul Reed Smith Custom 22/12

YEAR
2004

PRODUCTION
2004 to current

Mark Tremonti, lead guitarist with the rock band Creed, was only the second artist to have a PRS signature model (the first was the legendary Carlos Santana), and he was the first to embrace the PRS Singlecut design. The PRS Mark Tremonti model of 2001 was successful enough for PRS and Tremonti to create a limited-edition model in 2004.

The Mark Tremonti Tribal featured a large graphic design on the top of the guitar, along with a condensed version on the peghead. Although it had the general look of a ceremonial mask from a primitive culture, the specific inspiration was never noted. The basic specs of the Tribal were the same as Tremonti's regular model, built on a slightly-thicker-than-standard Singlecut body.

The PRS Custom Shop was around halfway through the announced limited run of 100 Tribals when production was suspended due to a lawsuit over the Singlecut design. More were made in 2006. In the meantime, Creed broke up in 2004 and Tremonti continued his career with the band Alter Bridge.

MODEL
Paul Reed Smith Mark Tremonti Tribal

YEAR
2004

PRODUCTION
2004 to 2006

Rickenbacker brought the first viable electric guitar to market in 1932. Moreover, its horseshoe-shaped pickup was the only pre-World War II pickup from any maker that, to today's ears, still needs no improvement. Surprisingly, though, the company all but ignored the "Spanish style" electric until 1953, when founder Adolph Rickenbacker sold his share to F.C. Hall (founder of Radio-Tel, Fender's exclusive distributor at the time).

Hall immediately switched focus from the fading Hawaiian models to the new solidbodies and introduced the Combo 800 and 600 in 1954. They featured a carved top, like the Gibson Les Paul that preceded them by two years, but with a more pronounced "lip" that would come to be known as the "German carve." The term was accurate; Roger Rossmeisl, the son of a German guitarmaker, brought it to Rickenbacker in 1954.

The Combo 800, with a double-coil pickup, and the Combo 600, with a single-coil horseshoe, lasted only until 1959, giving way to thinner bodies with more dramatic cutaway lines, but the German carve became a Rickenbacker signature feature on hollow as well as solidbody models.

207

MODEL
Rickenbacker Combo 800

YEAR
1955

PRODUCTION
1954 to 1959

RICKENBACKER

In contrast to the carved top and "sliced" cutaways of Rickenbacker's first solidbody models, the new Combo models of 1956 featured a thinner, flat body with upper bouts that curved symmetrically to their points – inspiring the nickname "tulip shape."

The Combo 1000 had the highest model number but was actually the lowest of the tulip-shapes, with a single pickup, three-quarter scale length (one of three short-scale models in the group), and three fewer frets than the higher models. The group's most important design element was revealed by a bit of light-colored wood peeking out just below the pickguard. It was the end of the neck – evidence of neck-thru-body construction – which made these Combo models unique in the guitar world at that time.

The tulip shape proved to be limiting for players, and shortly after this 1957 Combo 1000 was made, Rickenbacker widened the treble-side cutaway. Most of the models in this series changed to another new body known as the "cresting wave" in 1958, but the 1000 retained the modified tulip shape and was discontinued the next year.

MODEL
Rickenbacker Combo 1000

YEAR
1957

PRODUCTION
1957 to 1970

This Rickenbacker Combo 450 from 1957 still featured the tulip-shape body, but it already sported several upgrades. The pickup covers have two openings, earning them the nickname "toaster tops." And the old, pre-World War II knobs (aka "flying saucers") have been replaced by a larger, flashier style, affectionately known as "cooker" or "kitchen stove" knobs. An anodized aluminum pickguard set off the Jet Black finish – one of three eye-catching options, the other two being a golden Montezuma Brown and a blue-green Cloverfield Green.

Jean "Toots" Thielman played a tulip-shaped 450 with the George Shearing quartet and, in 1960, a photo of Thielman appeared on the cover of the American magazine Accordion and Guitar World. Although the tulip shape was two years out of date by then, the photo nevertheless inspired future Beatle John Lennon to one day own a Rickenbacker.

With the Combo 450's change in 1958 to the "cresting wave" body, characterized by a curled bass horn, it went on to become one of Rickenbacker's most popular and enduring solidbody models, lasting until 1984.

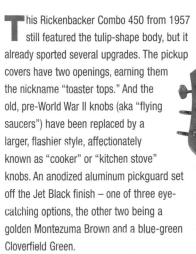

209

MODEL
Rickenbacker Combo 450 (tulip shape)

YEAR
1957

PRODUCTION
1957 to 1958

SUPRO

Supro's calling card in the 1950s was celluloid, particularly the simulated mother-of-pearl pattern that appeared on kitchen tables of the period and is affectionately known today in the guitar world as "mother of toilet seat." The Belmont, with its "sherry maroon" pearloid covering, replaced the lowly Ozark models in 1954.

Supro was owned by Valco, which evolved from the National and Dobro companies of the late 1920s. Although there were no Supro acoustics, this 1960 Belmont sports a piece of the company's acoustic history with its flared tailpiece, a style that originated on the earliest National and Dobro resonator guitars.

The Supros have a kitschy appeal today, and, true to their appearance, they were not very sturdily made. In addition, their pickups were weaker than those of other major makers. They did, however, maintain their aesthetic flair, as the celluloid look gave way to molded fiberglass in the early 1960s. The Supro brand also supported Valco's amplifier line, and the budget line lasted until 1967, when Valco acquired the Kay company and promptly went bankrupt.

MODEL

Supro Belmont (wood body)

YEAR

1960

PRODUCTION

1955 to 1961

The pointed horns of this 1968 Tokai Humming Bird were inspired by Gibson's SG models, but the rest of the body shape, including the "German carve" (the contoured "lip" around the top edge), was copied directly from Mosrite of California's most famous guitar – the Ventures signature model. It was available only to Japanese buyers, who also got such Mosrite features as the diagonally mounted neck pickup, the configuration of control knobs and selector switch, and the "zero fret."

Tokai, based in Hamamatsu, Japan, made its first electric models in 1967 and entered the U.S. and British markets in the 1980s. While Tokai was one of the leaders in copying classic American designs, the company was also at the forefront of a movement toward better quality from Japanese makers, and in 1982 the Houston-based Robin company contracted with Tokai to build its first guitars.

With rising labor costs in Japan and increasing competition in the global market, Tokai retreated to the Japanese market in the mid 1990s.

MODEL
Tokai Humming Bird

YEAR
1968

PRODUCTION
Late 1960s

With a body featuring a prominent "lump" that begged to be removed, the Apache was the first of a series of oddly shaped Vox solidbody guitars, but it represented the fourth genre of musical instruments that the Jennings Musical Instrument company offered.

Like many European guitar brands of the 1960s, JMI had roots in the accordion business – not a multi-generational family company but as a British import business founded by accordion player Tom Jennings in 1945. By the end of the 1940s, Jennings was in the electronic organ business with a model called the Univox. In the mid 1950s, as rock'n'roll was bringing the electric guitar to the forefront of pop music, Jennings began adapting organ amplifiers to guitars, and he teamed up with an Army buddy, Dick Denny, to create the first Vox amplifier in 1958.

A year later, JMI entered the guitar business with cheap models made by a British woodworking company. In 1961, the company added an in-house design team to create models worthy of the Vox brand name, and the Apache led this new wave of Vox guitars.

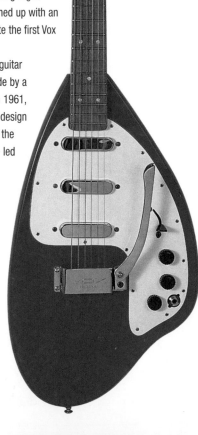

MODEL
Vox Apache

YEAR
Circa 1961

PRODUCTION
1961 to 1966

In early 1964, Vox designers rounded out the blob body shape of the Apache into a symmetrical teardrop shape – similar to that of a lute. Its official names were Phantom Mk III, then Mk VI, but guitarists around the world knew it as the Vox Teardrop that Brian Jones plays in The Rollings Stones.

By the mid 1960s, Vox was on top of the world – on top of three worlds, actually. Jones was one of several guitarists in "British Invasion" groups who were playing Vox's attention-grabbing guitars. Vox combo organs were featured in the sound of The Dave Clark Five and The Animals. And Vox amps were used by The Beatles.

Vox's fast growth led, ironically, to production and financial challenges that, in 1964, prompted JMI founder Tom Jennings to outsource Vox guitars to the Italian-based Eko company and to sell a controlling interest to the Royston group, a British holding company. It marked not only a high point for Vox guitars, but the beginning of the end. Vox guitars would be gone by the end of the decade.

MODEL
Vox Mk VI

YEAR
Circa 1965

PRODUCTION
1964 to 1967

In contrast to the classy, conventional look of Vox amps, with their diamond-stitched grille cloths, Vox guitars were among the most modernistic instruments of the early 1960s, and they fit the musical attitude of the era perfectly. The angular polygonal body of the Phantom series made it difficult, if not impossible, to play in a sitting position – a sign that Vox designers recognized the solidbody guitar as the instrument of rock'n'roll, where no guitarist would even think of sitting down.

Introduced in late 1961, the Phantom line grew to include a 12-string in 1963 and this stereo 12-string in 1966. The Phantom XII's three pickups were split, and each coil had its own volume and tone control. The 12 knobs of the stereo Phantom XII may have set a record, but the guitar did not find its way *onto* many records, and it was last made in 1968.

In 1969, Vox's parent company, Royston, folded, and while amplifier production continued under future owners, it was the end of the original Vox guitars.

214

MODEL
Vox Phantom XII (stereo)

YEAR
1966

PRODUCTION
1966 to 1968

Vox was better-equipped than any musical instrument company of the 1960s to combine a guitar with an organ. After all, JMI (Vox's parent company) had been making electronic organs since the late 1940s and electric guitars since the late 1950s. When Robert Moog demonstrated his first synthesizer in 1964 at the Audio Engineering Society convention, the timing must have seemed perfect for electronic sounds on a guitar.

Vox engineers wired the guitar's frets to tone generators from its highly successful Continental model combo organ. In addition to Octave, Organ Tone and Flute sounds, they also provided the guitarist with onboard rhythm sounds. Six pushbuttons controlled individual strings. The angular body of Vox's Phantom guitars provided aesthetically appropriate lines for the rows of controls.

The result was a modernistic instrument with which a guitarist could theoretically play a guitar along with a supporting organ part and a rhythm section (as well as in various other combinations), but in practice, the Phantom Guitar Organ was simply an electronic mess. It was introduced in 1966 and didn't last a year.

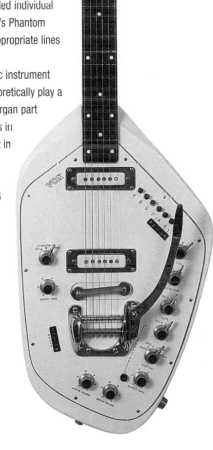

MODEL
Vox Phantom Guitar Organ

YEAR
1966

PRODUCTION
1966

215

Darrell Abbott, aka Dimebag Darrell, was associated with Dean guitars through most of his career, starting as a hotshot contest guitarist in his home state of Texas and continuing for over 20 years (1981-2003) with the heavy metal band Pantera. Washburn's growing reputation as a maker of heavy metal guitars was enhanced considerably when Dimebag Darrell switched his allegiance in 1996.

Washburn made nine different "Dime" models with body shapes based on a Flying V or a four-point star. The cherry stain finish on this 1999 model, the Dime Culprit, has one of the series' more subdued treatments; others featured green slime and lightning-bolt finish effects. Dimebag also had his own special humbucking pickups, called Dimebuckers made by the Seymour Duncan company.

In December 2004, just a few months after he renewed his association with Dean guitars, Dimebag Darrell was shot dead onstage at a concert in Columbus, Ohio. In 2004 Dean put a new line of Dimebag tribute guitars into production.

MODEL
Washburn The Dime Culprit

YEAR
1999

PRODUCTION
1996 to 2000

Washburn is one of the oldest guitar brands, dating back to 1887, and in the late 19th century its parent company Lyon & Healy was the largest musical instrument maker in America. The brand name was the middle name of founding partner George Washburn Lyon.

In the late 20th century, under ownership of the Chicago-based Fretted Industries Inc. (now called Washburn International), the Washburn brand returned to prominence with models endorsed by heavy metal guitarists.

Paul Stanley, founding member and rhythm guitarist of the rock band KISS, came over to Washburn in 1998 after a career of playing Ibanez guitars. In an ironic turn of events, an American company copied a Japanese guitar – and it wasn't just any model, it was the Ibanez Iceman, conceived as a sort of national guitar design of Japan – to create the Washburn Paul Stanley model of 1998. Although the model only lasted two years, Stanley and Washburn got back together in 2006 for a new line of seven signature models, none of which had the Iceman shape.

MODEL
Washburn Paul Stanley PS-500

YEAR
1999

PRODUCTION
1998 to 1999

WATKINS

Many aspiring British guitarists of the early 1960s learned to play on a Watkins Rapier. The London-based company was headed by Charlie Watkins, who specialized in amplifiers, while his brother Sid handled guitars. The Watkins Rapier line was easy to understand: Model 22 had two pickups, 33 had three pickups and 44 had four.

The Watkins brand debuted in the solidbody market in 1959 with Gibson-inspired models, but their inspiration switched to Fender in 1961. This Rapier 33 looks like a poor-man's Stratocaster, with its inelegant headstock shape and square-cornered pickups.

In 1965 the brandname changed to WEM (for Watkins Electric Music), and the company found greater success with amplifiers, P.A. systems, and effects than it had with guitars. The brand changed again by the end of the 1960s to Wilson (the maiden name of Watkins'mother), and Sid Watkins focused on semi-acoustic guitars, the inexpensive Ranger solidbody, and another Strat-inspired model, the Hand Made Mercury. Watkins/WEM/Wilson guitar production finally ended in 1985.

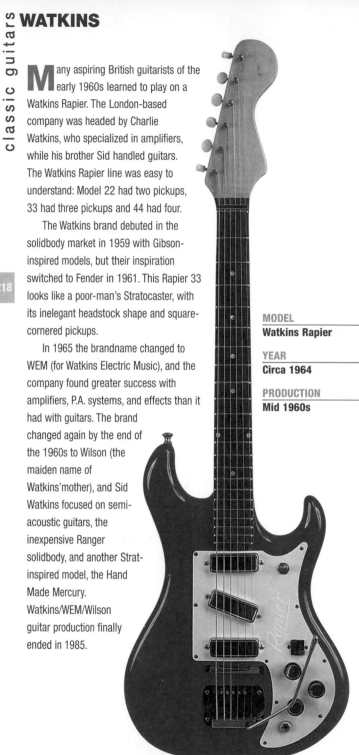

MODEL
Watkins Rapier

YEAR
Circa 1964

PRODUCTION
Mid 1960s

Like several other Italian guitar makers, Welson began as an accordion company. Founded in the town of Castelfidardo by Orlando Quagliardi in 1921, Welson introduced its first solidbodies in 1962. They were typical Italian guitars, featuring an array of pushbutton controls.

In the mid 1960s Welson switched its design themes to more conventional styles, such as the Jazz Vedette. The name was undoubtedly intended to connect with Fender's Jazzmaster, and the three-tone sunburst finish and tortoiseshell celluloid pickguard were typical Fender features. The three-piece pickguard design, however, was a clear nod to Londoner Jim Burns.

In French, "vedette" is an entertainment term for a star (it is also a small boat), and it underscoresd Welson's success outside of Italy. In addition to its own brand, the company made a full line of guitars under the Dynacord brand for the German market, while the U.S.-based Wurlitzer company markctcd Welson instruments under the Wurlitzer and Orpheum brands. In the 1970s, the company gravitated toward copies of Gibson models before going out of business in 1981.

MODEL
Welson Jazz Vedette

YEAR
Circa 1967

PRODUCTION
Late 1960s

YAMAHA

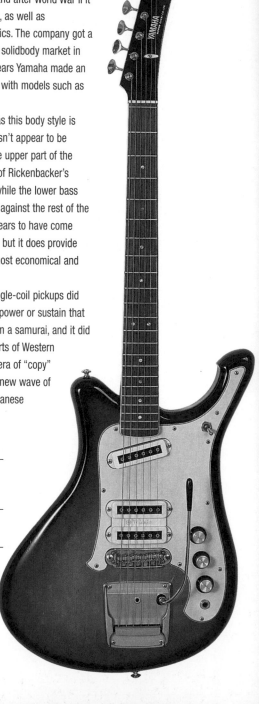

Yamaha was founded in Japan in 1887 as a piano company, and after World War II it branched out into guitars, as well as motorcycles and electronics. The company got a relatively late start in the solidbody market in 1964, but within a few years Yamaha made an unforgettable impression with models such as this 1967 SG-5A.

The Flying Samurai, as this body style is affectionately called, doesn't appear to be particularly airworthy. The upper part of the body is a reverse image of Rickenbacker's "cresting wave" shape, while the lower bass bout seems to be pulling against the rest of the body. The headstock appears to have come from a different designer, but it does provide straight string-pull in a most economical and minimalist way.

The SG-5A's three single-coil pickups did not generate the level of power or sustain that players would expect from a samurai, and it did not cause fear in the hearts of Western guitarmakers. But in the era of "copy" imports, it represented a new wave of original designs from Japanese makers.

MODEL

Yamaha SG-5A "Flying Samurai"

YEAR

1967

PRODUCTION

Mid 1970s

I n the 1970s, Yamaha joined other Japanese makers in copying American designs, but in the case of this SG-60T from 1973, they picked an unlikely model.

The body did feature a routed "lip" around the top edge that was known as the "German carve," in part because it had been introduced in America on Rickenbacker guitars designed by German-born luthier Roger Rossmeisl. However, the Yamaha SG 60T (T for tremolo; it was also available without tremolo) did not copy the Rickenbacker so much as the cheap National and Supro guitars made in the early 1960s by the Chicago-based Valco company. National had gone out of the business in 1967, unable to compete with inexpensive Japanese imports; perhaps Yamaha somehow thought the National/Supro designs still viable.

While the SG 60T did not raise Yamaha to the level of Fender or Gibson, it was part of a second wave of Yamaha solidbodies that sported better tuners and more powerful humbucking pickups, and it served notice that Yamaha might soon be a formidable player in the solidbody market.

MODEL
Yamaha SG 60T

YEAR
Circa 1973

PRODUCTION
Early 1970s

YAMAHA

In 1976, Yamaha changed the reputation of Japanese-made guitars with the SG2000. Most players familiar with the original models, made from 1976–88, consider the workmanship as well as the performance of the guitar to be superior to anything Gibson offered at that time.

The body design looks Gibson-esque, and the shape did come from a somewhat obscure double-cutaway version of the Gibson Melody Maker, made from 1963–64. The top cap was three-piece maple, like that of Gibson's Les Paul in the 1970s, but under the top was a fundamental difference. Where the Gibson had slab of mahogany, the Yamaha had a neck-thru-body design. The extra rigidity of the three-piece mahogany and maple neck gave the SG2000 more sustain than any other popular guitar on the market, a factor that won over Carlos Santana for a brief period (before he endorsed Gibson's L-6S).

Yamaha moved production of most of its models to Taiwan in 1984 but kept the SG2000 in Japan until it was discontinued in 1988. It was reissued as the SBG2000 in 2007.

MODEL
Yamaha SG 2000 (SBG 2000)

YEAR
Circa 1984

PRODUCTION
1976 to 1988

The metal front plate is the most familiar sign of a guitar by British maker Tony Zemaitis. He was already a well-known maker of acoustic guitars when, around 1970, he was shielding some pickups on an electric guitar with aluminum foil and decided to take the concept to the extreme.

His first guitar with a full metal top went to bluesman Tony McPhee. His next was the first of many made for Ronnie Wood (then of The Faces, later of The Rolling Stones). He enlisted the help of gun engraver Danny O'Brien for the elaborate ornamentation of the metal top plates, and his clients quickly grew to include Keith Richards, Ronnie Lane and Eric Clapton.

Zemaitis also made instruments with intricate pearl and mosaic inlays, and he was known as the father of the "boutique" guitar by the time he retired in 2000. He died two years later, but his designs are carried on today by his son, Tony Zemaitis Jr.

MODEL
Zemaitis Metal Front

YEAR
Circa 1975

PRODUCTION
Circa 1970 to current

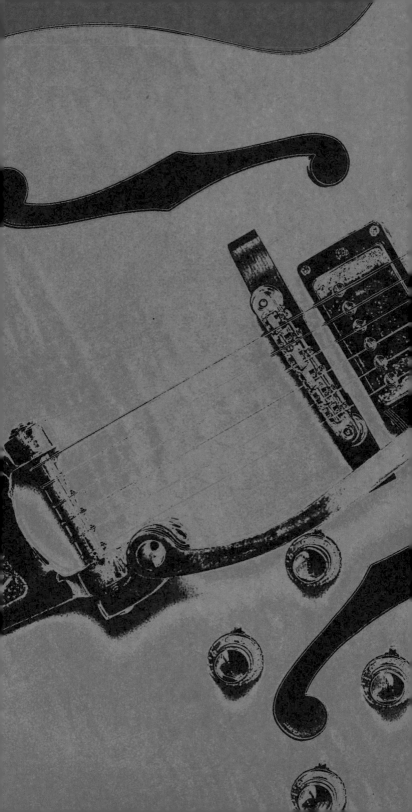

classic guitars

HOLLOWBODY
GUITARS

ELECTRIC HOLLOWBODY

Within a few years of the earliest attempts at electrifying stringed instruments, guitar makers and players realized that the amplification system – not the volume produced by the vibration of the top nor the tone shaped by the body – was the key element to the sound of the electric guitar. In 1950, Leo Fender seemed to drive that point home decisively with his innovative solidbody guitars. However, not everyone bought into the concept that a hollowbody was no longer necessary to the electric guitar.

Given the personal relationship that guitarists have with their instruments, it's not surprising many players feel that a guitar, like any living being, needs air. The effect that hollow areas of the body have on the sound of an electric guitar is subtle but, to the ears of players, critical. Adding or subtracting the right amount of air, finding the perfect degree of natural resonance to temper and shape the electric sound, is much like creating an alloy to make a base metal stronger or more malleable. Opinions vary widely as to the optimal configuration, and the debate is played out in these pages, from traditional body styles that are essentially all-acoustic with an unintrusive "floating" pickup, to bodies that are functionally solid with only the perception of hollowbody construction.

Just as the human voice extends over a wide range, so does the voice of the electric guitar. As these classic guitar models illustrate, there is no single perfect combination of acoustic and electric qualities, but in pursuit of that goal, guitar makers have created a fascinating spectrum of hollowbody models, some of them influential, some simply interesting, all classics.

While the guitars of John D'Angelico in New York and the Strombergs in Boston dominated the East Coast jazz scene, in Chicago a Swedish immigrant named Carl Albanus Johnson quietly emerged in the late 1950s with carved-top guitars that rivaled those of the more legendary makers.

Albanus guitars featured a carved ebony tailpiece that was a carryover from Johnson's training as a violin maker, and it preceded the more widely publicized ebony tailpieces of James D'Aquisto by as much as a decade. His distinctive, asymmetrical headstock, inspired by Gibson's "dove-wing" design, proved to be perfect for the extra tuner on this seven-string model. Seven-string guitars were popularized by jazz stylist George Van Eps, who tuned the seventh string to a B below the standard low-E. When rockers discovered the seven-string in the 1980s, thanks in large part to Steve Vai, they tuned down to A to get a powerful root-fifth-octave configuration on the lower strings.

Johnson died in 1973. His total production is estimated at less than 100 guitars.

MODEL
Albanus 7-string

YEAR
Late 1950s

PRODUCTION
Late 1950s to 1973

ANTORIA

The Antoria brand appeared in England by the late 1950s on guitars imported by distributors J.T. Coppock Leeds Ltd. and later CSL Charles Summerfield. Some Antorias looked very much like Ibanez models; not coincidentally, they came from the same Japanese factory – Fuji Gen-Gakki.

The Rockstar drew its inspiration from two classic Gibsons. The most obvious influence was the double-cutaway body of the ES-335, the original semi-hollow electric, although Antoria claimed the Rockstar had a "double sustain block" rather than the one-piece center block of the 335. The two humbuckers, four knobs, placement of the controls, dots on the fingerboard – all signs pointed to the 335. And to ensure a Gibson connection in the mind of the buyer, the Rockstar sported a cherry sunburst finish – not found on the ES-335 but the signature look of Gibson's most famous electric, the Les Paul Standard.

The Rockstar design was appealing enough that in later years, after production moved to Korea, the supplier pitched the same model to other importers, and a similar guitar appeared in the line of the Chicago-based Harmony company.

MODEL

Antoria Rockstar EG1935

YEAR

1989

PRODUCTION

Late 1980s

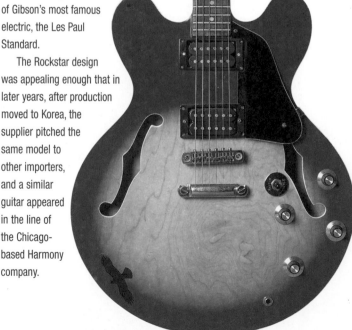

In the 1980s, a time when the quality of Gibson guitars was slipping and the quality of Japanese guitars was rising, the Aria Pro II TA60 offered guitarists all of the features of Gibson's semi-hollowbody ES-335 at a lower price.

The Aria company was founded by Japanese classical guitarist Shiro Arai in the early 1950s and made its first electrics in 1960. By the end of the decade Aria was leading Japanese makers into the "copy era," where the most successful Japanese guitars looked very much like the most successful American guitars. By the end of the 1970s, however, Aria had begun developing its own designs, and the brand name was upgraded to Aria Pro II in 1975.

The Titan Artist semi-hollow series appeared in 1981. The TA-60's double-cutaway shape with rounded horns was a slightly elongated and sleeker version of Gibson's ES-335, which had been introduced in 1958 and by this time would qualify as a traditional style. The headstock shape was distinctive, but otherwise the TA60 appealed strictly to the Gibson crowd.

229

MODEL
Aria Pro II TA60

YEAR
1989

PRODUCTION
1981 to 1999

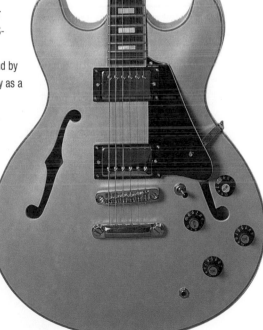

BARKER

William Barker began his guitar-making career in the employ of Carl Albanus Johnson, the Chicago maker whose archtops rivaled the legendary D'Angelicos and Strombergs in the 1950s and 1960s. By the late 1960s, Barker and his brother had set up their own shop in Peoria, Illinois, a few hours southwest of Chicago.

Barker died in 1991 at age 66, after making somewhere between in 105 and 120 instruments, only a handful of which were seven-string guitars, and only one of which – this one – was a seven-string with an 18-inch body. Barker's headstock, with a slightly longer bass side, shows an Albanus influence, but curiously, Barker chose to put the extra tuner on this seven-string guitar on the treble side.

In the same manner that John D'Angelico passed the torch in New York to his assistant James D'Aquisto, the guitarmaker's torch was passed two times in northern Illinois – from Johnson (Albanus) to Bill Barker and then to Barker's longtime assistant Bill Hollenbeck, who went on to become a respected archtop maker in his own right.

MODEL
Barker 7-string

YEAR
1985

PRODUCTION
Late 1960s to late 1980s

Born in New York City in 1905, John D'Angelico learned the luthier's trade from a grand-uncle who made violins, mandolins and flat-top guitars. He established his own shop in 1934, and his earliest archtop guitars were modeled on Gibson's 16-inch L-5 model – the first f-hole archtop. When Gibson increased the size of its guitars, D'Angelico did, too. By 1936 he had three 17-inch models and, at the top of the line, the 18-inch New Yorker, and by the end of the 1940s, only the Excel and New Yorker remained.

This New Yorker features the most easily identifiable mark of D'Angelico's high-end models – the oversized headstock with the "broken-scroll pediment" (the squashed cutout) framing an ornamental cupola (the button).

The truss-rod cover took its inspiration from the skyscrapers of New York. The slashed-block fingerboard inlays distinguished the New Yorker from the Excel, which had solid pearl blocks on its fingerboard. The body of a D'Angelico had its own identifying features, too, including a massive tailpiece with a stairstep motif that was repeated in the pickguard design.

MODEL
D'Angelico New Yorker

YEAR
1955

PRODUCTION
1936 to 1964

D'ANGELICO

D'Angelico's model offering of the 1930s encompassed five basic models. The plainer A, A-1 and B models appeared often in his ledger book and were apparently a favorite of music store clients. As the maker's reputation grew, more and more individual players ordered guitars, and by the end of the 1940s, the Excel had emerged as the most popular D'Angelico model. The larger, fancier Excel New Yorker may have produced a bit more volume, but as guitarists began putting pickups on their instruments, acoustic volume became less of an issue, and the comfort of the smaller Excel made it more attractive to many players.

D'Angelico was somewhat of a latecomer to the cutaway. Although Gibson offered its first cutaway guitars in 1939, it was 1947 before D'Angelico first noted a cutaway in his ledger book. Among his cutaways, the Excel maintained its popularity over the New Yorker.

John D'Angelico died September 1, 1964, leaving ten guitars unfinished. His apprentice James L. D'Aquisto finished those ten and carried the art of the carved-top guitar to even greater heights.

MODEL
D'Angelico Excel Cutaway

YEAR
1950

PRODUCTION
1947 to 1964

Working out of a small shop in New York, John D'Angelico made archtop guitars for some of the greatest musicians from the late 1940s through the early 1960s. He was the first individual luthier to gain a legendary reputation, and he established the idea that fine archtop guitars required the focused attention of an individual artisan, who could make guitars to a higher standard of quality than a factory.

Although D'Angelico had standardized models, every guitar was, in effect, a custom order, and this Excel cutaway is a case in point, with a smaller body than the Excel's typical 17-inch width.

Except for some electrics with laminated bodies, D'Angelico's guitars were acoustic. However, many players fitted them with a "floating" pickup, so-called because it was installed with no drilling or routing into the top. The DeArmond Rhythm Chief on this Excel cutaway model was the most popular aftermarket pickup in the 1940s and '50s. It attached by way of an extension arm to the side of the fingerboard, and the controls (including a jack) attached to the pickguard.

MODEL
D'Angelico Excel Cutaway

YEAR
1950

PRODUCTION
1947 to 1964

D'ANGELICO

Although many D'Angelico instruments were fitted with floating pickups, not one of the 1,164 guitars entered into his ledger book was noted as being electric. Nevertheless, a fair number of true electric guitars – with electronics mounted directly into the top – appeared in the 1950s and early 1960s with D'Angelico's name prominently engraved on the tailpiece and inlaid in the headstock.

234

This left-handed example shows the distinctive wood grain of a maple top, and it lacks a center seam – clear evidence that the top was laminated rather than solid and was pressed into an arched shape rather than carved. It seemed beneath D'Angelico – and it was. The body was made by United Guitars or Codé, both located across the river from New York City in New Jersey.

D'Angelico made the neck and the tailpiece, but the knobs and toggle switch look as if they came off a Harmony or some other inexpensive model. The pickups, however, were the best available at the time – Gibson humbuckers.

MODEL
**D'Angelico Electric
(left-handed)**

YEAR
Late 1950s

PRODUCTION
1950s to early 1960s

New York luthier John D'Angelico never felt his electric guitars were worthy of entry into his ledger book, but they helped him through chronic hard times. His apprentice James D'Aquisto (who would become a renowned maker in his own right) said that D'Angelico felt lucky if he could get $500 for one of his carved-top acoustics, so the electrics – which required him to make only the neck and then to assemble and finish the instrument – were quick jobs for quick cash.

This D'Angelico electric has several upgrades over the typical example with a D'A neck and a body by United or Codé. The spruce top is undoubtedly laminated but is a higher-quality element than the typical laminated maple top on these models. And the pickguard has the stairstep shape and multi-layered binding of a "real" D'Angelico. The pickups may have come from Magna Electronics, makers of budget-line Magnatone guitars and amplifiers.

These laminated-body electric D'Angelicos are fairly rare though not nearly as prized by collectors or players as those with bodies actually made by D'Angelico.

MODEL
D'Angelico Electric

YEAR
Circa 1955

PRODUCTION
1950s to early 1960s

D'ANGELICO

Like D'Angelico's legendary acoustic archtops, his more mundane, laminated-body electrics were typically built to order for individual customers, so they, too, varied in specifications.

This 1960 guitar is 16.75 inches wide, which is a quarter-inch larger than many others. Unlike the two-pickup examples, which typically had only two control knobs, this one has four knobs providing individual volume and tone controls for each of the humbucking pickups. The "Rhythm/Treble" ring around the pickup selector switch on the cutaway bout, along with the mottled-pattern pickguard, suggest that D'Angelico grabbed parts from wherever he could find them. The switch ring was probably lifted directly from a Gibson Les Paul solidbody and the pickguard from a Gibson Super 400 archtop.

D'Angelico had kept a close eye on Gibsons in the 1930s, and it's likely that his production of laminated models peaked in the mid 1950s along with the popularity of Gibson's laminated-maple ES-175 and ES-5 models. Examples with humbuckers would be among the last of his true-electric guitars.

MODEL
D'Angelico Electric

YEAR
Circa 1960

PRODUCTION
1950s to early 1960s

Like D'Angelico, D'Aquisto made many custom models, and one of his most popular – a New Yorker with a 17-inch body rather than the standard 18-inch width – became a standard model called the New Yorker Special.

Although D'Aquisto continued the basic construction and, to some degree, the ornamentation of D'Angelico guitars, he quickly began adding his own design touches, and by the time of this 1978 New Yorker Special, there was no mistaking a D'Aquisto for a D'Angelico. The S-shaped soundholes replaced traditional f-holes. A sleek, narrow pickguard, made of ebony, replaced the tortoiseshell celluloid style with the stairstep design. A large ebony tailpiece replaced the metal stairstep design. The peghead cutout of D'Aquisto's 1970s guitars was the only conceptual feature that linked him to tradition, and the ebony tailpiece and pickguard were a signal of more radical departures ahead.

D'Aquisto called his regular, 18-inch model the New Yorker Deluxe, and unlike D'Angelico, whose production was fairly evenly divided between Excels and New Yorkers, D'Aquisto's clientele overwhelmingly preferred the New Yorker models.

237

MODEL
D'Aquisto New Yorker Special

YEAR
1978

PRODUCTION
1965 to 1995

D'AQUISTO

James L. D'Aquisto started working for John D'Angelico as a teenager in the 1950s, and he had D'Angelico's legacy suddenly thrust upon him when his mentor died in 1964. Ten guitars were left as works in progress, and by the time D'Aquisto finished them, the apprentice had established himself as a master luthier.

In addition to following in D'Angelico's footsteps as the premier maker of traditional archtop guitars, D'Aquisto also followed D'Angelico's lesser-known habit of making a less-expensive, true electric guitar, with pickups and controls mounted directly in the top of a ready-made, laminated maple body.

The tailpiece on this example (believed to be one of the earliest made by D'Aquisto on his own) appears to be the same as those on D'Angelico's electrics, except that it's engraved *D'Aquisto*. However, the S-shaped soundholes (without the central points of traditional f-holes) and the circular peghead cutout, show that D'Aquisto was already adding his own signature design features. With the engraving on the pearl scroll peghead, D'Aquisto christened this model with the unimaginative name "D'Aquisto Electric."

MODEL
D'Aquisto Electric

YEAR
Circa 1965

PRODUCTION
Circa 1965

As James D'Aquisto was becoming America's premier maker of traditional archtop guitars, he was also stretching his designer wings with electric hollowbody models created for Hagstrom in the late 1960s (put into production in the mid 1970s) and for Fender in 1984. In the meantime, he brought what were essentially mass-market design ideas into his own shop with such models as the Jazz Master.

The Jazz Master's lack of soundholes indicated that acoustic qualities were of no concern to the maker. That alone was a departure for D'Aquisto; even his true electric models had had soundholes. The figured maple top reflected the growing market for vintage reissues of Gibson's Les Paul Standard or the newly introduced PRS solidbodies. (The Jazz Master was not solid, however; it had only a solid center block.)

The Jazz Master name was familiar, of course, as a Fender model, but Fender had dropped its Jazzmaster in 1980. Not only did the D'Aquisto bear no resemblance to the solidbody Fender, it was more appealing to jazz players than the Fender had ever been.

MODEL
D'Aquisto Jazz Master

YEAR
1987

PRODUCTION
Late 1970s to late 1980s

ELECTAR

The Epiphone company created a new brand, Electar, to introduce its first electric model in 1935. Not coincidentally, the name was similar to the Electro brand on the very first viable electrics made by Rickenbacker (which was officially the Electro String Instrument company).

The term "Spanish" distinguished guitars played in the conventional position from those played Hawaiian style (in the lap). While Rickenbacker had offered a Spanish-electric along with its original "Frying Pan" Hawaiian in 1932, the Rick bodies were cheap instruments furnished by the Harmony company. National's Electric Spanish model, introduced in early 1935, was also built on a budget guitar, in this case made by Regal. Epiphone was the first company to offer a pickup on a guitar that was made by the company whose name was on the headstock.

Among the most successful aspects of the Electar Model M and the smaller-bodied Model C that was introduced with it, was the simple fact that Epiphone beat its arch-rival Gibson into the electric Spanish market by a full year.

MODEL
Electar Model M Spanish

YEAR
Circa 1935

PRODUCTION
1935 to 1937

By 1939, Epiphone had dropped the Electar brand and introduced three new models under the Epiphone name. The top model of 1939 was the Zephyr, available in a striking natural finish that showed off its maple top.

A laminated maple top, bent into an arched shape, was a departure from the carved spruce top of acoustic archtops – a sign that guitarmakers were beginning to recognize the fact that an electric guitar need not have a great acoustic sound. Although the laminated top was cheaper to make, Epiphone was willing to invest some money in the electric guitar, as evidenced by the Zephyr's triple-bound body and bound fingerboard.

Epiphone also invested in an electrical engineer – Herb Sunshine, who was shown in literature dressed in a white lab coat. Sunshine's greatest contribution was the pickup that the Zephyr sported. It was the first with height-adjustable polepieces, and although these pickups did not have the power of Rickenbacker's or Gibson's pickups, Sunshine's screw-polepiece concept would become an industry standard that endures today.

MODEL
Epiphone Zephyr

YEAR
1939

PRODUCTION
1939 to 1956

EPIPHONE

Epiphone and Gibson had engaged in a battle of one-upsmanship in the acoustic market prior to World War II, and the rivalry resumed in the postwar years. Following close on the heels of Gibson's ES-5 (a three pickup version of Gibson's venerable L-5), Epiphone introduced a three-pickup, six-pushbutton version of its top model, the Emperor.

Epiphone already had a Zephyr model, but the company also used the term to signify an electric version of any acoustic model. "Regent" was used in a similar manner to denote any model with a cutaway. So the new electric cutaway model was called the Zephyr Emperor Regent.

Although in name as well as appearance, this model appears to be an acoustic Emperor with pickups, the Zephyr Emperor Regent was in fact designed with a laminated maple top – like Gibson's ES-5 and *not* like Gibson's electric Super 400 and L-5 models, which would be introduced a year later. It was an electric guitar from the very beginning and was never intended to be played acoustically.

MODEL
Epiphone Zephyr Emperor Regent

YEAR
1950

PRODUCTION
1950 to 1956

Although the Epiphone line was intended to be almost-but-not-quite equal to the Gibson line, models such as the Sheraton gave Epiphone its own distinct identity. Not only was there no equivalent to the Sheraton's ornamentation in the Gibson line, some of the Epis – like this 1961 Sheraton – featured an improved vibrato design that was never available on a Gibson. On the Epi unit, the strings wrapped around a tapered bar – thinner for the bass strings, thicker for the treble – that compensated for the differences in string diameter and made for a more uniform pitch change.

Non-vibrato models had Epi's traditional Frequensator tailpiece, whose double-trapeze design also took into account the different vibrating qualities between treble and bass strings. Like the Epi vibrato, the Frequensator was unavailable on a Gibson.

By 1961, high-end models such as the Sheraton sported "humbucking" pickups. They were probably designed to have the same size and look as the earlier Epiphone "New York" pickups, but they were smaller than the humbuckers on Gibsons, and the Epi pickups got the diminutive nickname "mini-humbuckers."

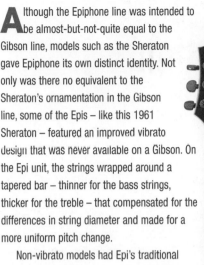

MODEL
Epiphone Sheraton
E-212T

YEAR
1961

PRODUCTION
1959 to 1969

EPIPHONE

The Sheraton's semi-hollow, double-cutaway body and high-end ornamentation pumped new life into the Epiphone line in 1958 and served notice that although the company was now owned by Gibson, the Epiphone brand still had its own unique personality.

Gibson had bought Epiphone in 1957 to gain Epiphone's acoustic bass production capabilities, but Gibson quickly applied the well-known brand name to a new line of guitars. The Epis carried the prestige of being made in Gibson's factory in Kalamazoo, Michigan, and were, for the most part, near-equivalent to Gibson models, but they could be sold by a new dealer network that would not dilute the territorial exclusivity that Gibson's established dealers enjoyed.

While some of the new electrics continued with such familiar and traditional Epiphone model names as Zephyr and Emperor, the Sheraton was new – based on Gibson's ES-335 semi-hollowbody (introduced the same year). The Sheraton's multi-ply binding, fancy inlays, and gold-plated hardware put it a step above the 335, but Gibson always kept the Epiphones in their place by reserving full-sized humbucking pickups for Gibsons only.

MODEL
Epiphone Sheraton E-212TN

YEAR
1962

PRODUCTION
1959 to 1969

The Epiphone Sorrento of 1960 appeared to adhere to Gibson's philosophy of keeping the Epiphone line slightly below the Gibson line by equipping Epis with "mini-humbuckers" – slightly smaller in size and less robust in sound than the full-size humbuckers on Gibson's top models. However, in the case of the Sorrento, the equivalent Gibson had single-coil pickups and was, in that respect, inferior to the Epiphone.

The Sorrento illustrates how quickly Gibson's new Epiphone line of 1958 was accepted. Gibson expanded the archtop electric line in 1959 with a model called the Wilshire, which was basically the Epi version of Gibson's popular ES-125CT, a fully hollow thinbody with a single cutaway. The Sorrento, initially offered with dot fingerboard inlays, sported mini-humbuckers and quickly replaced the Wilshire, adopting the Wilshire's oval fingerboard inlays.

Throughout the 1960s the Sorrento held a unique spot in the Gibson and Epiphone lines as the only thinline hollowbody with a pointed cutaway and humbucking pickups. A similar model did not appear under the Gibson brand until the ES-175T of the 1970s.

MODEL
Epiphone Sorrento

YEAR
1968

PRODUCTION
1960 to 1969

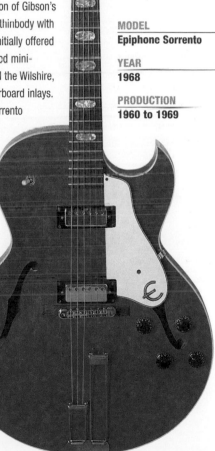

EPIPHONE

The Casino has gained the most fame of any of the Epiphone electric models of the 1960s, thanks to Beatles John Lennon, Paul McCartney and George Harrison, who each owned one.

Surprisingly, in light of the fact that The Beatles could afford any guitar in the world by the end of 1964, the Casino was only a midline model. It had been introduced in 1961 as the Epiphone version of Gibson's ES-330, a fully hollow, double-cutaway model with single-coil pickups. McCartney bought this Casino – a right-handed model that he re-strung for left-handed play – because it was the only hollowbody in the dealer's inventory that had a Bigsby vibrola. The model was offered in sunburst or natural finish, but all three of The Beatles' instruments were originally sunburst.

Among The Beatles' many uses of their Casinos were McCartney's lead part on "Paperback Writer," Harrison in the video promo for "Hello Goodbye," and Lennon with his stripped-finish Casino on the rooftop of Apple headquarters for The Beatles' last performance together in 1969.

MODEL
Epiphone Casino

YEAR
1962

PRODUCTION
1961 to 1969

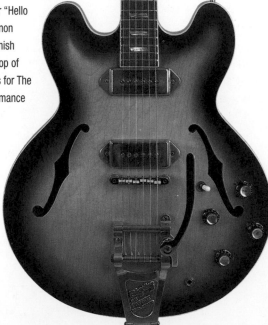

The Epiphone Professional appears to have far more controls than a single-pickup guitar would need, and indeed, the volume and tone knobs on the treble side of the pickguard are the only actual controls for the guitar. All of the other knobs and switches are for the guitar's amplifier.

With Gibson's purchase and makeover of Epiphone in the late 1950s, Epiphone was less bound by tradition than Gibson, and the Professional represented a continuing effort within the Epiphone division to use imaginative designs to circumvent the one-step-below-Gibson status that Epiphones were supposed to maintain.

While it was a great idea, in theory, to give a guitarist a remote control over his amplifier settings, in practice the Epiphone Professional severely limited the guitarist's choices of amplifiers to the matching Professional amplifier. The control-less amp was useless without the guitar, and the guitar cord would only connect with the matching amp. Consequently, the Professional only lasted until 1966 and was a rare failure in the Epiphone line of the 1960s.

247

MODEL
Epiphone Professional

YEAR
1962

PRODUCTION
1962 to 1966

EPIPHONE

Prior to its acquisition by Gibson, Epiphone had been based in New York, so it was only natural that New York-based guitarist Al Caiola would become Epi's first signature artist of the 1960s.

Caiola began his career after World War II as a staff musician for CBS radio, and through the 1950s he played numerous recording sessions in Manhattan. He became one of the best-known guitarists in America in 1961, when his recording of the theme song from the film *The Magnificent Seven* hit the Top 40 of the pop charts, followed by his Top 20 single of the theme from the TV show *Bonanza*.

Within two years Caiola had his own Epiphone signature model, which featured a 25.5-inch scale length (most Gibsons and Epis were 24.75 inches) and five tone switches. The Caiola model was unique among Gibsons and Epis of the period in that it had only a single humbucker (a mini, as all Epis had). It became the Caiola Custom when the Caiola Standard, a plainer version with two single-coil pickups, appeared in 1966.

MODEL
Epiphone Caiola Custom

YEAR
1967

PRODUCTION
1963 to 1969

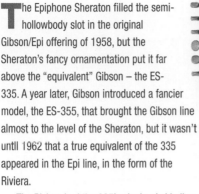

The Epiphone Sheraton filled the semi-hollowbody slot in the original Gibson/Epi offering of 1958, but the Sheraton's fancy ornamentation put it far above the "equivalent" Gibson – the ES-335. A year later, Gibson introduced a fancier model, the ES-355, that brought the Gibson line almost to the level of the Sheraton, but it wasn't until 1962 that a true equivalent of the 335 appeared in the Epi line, in the form of the Riviera.

The Riviera had the 335's single-ply binding and nickel-plated (later chrome-plated) hardware, and although it had slightly better fingerboard inlays – parallelograms compared to the 335's dots – it had the mini-humbucking pickups that kept it in line, a step below a Gibson.

When a 12-string version of the ES-335 appeared in the Gibson line in 1965, Epiphone kept apace with a 12-string Riviera. It would be the only 12-string electric among the American-made Epiphones of the 1960s, and it would last until Gibson moved Epiphone production to Japan in 1970. Epiphone reissued the Riviera 12-string in 2003 in its high end, Japanese-made Elitist Series.

249

MODEL
Epiphone Riviera 12-string

YEAR
1968

PRODUCTION
1965 to 1969

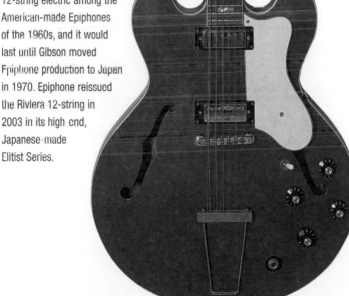

FENDER

For the entire period of Leo Fender's ownership (until January 1965), Fender made solidbody electrics exclusively. Shortly after the CBS broadcasting conglomerate bought Fender, however, the new owners tried to tap into the archtop electric market. To that end the Fender Coronado was created.

German-born designer Roger Rossmeisl, who had been designing Fender acoustics since 1962, designed the Coronados. Their laminated top did not have the elegant "German carve" that was Rossmeisl's signature on his earlier Rickenbackers and his later Fenders, but his touch was evident in the Coronado's smoothed-out peghead shape and thin f-holes. The Coronado II had two pickups; the Coronado I had a single pickup and a dot-inlaid fingerboard.

The Coronado's pickup (made by DeArmond), bridge, and tremolo designs were distinct from Fender's solidbodies. In addition, they were available in Wildwood colors. Wildwood was actually beechwood with dye injected into the tree before it was cut. Fender organized the colors, which ranged from green to orange to blue, under a Roman-numeral system, and the greenish Wildwood II was the most commonly seen.

MODEL

Fender Coronado II Wildwood II

YEAR

1966

PRODUCTION

1966 to 1969

Electric 12-string guitars appeared to be the "next big thing" in rock'n'roll music after The Beatles used a Rickenbacker on "A Hard Day's Night" in 1964 and the Byrds made it the signature sound of "Mr. Tambourine Man" in 1965. Gibson introduced semi-hollow 12-strings under the Gibson and Epiphone brands in 1965, and when Fender announced its forthcoming semi-hollowbody electrics late in that year, the new series included a Coronado XII 12-string.

Introduced in 1966, the Coronado XII did not fare as well as Fender's solidbody Electric XII (introduced in mid 1965), and 12-string electrics in general quickly became more of an effect rather than a vital element of rock'n'roll music.

Perhaps it was the DeArmond pickups – Fender's first outsourced pickups – or maybe it was the incongruity of Fender's standard bolt-on neck on a traditional-style archtop electric, but something about the Coronados did not sit right with guitarists, and all the Coronados were gone by the end of 1970.

MODEL
Fender Coronado XII

YEAR
Circa 1968

PRODUCTION
1966 to 1969

FENDER

Roger Rossmeisl had been with Fender for seven years, designing acoustic flat-tops as well as the Coronado semi-hollow electrics, before Fender gave his creative talent free rein in 1969. The result was the LTD model.

Fender's first hollowbody electric featured a spruce top that was personally carved by Rossmeisl. It sported the elegant "German carve" – the pronounced "lip" around the edge of the top that Rossmeisl had brought with him from his native Germany (where his father was a noted guitarmaker). The neck-position pickup with controls in the pickguard, the height adjustable ebony bridge, the gold-plated tailpiece, the ebony fingerboard with fancy inlays, the flared headstock – everything about the LTD (except, significantly, the bolt-on neck) exuded traditional artisanship in a way no Fender ever had before.

Unfortunately, no matter how great a designer Rossmeisl may have been, guitar buyers were still hesitant to buy a Fender that didn't have a solidbody. The LTD's name proved prophetic. Production was quite limited, estimated at no more than a dozen guitars.

MODEL
Fender LTD

YEAR
1968

PRODUCTION
1968 to 1975

Fender's Telecaster was the first commercially successful electric solidbody guitar, but despite its historical importance, it languished in the shadow of the Stratocaster and other more modern Fenders in the 1960s.

One of the Telecaster's problems was the weight of the ash body that Fender still used for the Tele's standard "blond" finish (most other Fenders had a lighter alder body).

The solution to the weight problem was simply to remove some of the wood from the body, and rather than hide the cavity, Fender designer Roger Rossmeisl called attention to it with an f-hole. He also redesigned the Telecaster's pickguard into a flowing shape that encompassed the controls, eliminating the need for a separate control plate. A pearloid pickguard added flair to what was, by the late 1960s, the Telecaster's dated look. Most Thinlines had a natural-finish ash body but mahogany was also offered.

In 1971, Fender replaced the Thinline's single-coil pickups with humbuckers. It was reissued in Japanese production in 1997, featuring a mahogany body and the model name '69 Thinline.

253

MODEL

Fender Telecaster Thinline (single-coil pickups)

YEAR

1968

PRODUCTION

1968 to 1971

FENDER

Except for its lighter weight, the Telecaster Thinline of 1968 was essentially no different than the standard Telecaster that Fender had been making since 1950, and most Telecaster buyers stayed with the tried-and-true version. Consequently, after three years of unimpressive Thinline sales, Fender created a fundamentally different guitar by abandoning the Tele's traditional single-coil pickups for a pair of humbuckers.

One humbucker on a Fender was good. The Rolling Stones' Keith Richards, for example, installed a neck-position humbucker in his Telecasters, as did bluesman Albert Collins, and many Stratocaster players of the 1980s would add a bridge-position humbucker. But two humbuckers were one too many. In the 1970s, and still today, dual humbuckers were associated with Gibson (the company that invented the humbucker), and most guitarists who wanted a semi-hollowbody – or solidbody, for that matter – with two humbuckers simply bought a Gibson.

The humbucker-equipped Thinline lasted through 1979, and like the original, single-coil version, it was reissued in Japanese production in 1997, featuring an ash body and the model name '72 Thinline.

MODEL

Fender Telecaster Thinline (humbucking pickups)

YEAR

1977

PRODUCTION

1971 to 1979

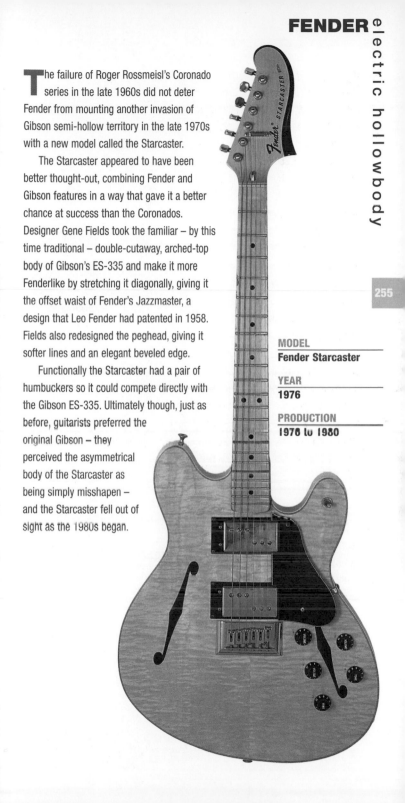

The failure of Roger Rossmeisl's Coronado series in the late 1960s did not deter Fender from mounting another invasion of Gibson semi-hollow territory in the late 1970s with a new model called the Starcaster.

The Starcaster appeared to have been better thought-out, combining Fender and Gibson features in a way that gave it a better chance at success than the Coronados. Designer Gene Fields took the familiar – by this time traditional – double-cutaway, arched-top body of Gibson's ES-335 and make it more Fenderlike by stretching it diagonally, giving it the offset waist of Fender's Jazzmaster, a design that Leo Fender had patented in 1958. Fields also redesigned the peghead, giving it softer lines and an elegant beveled edge.

Functionally the Starcaster had a pair of humbuckers so it could compete directly with the Gibson ES-335. Ultimately though, just as before, guitarists preferred the original Gibson – they perceived the asymmetrical body of the Starcaster as being simply misshapen – and the Starcaster fell out of sight as the 1980s began.

255

MODEL
Fender Starcaster

YEAR
1976

PRODUCTION
1976 to 1980

FENDER

In 1984, after almost 20 years of disappointment with in-house archtop designs, Fender went outside the company and enlisted James D'Aquisto, the legendary maker of acoustic archtop guitars, to create a new Fender model.

D'Aquisto's design hand was obvious in the massive ebony tailpiece and sleek pickguard shape, along with soundholes that had a traditional f-shape on one edge and D'Aquisto's S-shape on the other. The large headstock was a refinement of Roger Rossmeisl's design on the Fender LTD of the late 1960s (which itself had been a refinement of the large headstocks of D'Angelico and D'Aquisto). Because the top was laminated, there was no pretense of equipping it with a floating pickup; the humbucker and control knobs were mounted directly into the top.

The original Fender D'Aquistos – a Standard and an Elite – were produced only briefly by the newly formed Fender Japan division. In 1994, a year before D'Aquisto's death, Fender's Custom Shop revived the design in the form of the D'Aquisto Deluxe. In 2002, Fender's agreement with D'Aquisto's estate ended and the name was licensed to Aria.

256

MODEL
Fender D'Aquisto Deluxe

YEAR
1995

PRODUCTION
1994 to 2002

Although Japanese makers became infamous for copying successful American guitars in the late 1960s, this Framus Hollywood 5/132 shows that German makers were blazing that trail a decade earlier. The general body shape and the cherry sunburst finish of this guitar were obviously intended to appeal to players who aspired to own a Gibson Les Paul Standard.

The Framus differed from the Les Paul in many obvious ways, including its three pickups, large pickguard, tailpiece, and control knobs. And under the top, the difference was even more significant, as the Framus was actually a semi-hollowbody rather than a solidbody guitar.

Framus, founded in Germany in 1946, was the leading European maker of electric guitars by the mid 1950s, and the Hollywood series of simulated solidbodies – available with one, two, or three pickups – appeared in 1958. Although Framus guitars never gained a strong international following, they were still considered in the U.S. to be a quality import, a step above the flashier but more cheaply made guitars from Japan and Italy.

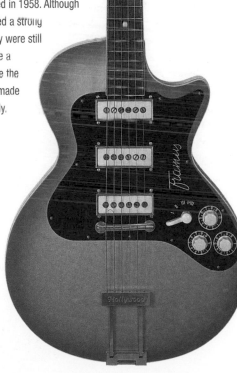

MODEL
Framus Hollywood 5/132

YEAR
1959

PRODUCTION
1958 to mid 1960s

GIBSON

Gibson's ES-150 was not the first electric guitar, but it might as well have been. It was the first professional-quality model, and moreover, it was the guitar Charlie Christian played when he revolutionized the role of the electric guitarist as a member of Benny Goodman's band from 1939 until his death in 1942.

Gibson employee Walt Fuller, an amateur radio enthusiast, developed a distinctive hexagonal pickup for the company's first model, the EH-150, introduced in late 1935. E stood for Electric, and H stood for Hawaiian (as opposed to conventional "Spanish" style guitars); 150 denoted the $150 price of guitar and its companion amplifer. It took a year for Gibson to gain enough confidence in electrics to introduce an Electric Spanish version, the ES-150.

Any doubt about the future of electric guitars was smashed by Charlie Christian, who used an ES-150 and later a fancier Gibson ES-250 to free the electric guitar from a rhythmic role, establishing it as a lead instrument with its own unique voice.

MODEL
**Gibson ES-150
(pre-WWII version)**

YEAR
1937

PRODUCTION
1936 to 1942

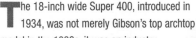

The 18-inch wide Super 400, introduced in 1934, was not merely Gibson's top archtop model in the 1930s, it was an industry leader in a movement toward larger-bodied guitars – acoustic guitars, that is. On the electric side, the first Gibson electrics, which appeared in 1936, were not as big, not as highly ornamented, and did not require the same level of craftsmanship as the acoustic models.

A standard Gibson electric was apparently just not good enough for the player who custom-ordered this Super 400 with a pickup in 1940. Gibson had recently developed its first pickup with height-adjustable polepieces for the ES-300 model, and it was easy enough to rout the top of a Super 400 for the electronics. The model name on the label, Super 400 Premier EN, includes all of this guitar's special features: Premier for cutaway body, an option introduced in 1939; E for Electric; and N for Natural finish, introduced in 1938.

Despite the obvious potential, it would be over a decade before Gibson offered an electric Super 400 as a catalog model.

MODEL

Gibson Super 400 Premier NE

YEAR

1940

PRODUCTION

1940

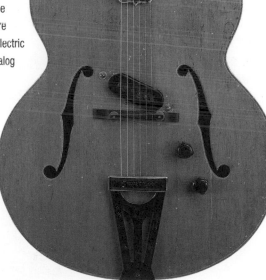

GIBSON

Gibson's original pickup, nicknamed the "Charlie Christian," is still prized by some jazz guitarists today, but its one-piece bar polepiece had severe limitations. To allow players to adjust the signal level for each individual string, Gibson appropriated a concept from its arch-rival Epiphone and developed a pickup with height-adjustable screws for polepieces.

The new pickup got a new housing – an oval, tortoiseshell-pattern celluloid cover – as well as a new model to introduce it. The ES-300 of 1940 featured this new design in what may be a record for pickup length: over seven inches. The slanted configuration made the low strings more bassy sounding and the treble strings more brilliant, but amplifiers of the day weren't equipped to exploit the increased tonal spectrum, and a more economical-sized pickup quickly appeared.

The ES-300 introduced two new visual elements to the Gibson line: double-parallelogram fingerboard inlays and the "crown" inlay on the peghead. It continued in the postwar years but was soon overshadowed by a cutaway version, called the ES-350.

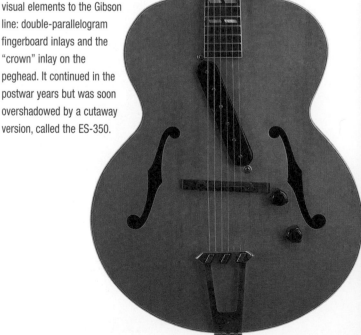

MODEL
**Gibson ES-300N
(pre-World War II)**

YEAR
1941

PRODUCTION
1940 to 1942

Gibson moved fast in the post-World War II electric guitar market, introducing in quick succession an improved pickup (the P-90, with its distinctive "dog-eared" black plastic cover), its first cutaway electric (the ES-350), and its first two-pickup guitar (again, the ES-350). The versatility of a neck pickup and a bridge pickup quickly won over many guitarists, and the next step was obvious – if two pickups were good, three would be better.

In 1949, Gibson began building ES-350s with three P-90s. The two-pickup ES-350 had individual volume controls for each pickup but only one master tone control, and that concept was extended on the experimental three-pickup models, which featured three volume controls and one master tone.

Gibson put together a dozen of these models, labeled "ES-350 Sp.," in June and July of 1949 and then decided that a three-pickup guitar deserved a fancier look and more sophisticated controls. Although the ES-5 that debuted later in 1949 would be a step above the ES-350 Specials, Gibson nevertheless went back in serial number logbooks and ink-stamped "ES-5" over the original ES-350 entries.

261

MODEL
Gibson ES-350 Special
(3 pickups)

YEAR
1949

PRODUCTION
1949

GIBSON

Gibson's ES-5 might seem to have had a lowly model designation in the company of Gibson's other postwar electrics – the ES-125, 150, 300 and 350. But in Gibson tradition, Style 5 signified one of the highest levels of importance as well as ornamentation. The L-5 acoustic, introduced in 1922, had been the first archtop with f-holes, and an ES (Electric Spanish) version of the L-5 would command instant recognition and respect.

The ES-5 was the first guitar – by Gibson or anyone else – with three standard pickups, each with its own volume control, plus a master tone control on the cutaway. The neck ornamentation was similar to that of an L-5, but instead or the L-5's flowerpot peghead ornament, the ES-5 had a "crown" inlay.

The beautiful wood grain of the top of this natural finish ES-5 from 1952 illustrates another fundamental difference between the ES-5 and the L-5. Like all of Gibson's postwar electrics, it had a laminated maple body rather than the carved spruce top and solid maple body of the acoustics.

MODEL
Gibson ES-5

YEAR
1952

PRODUCTION
1949 to 1955

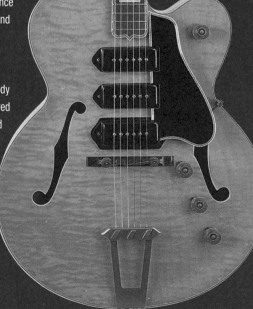

In 1949, two years after Gibson added a cutaway to its 17-inch ES-300, making it the ES-350, Gibson did the same with its 16-inch ES-125. For the cutaway version, Gibson once again added 50 "points" to the model number and called the new guitar the ES-175. The model's pointed "Florentine" cutaway made it unique among Gibson's electric archtop models of the 1950s.

Continuing to follow the ES-350's example, Gibson introduced a two-pickup version of the ES-175 in 1951, and this comfortable, 16-inch, laminated-maple electric hollowbody quickly became one of Gibson's more successful electrics. The two-pickup ES-175D has been in continuous production longer than any other Gibson.

In the meantime, the single-pickup ES-175 gained a reputation as the workhorse guitar of the jazz guitar world. Some of the most prominent jazzmen of the 1950s, such as Kenny Burrell and Jim Hall, played single-pickup ES-175s, and Herb Ellis was so closely identified with his single-pickup ES-175 that it became the ES-165 Herb Ellis signature model in 1991.

263

MODEL
Gibson ES-175

YEAR
1953

PRODUCTION
1949 to current

GIBSON

Gibson's ES-5 was modeled after the company's legendary L-5 acoustic – but only to a point. Despite such high-end features as three pickups and gold-plated hardware, it had a laminated maple body that left some guitarists longing for a true electric version of the L-5. And that's exactly what Gibson gave them in 1951.

The L-5CES (Cutaway Electric Spanish) was built as an acoustic guitar, complete with carved spruce top and solid maple back and sides. Gibson simply cut holes in the top for pickups and controls. The holes severely compromised the guitar's acoustic qualities, but players did not seem to care.

Although the L-5 had always been a favorite of big band and jazz players, the L-5CES gained a higher level of notoriety in the hands of Elvis Presley's guitarist Scotty Moore. Moore bought a natural finish L-5CESN in 1955, just as Presley was leaving Sun Records for RCA, and Moore played it the biggest hits from the biggest pop star of the era, including "Hound Dog," "Heartbreak Hotel," "Blue Suede Shoes" and "Don't Be Cruel."

MODEL
Gibson L-5CES

YEAR
1951

PRODUCTION
1951 to current

In 1951, Gibson introduced electric versions of its two most famous acoustic archtop guitars, the Super 400 and L-5.

From a practical point of view, it made little sense to go to the trouble and expense of carving a solid spruce top and then cutting holes in it for pickups and controls, but guitarists who bought the Super 400CES didn't really care about its performance quality as an acoustic; they simply wanted a Gibson electric that was as fancy and prestigious as any Gibson acoustic model.

Like the L-5, the 18-inch Super 400 had been a favorite of big band jazz players since its introduction in 1934, but like the L-5CES, the Super 400CES gained its greatest exposure in the hands of the most influential rock'n'roll player of the 1950s – Scotty Moore, Elvis's guitarist. Moore bought a natural-finish model in January 1957 and used it into the 1960s, a period that encompassed such No. 1 Elvis hits as "All Shook Up," "Teddy Bear," "Hard Headed Woman," and "Good Luck Charm."

MODEL
Gibson Super 400CES (P-90s)

YEAR
1953

PRODUCTION
1951 to 1957

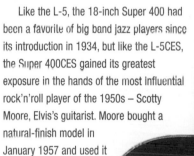

GIBSON

As Gibson was introducing its first solidbody electric, the "goldtop" Les Paul Model of 1952, the company also offered the expensive-looking gold finish to players of hollowbody electrics with the ES-295.

Essentially a gold version of the ES-175, the ES-295 took the concept a step beyond the gold top of the Les Paul by sporting gold finish on the neck, back, and sides, as well as the top. The connection to the solidbody model was evident in the ES-295's combination bridge tailpiece, which was invented by Les Paul and featured on his signature guitar as well (but never on the ES-175).

One musician who couldn't resist the allure of an all-gold guitar was Memphis guitarist Scotty Moore, who was playing in a country band in 1953 when he saw an ES-295 in a store window and had to have it. In 1954, Moore brought it to a session with Elvis Presley and played it on "That's All Right," and popular music was never the same again.

MODEL
Gibson ES-295

YEAR
1952

PRODUCTION
1952 to 1958,
1990 to 1994

The Super 400CES never set any sales records for Gibson, but the 18-inch archtop electric has remained in production since its introduction in 1951 as a symbol of the highest level of the guitarmaker's art. If a guitarist wanted the best guitar Gibson made – in terms of price – it had to be a Super 400.

Scotty Moore, Elvis Presley's guitarist, bought his first Super 400, which was equipped with single-coil P-90 pickups, in the mid 1950s during Elvis's "Hound Dog" era. Gibson upgraded the Super 400 (and all its other high-end electrics) with humbucking pickups in 1957, and in 1963 Moore upgraded to the newer version, which had also received a Florentine pointed cutaway.

The Super 400CES may have gotten its greatest exposure of the 1960s on Elvis's 1968 "comeback" TV Special when Elvis took the black finished guitar from Moore's hands to accompany himself solo on "One Night With You." The Super 400 was Moore's main guitar well into the 1980s, and it remains the flagship of Gibson's high-end electric archtop line today.

MODEL
Gibson Super 400CESN
(humbuckers)

YEAR
1958

PRODUCTION
1957 to current

GIBSON

While Gibson's L-5CES and Super 400CES, with their carved spruce tops, represented the highest level of artisanship in the Gibson electric line of the mid 1950s, the three-pickup ES-5 was Gibson's showcase for electronic advancement.

The original version of the ES-5 had a single volume control for each pickup, plus a master tone control, which allowed the player easily to "dial in" a preferred pickup combination but made it difficult to switch quickly and accurately to other settings. In 1955, Gibson added a tone control for each pickup, along with a slotted switch with four settings that let the player select each pickup alone or all three together. The ES-5 Switchmaster, as the new version was named, did not allow any combinations of two pickups, but the six knobs and large switch made it appear, at least, as if it could outperform any other electric guitar.

Gibson changed the cutaways on its electric models to a pointed Florentine shape in 1961, and a handful of Switchmasters were made with the new shape before production ended in that same year.

MODEL
Gibson ES-5
Switchmaster

YEAR
1957

PRODUCTION
1955 to 1961

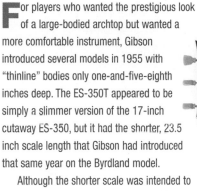

For players who wanted the prestigious look of a large-bodied archtop but wanted a more comfortable instrument, Gibson introduced several models in 1955 with "thinline" bodies only one-and-five-eighth inches deep. The ES-350T appeared to be simply a slimmer version of the 17-inch cutaway ES-350, but it had the shorter, 23.5 inch scale length that Gibson had introduced that same year on the Byrdland model.

Although the shorter scale was intended to appeal to jazz players, the ES-350T will forever be remembered as the guitar Chuck Berry used as he "wrote the book" on rock'n'roll guitar licks on such hits as "Maybellene," "School Days" and "Roll Over Beethoven." Berry's natural-finish ES-350T was immortalized in early photos of the artist in a crossed-knees stance or duck-walking across a stage.

After Gibson's introduction of semi-hollowbodies in 1958, Berry switched to the ES-355, and the ES-350T never recovered. Gibson dropped it after 1962, and although Gibson reintroduced it several times (beginning in 1977), the newer versions always had a standard scale length.

MODEL
**Gibson ES-350T
(23.5-inch scale)**

YEAR
1957

PRODUCTION
1955 to 1962

GIBSON

With a 16-inch body, the ES-175D (D for Double-pickup) was barely even a midline model, but Gibson gave it an important, high-end upgrade in 1957 by replacing the ES-175's single-coil P-90 pickups with the new double-coil humbuckers.

Gibson engineer Seth Lover invented the humbucker to literally "buck the hum" that plagued single-coil pickups whenever they were near a rheostat, fluorescent light or some other source of electrical interference. The greater power of humbuckers would not be exploited until the 1960s, but they were nevertheless welcomed by players as soon as they were introduced.

While the ES-175 had been the preferred model of many jazz players in the 1950s, the humbucker-equipped model was attractive to rock'n'roll players in later decades. The jazz and rock appeal made it especially suitable for the eclectic musical output of Steve Howe, guitarist with the British group Yes. This 1964 ES-175 is his personal instrument. He became so closely identified with it that Gibson gave him a signature ES-175 (albeit fancier) in 2001.

MODEL
Gibson ES-175D

YEAR
1964

PRODUCTION
1951 to current

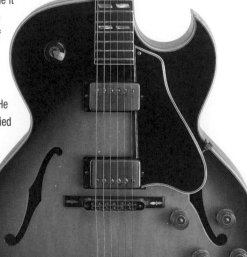

Doubleneck Hawaiian electric guitars appeared within a few years of the first electric guitars, but it was another 20 years before the doubleneck concept migrated to conventional electrics. In 1958, prompted by the popularity of hot-picking southern California guitarists Joe Maphis and Larry Collins (who both played custom-made doublenecks), Gibson began offering guitars with any combination of guitar, banjo, mandolin, and bass necks. The most popular was the 6/12 configuration of the EDS-1275.

The most remarkable aspect of these first Gibson doublenecks was the body. It was hollow, with a top carved spruce top, like Gibson's acoustic archtops. It was unique in that it had no soundholes – a design that had only been used on two electric basses made by Gibson in the pre-World War II years.

Within a few years, Gibson decided that the subtle tonal differences of the spruce top and hollow design were not as important as bringing the cost within the range of more guitar buyers, and by 1962, the EDS-1275 had become a solidbody based on the design of Gibson's SG series.

MODEL
Gibson EDS-1275 Double 12

YEAR
Circa 1959

PRODUCTION
1958 to 1961

271

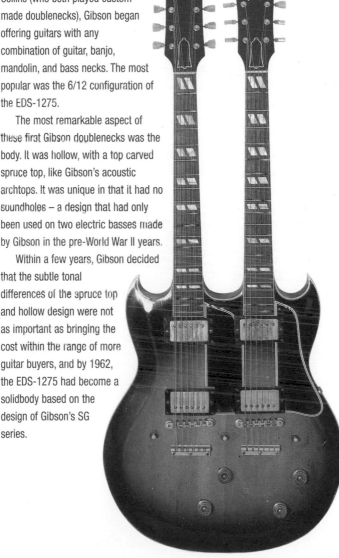

GIBSON

More than any other guitarist of the 1950s and '60s, Barney Kessell easily moved back and forth between jazz to pop music. In the jazz world, his Charlie Christian-inspired style gained him recognition as a member of the Oscar Peterson Trio, and in pop music, he played a prominent solo on Julie London's 1955 hit "Cry Me a River."

Gibson thought enough of Kessel to give him two signature models in 1961. Both featured a new body style – a full-depth archtop body with double cutaways that came to a point. The body was laminated maple, but through the first few years of production the tops were laminated spruce. The Kessel Regular had double-parallelogram inlays while the Kessel Custom sported bowtie inlays and a musical note on the peghead.

In the 1960s, Kessel was a member of the "The Wrecking Crew," who played on hits by the Beach Boys and the Monkees, but by the end of the decade, he was spending more time running a music store and refocusing on jazz. Gibson last produced his models in 1973.

272

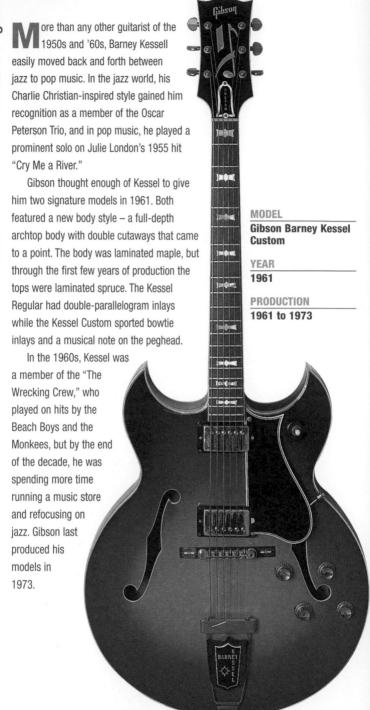

MODEL

Gibson Barney Kessel Custom

YEAR

1961

PRODUCTION

1961 to 1973

Johnny Smith brought an impeccable reputation to Gibson's artist roster in 1961, and his signature model featured the classic jazz setup – an acoustic archtop guitar with a "floating" pickup.

Smith's 1952 album *Moonlight in Vermont* set the standard for "chord melody" style, and he gained even greater fame from writing "Walk Don't Run," which was covered first by Chet Atkins and then in 1960 by The Ventures, whose version became a surf music classic.

After an endorsement agreement, and then a disagreement, with Guild, Smith signed with Gibson in 1961. The Gibson Johnny Smith model was based on Smith's personal D'Angelico guitar, which had a non-standard 25-inch scale length. It featured a smaller "mini" version of Gibson's humbucking pickup. It remained a symbol of class at the top of Gibson's archtop electric line until Gibson moved headquarters from Kalamazoo, Michigan, to Nashville, Tennessee, in 1984. Smith remained loyal to the Kalamazoo workers who stayed behind to form the Heritage company, and he left Gibson in 1988, although Gibson continued to offer the same model as the LeGrand.

MODEL
Gibson Johnny Smith

YEAR
1962

PRODUCTION
1961 to 1988

GIBSON

Following close on the heels of the Johnny Smith and Barney Kessel models, Gibson's Tal Farlow model secured Gibson's image as the preferred guitarmaker for elite jazz musicians. Farlow was inspired by the recordings of Charlie Christian, who practically invented electric jazz guitar, and pianist Bud Powell. The speed, accuracy and complexity of Farlow's style – demonstrated on a series of solo albums in the mid 1950s – put him in the upper echelon of bebop jazz guitarists.

Farlow's signature model was built on the familiar single-cutaway body of Gibson's 17-inch ES-5 model but with some unconventional features, including a scrolled cutaway bout (simulated with inlaid binding material), fingerboard inlays that were the "crest" of the J-200 flat-top turned upside-down, and a double-crown peghead ornament.

Ironically, Farlow (like Johnny Smith) had gone into semi-retirement shortly before Gibson debuted his signature model, not to emerge until the late 1970s. In the meantime, his namesake guitar sold less than 100 units, making it the rarest of Gibson's artist models of the 1960s.

MODEL
Gibson Tal Farlow

YEAR
1964

PRODUCTION
1962 to 1970

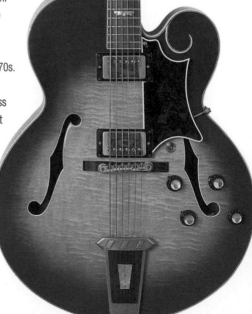

Despite the invention of powerful humbucking pickups in 1957 and the availability of a "floating" humbucker like the one Gibson used on its Johnny Smith model in the 1960s, some players preferred to stick with the old ways. The classic electric jazz guitar of the 1940s and early 1950s was a fully acoustic archtop with a DeArmond pickup, and that's how the owner of this 1969 Gibson Super 400 set up his guitar.

The unusual feature of this guitar, signified by "WAL" in the model designation, is a walnut-stained finish on the back, sides and neck. Numerous low-end Gibson models – solidbody as well as hollow – with a sunburst top finish had the dark brown stain over the rest of the guitar, but it was unheard of on any maple-body electric model with a natural top finish.

On the other hand, this guitar was made in 1969, and Gibson was struggling in a market overrun with cheap Japanese-made imports. Any new variation might have attracted attention to traditional Gibsons, but the walnut finish did not catch on.

MODEL
Gibson Super 400 CN WAL

YEAR
1969

PRODUCTION
1969

GIBSON

The model name of the Gibson's ES-135 of 1991 might have been vaguely familiar to veterans of the guitar industry – it had been a full-depth, non-cutaway archtop that made a brief appearance in the mid 1950s – but the single-cutaway body of the 1991 version was something new for Gibson's semi-hollowbody line. Until that time, all of the semi-hollows had had the ES-335's double-cutaway shape.

With a center block of lightweight – but strong – balsa wood, the ES-135 was Gibson's first new idea in archtop electric design since the 1970s, and Gibson's CEO Henry Juszkiewicz (whose ownership group had acquired the company in 1986) added a touch of mystique by coining the term Chromyte for the balsa wood.

The ES-135 was moderately successful and led to two offshoots, the all-black, humbucker-equipped ES-135 Gothic (1998–99) and the Swingmaster ES-135 (1999), which featured dog-eared P-90s and such "hip" finishes as Outa-Sight White and Daddy-O Yellow. Although the ES-135 was last made in 2003, the basic model style continues in Gibson's ES-137 series.

276

MODEL
Gibson ES-135

YEAR
1993

PRODUCTION
1991 to 2003

Gibson opened a new facility in Nashville in 1974, intending to move solidbody electric production there. The craftsmen who made Gibson archtops – a style of guitar that Orville Gibson had invented in the 1890s – stayed in Kalamazoo, Michigan, and in 1978 they demonstrated their skills with an elaborately ornamented creation called the Kalamazoo Award.

The pickguard alone set the Kalamazoo Award apart from all previous Gibsons. Instead of celluloid, it was birdseye maple, inlaid with an abalone flying bird and branch. The figures were repeated on the peghead and tailpiece insert, and the large block fingerboard inlays were also abalone. The floating mini-humbucking pickup, with controls mounted in the pickguard, indicated that this guitar was designed to perform equally well as an acoustic or an electric.

Made in very limited numbers during a period when Gibson quality was falling fast, the Kalamazoo Award offered the guitar world a glimmer of reassurance that the tradition of fine, hand-crafted guitars was still alive and well at Gibson.

277

MODEL
Gibson Kalamazoo Award

YEAR
1979

PRODUCTION
1978 to 1984

GIBSON

Wes Montgomery gained fame in the mid 1960s for recording popular songs, such as "Goin' Out of My Head," in a smooth, mellow style that featured the melody played in octaves, but few pop fans knew that the Indianapolis native was a highly respected jazz guitarist who had carried the standard for bebop guitar in the early 1960s.

The classic jazz guitar of the 1950s was an archtop with a single pickup, but after the introduction of the humbucking pickup in 1957, Gibson only offered the 16-inch, laminated-body ES-175 with that configuration. Montgomery preferred the larger, fancier Gibson L-5, with its carved spruce top, and he custom-ordered several L-5s with a single humbucker.

Montgomery died unexpectedly from a heart attack at age 43 in 1969, but he remained closely identified with the single-pickup L-5, and Gibson's Custom Shop introduced it as a Wes Montgomery signature model in 1993. The Custom Shop also restored a fire-damaged Montgomery guitar that had his name engraved on a heart-shaped pearl inlay, and that version was offered in a limited edition in 1997.

278

MODEL
Gibson Wes Montgomery

YEAR
1997

PRODUCTION
1993 to current

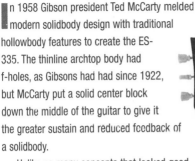

In 1958 Gibson president Ted McCarty melded modern solidbody design with traditional hollowbody features to create the ES-335. The thinline archtop body had f-holes, as Gibsons had had since 1922, but McCarty put a solid center block down the middle of the guitar to give it the greater sustain and reduced feedback of a solidbody.

Unlike so many concepts that looked good on paper, the semi-hollow guitar worked perfectly. The ES-335 not only bridged solid and hollow designs, it bridged musical genres from blues to rock to jazz. Eric Clapton and Alvin Lee (of Ten Years After) were among the influential rockers of the 1960s who played a 335. In jazz, Larry Carlton was so closely identified with the model that he became known as "Mr. 335." And iconic artists Chuck Berry and B.B. King are well known for playing fancier versions of the ES-335.

Of all the models introduced in the McCarty era – a Golden Era that includes Les Pauls, SGs, Firebirds, the Flying V and the Explorer – only the ES-335 has remained in continuous production.

MODEL
Gibson ES-335
(dot inlay)

YEAR
1959

PRODUCTION
1958 to 1962,
1981 to current

GIBSON

In 1959, only a year after Gibson had introduced the concept of a semi-hollowbody guitar, the ES-335 was well-established as the basic model, and the fancier ES-355 had found a market among more affluent buyers. Still, Gibson saw room in the middle for a third model, and the company filled that spot in 1959 with the ES-345.

Where the 335 had single-ply binding around the top, the 355 had seven-ply binding, so the 345's top was triple-bound. The 335 was nickel-plated, the 355 was gold; there was no middle ground so the 345 was given gold plating and the 355 was given a vibrato unit to make up for it. In between the dot fingerboard inlays and the large pearl blocks, the 345 sported double-parallelograms, a well-established inlay pattern on midline Gibsons.

Like the ES-355, the ES-345 was equipped with stereo output, which was a seldom-used but benign feature. However, the Varitone control ultimately made the 345 less desirable than the basic 335, and many players had their 345s rewired to bypass the Varitone.

MODEL
Gibson ES-345

YEAR
1959

PRODUCTION
1959 to 1982

Among the new features of Gibson's 1958 thinline, semi-hollowbody ES-335 was its double-cutaway body, a first for Gibson f-hole archtop models. It was so well-received that, a year later, Gibson tried the double-cutaway on a fully hollow thinline model.

The model number of the hollow version, ES-330, showed that, from the very start, Gibson considered it to be a little below the semi-hollow 335. And the 330's single-coil pickups secured its place as "poor relation" to the humbucker-equipped 335. The hollowbody precipitated another fundamental difference; without the support of the 335's center block, the neck had to extend farther into the body, leaving ES-330 players with less access to the upper register than the ES-335 provided.

The ES-330 did initially have one feature that the 335 lacked – a single-pickup version – but that only lasted through 1962. Not all musicians thought the hollowbody and shorter neck were too limiting. The ES-330 was reasonably successful, and the Gibson-made Epiphone version, the Casino, gained considerable fame in the hands of The Beatles.

281

MODEL
Gibson ES-330

YEAR
1961

PRODUCTION
1959 to 1971

GIBSON

Eric Clapton's 1964 Gibson ES-335 shows that despite the unqualified success of the ES-335, Gibson could not resist "upgrading" its basic semi-hollowbody model.

Late in 1959, little more than a year after the ES-335's introduction, Gibson added an optional cherry stain finish. Early in 1961, the pickguard was shortened by a few inches. Also in 1961, white nylon saddles replaced the metal saddles in the tune-o-matic bridge. And in mid 1962, small pearloid block inlays replaced the original dots on the fingerboard. For the most part, the changes were small and insignificant from a player's point of view, and they did not impede Clapton's performance with this guitar on Cream's recording of "Crossroads."

Gibson continued to meddle with the 335. Unlike the cosmetic upgrades, the replacement of the stopbar tailpiece with a trapeze in late 1964 was detrimental, and the addition of a coil tap in 1977 was gratuitious. Gibson finally came to its senses in 1981 and reverted to the original "dot-neck" version, and the ES-335 DOT continues to be a mainstay of Gibson's electric lineup.

MODEL
**Gibson ES-335
(block inlays)**

YEAR
1964

PRODUCTION
1962 to 1980

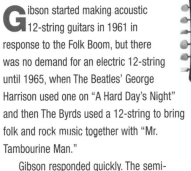

Gibson started making acoustic 12-string guitars in 1961 in response to the Folk Boom, but there was no demand for an electric 12-string until 1965, when The Beatles' George Harrison used one on "A Hard Day's Night" and then The Byrds used a 12-string to bring folk and rock music together with "Mr. Tambourine Man."

Gibson responded quickly. The semi-hollow ES-335, with its solid center block, was better suited than a hollow archtop to support the extra string tension of 12 strings, and the ES-335-12 debuted by the end of 1965.

ES-335-12 sales were respectable for two years, but despite the familiarity of the 12-string's unique sound, the market was apparently driven almost entirely by The Byrds. In 1968 The Byrds took a turn toward country music, and the era of the electric 12-string ended as suddenly as it had started. Sales of the ES-335-12 dropped by more than two-thirds that year and then by an even greater amount in 1969. Gibson shipped the last ES-335-12s in 1970.

283

MODEL
Gibson ES-335-12

YEAR
1965

PRODUCTION
1965 to 1970

GIBSON

From the front, the ES-340 was indistinguishable from Gibson's classic semi-hollowbody model, the ES-335, but a back view would reveal a three-piece maple neck on the 340, where the neck of the 335 was mahogany during the 340's production run.

The real difference between the two models was in the wiring. Gibson's traditional wiring system for two pickups was simple: separate tone and volume controls for each pickup plus a three-way switch that selected neck pickup alone, bridge pickup alone, or both pickups. That was more than enough for most players, but for those who liked a certain blend of the two pickups together, a seemingly simple adjustment in volume would cause both pickups to be changed by the exact same amount. It was difficult, if not impossible, to maintain the same pickup mix at different volumes.

Gibson solved the problem by rewiring the two individual volume knobs to function as a pickup blend control and a master volume. As it turned out, there really wasn't such a great demand for the ES-340's system, and the model only lasted in production for five years.

MODEL
Gibson ES-340

YEAR
1969

PRODUCTION
1969 to 1973

Ironically, in light of Gibson's phenomenal success with Les Paul's endorsement, Les Paul himself had very little input into the design of his classic 1950s models. That changed in the late 1960s when Gibson revived the solidbodies and brought Paul back into the fold.

This time around, Paul's ideas were implemented in every style of electric guitar, including a solidbody, an electrified flat-top acoustic, and an oddly shaped semi-hollow model – the Les Paul Signature. Paul had intended for the Signature to have neck-thru-body construction – essentially a continuation of the ideas he had introduced in 1941 with his homemade guitar, The Log. However, when it went into production, Gibson gave it a conventional set neck and a T-shaped center support block.

The Signature also sported the low-impedance humbucking pickups preferred by Paul but, unfortunately, not by most other guitarists. The bass version gained a cult following (and was eventually reissued in Gibson's Epiphone line as the Jack Casady signature model), but the Les Paul Signature guitar barely lasted five years in production.

MODEL

Gibson Les Paul Signature

YEAR

1976

PRODUCTION

1973 to 1977

GRETSCH

Tenor guitars were prevalent in the 1930s as they provided tenor banjo players with an easy way to switch to the increasingly popular guitar. By the 1950s most companies would still make almost any model as a tenor, but only by custom order.

This Gretsch electric tenor is a Synchromatic 6031, featuring the cat's eye soundholes that appeared on the Synchromatic acoustic series in 1939 and were the first of many design flairs that would set Gretsch apart from its competitors. Although this instrument is technically an acoustic model with an added pickup, the pickguard has the shape and tortoise pattern of a standard Gretsch guard, and the cutout for the pickup is bound, indicating that it was probably original, factory-installed equipment on this guitar.

As part of Gretsch's across-the line overhaul in 1955, the Synchromatic 6030 (sunburst finish) and 6031 (natural) received a new name – the Constellation – but Gretsch's focus was almost completely on electrics by that time, and the Constellation only lasted to the end of the decade.

MODEL
Gretsch Synchromatic 6031 electric tenor

YEAR
Circa 1954

PRODUCTION
1951 to 1954

Gretsch's Corvette hollowbody model was never as famous as the later solidbody Corvette, and with good reason. It was really just a re-named version of Gretsch's original electric model, introduced in 1940 just before World War II brought a halt to electric guitar production, and until 1955 it was still known by its unimaginative, generic but typical prewar model name: Electromatic Spanish.

The Corvette retained the earlier model name on the peghead. The "matic" part tied it in with Gretsch's high-end Synchromatic acoustics, but the 16-inch Corvette was a step below Gertsch's prestigious archtop line. The DeArmond pickup on the Corvette also tied it to an established tradition; DeArmond made the most popular add-on pickups that electric guitarists used to convert acoustic archtops to electric.

The DeArmond pickup, featured on all early- and mid-1950s Gretsch electrics, was (theoretically, at least) a step above Gibson's P-90, with height-adjustable magnet-slug polepieces rather than the simpler screw-poles used by Gibson. It didn't help the Corvette, however, which was left in the dust of Gretsch's more modern designs of the late 1950s.

287

MODEL
Gretsch Corvette

YEAR
1955

PRODUCTION
1955 to 1959

The Country Club started life with the generic name Electromatic II in 1951, but in 1954, it received a new name that was the first sign of an across-the-line upgrade in store for the Gretsch line a year later.

The 1955 Grestch catalog abandoned its traditional slogan – That Great Gretsch Sound – and replaced it with the hipper-sounding "Guitars for Moderns." The cover was printed in full color to show off what was, for the time, a radical selection of finish colors, including a Country Club in Cadillac Green.

Jimmie Webster, a pioneer of the fingerboard-tapping technique (that Eddie Van Halen would later appropriate for rock'n'roll), was the man responsible for the vibrant colors, as well as various electronic features and eye-catching ornamentation, that would set Gretsch apart from the competition in the late 1950s. To enhance the special treatment represented by a colorful finish, Gretsch gave each color its own model number. The Country Club in Cadillac Green was Model 6196.

MODEL
Gretsch Country Club

YEAR
1955

PRODUCTION
1954 to 1981

The Streamliner was essentially an upgraded version of Gretsch's original Electromatic Spanish (aka Corvette). In fact, its original model name was the boring but accurate Electromatic 16" Cutaway. In addition to the cutaway, it was distinguished from the basic Electromatic by its block inlays, and it was available with one or two DeArmond pickups.

The Streamliner name was adopted in 1955, although a sign of its Electromatic origins remained on the headstock. In keeping with other new colors of 1955, such as the White Falcon or the Cadillac Green Country Club, Gretsch offered the Streamliner not only in sunburst and natural finish but also in exotic – exotic-sounding, at least – Jaguar Tan. Although it was listed as being available only by special order, Jaguar Tan had its own special model number, Model 6189.

In 1958, Gretsch celebrated its 75th anniversary by appropriating the basic Streamliner for a new model called the Anniversary. Most of the Streamliner features continued, but the Jaguar Tan finish option did not survive the transition.

MODEL
Gretsch Streamliner

YEAR
1955

PRODUCTION
1955 to 1959

In 1955, Gretsch abandoned its established image as a maker of traditional archtops and gave itself a complete makeover. The new and improved guitarmaker introduced itself with a splashy array of finish colors and new models. At the top of the line, in gleaming white with gold trim, was the White Falcon.

Gretsch literature explained that this "luxurious styling" was created for the player "who is willing to pay the price," and at $600, the White Falcon was $200 more than the next most expensive model. But no other Gretsch matched its features, starting with a unique "Cadillac" tailpiece, so nicknamed because its V-shaped motif was similar to the V used with the automotive logo. The V was repeated in the truss-rod cover design, the headstock shape, and the gold sparkle wings framing the logo.

The Falcon is one of the more desirable Gretches on today's vintage guitar market, due in part to its use by rockers Stephen Stills and Neil Young and also due to the rarity that its high price ensured.

MODEL
Gretsch White Falcon
(single cutaway)

YEAR
1955

PRODUCTION
1955 to 1961

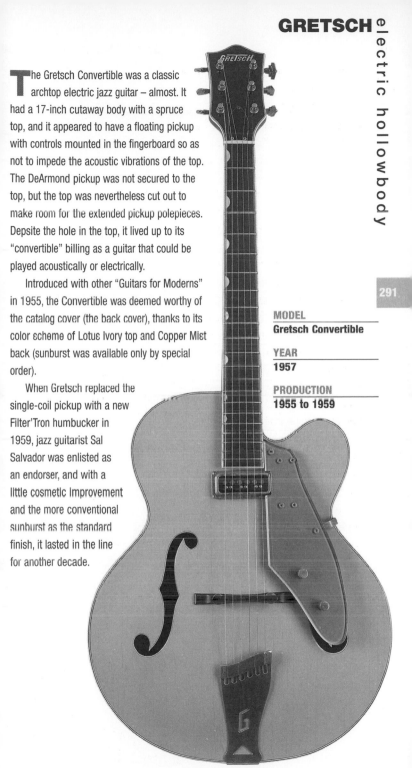

The Gretsch Convertible was a classic archtop electric jazz guitar – almost. It had a 17-inch cutaway body with a spruce top, and it appeared to have a floating pickup with controls mounted in the fingerboard so as not to impede the acoustic vibrations of the top. The DeArmond pickup was not secured to the top, but the top was nevertheless cut out to make room for the extended pickup polepieces. Despite the hole in the top, it lived up to its "convertible" billing as a guitar that could be played acoustically or electrically.

Introduced with other "Guitars for Moderns" in 1955, the Convertible was deemed worthy of the catalog cover (the back cover), thanks to its color scheme of Lotus Ivory top and Copper Mist back (sunburst was available only by special order).

When Gretsch replaced the single-coil pickup with a new Filter'Tron humbucker in 1959, jazz guitarist Sal Salvador was enlisted as an endorser, and with a little cosmetic improvement and the more conventional sunburst as the standard finish, it lasted in the line for another decade.

291

MODEL
Gretsch Convertible

YEAR
1957

PRODUCTION
1955 to 1959

GRETSCH

In 1952, when Gibson signed Les Paul to an endorsement agreement, Gretsch signed its first endorser, folksinger Burl Ives, for a flat-top acoustic model, and the results couldn't have been more disparate. By 1954, Les Paul's star was still rising, carrying Gibson guitar sales along with it, and Gretsch went looking for their own guitar star. They found Chet Atkins.

Atkins had been playing his distinctive, smooth, country-influenced style on a D'Angelico archtop equipped with a floating DeArmond pickup and a vibrato. For his Gretsch model, all he asked for were a brass nut, Bigsby vibrato and heavier bracing under the top (for more sustain). Gretsch staffer Jimmie Webster, the man responsible for the aesthetic flair that took over the entire Gretsch line in the mid 1950s, came up with the Western ornamention.

From this first Chet Atkins model, commonly known today simply as Model 6120, Gretsch expanded the Atkins line as Atkins's fame grew – to the point that his models carried Gretsch through the 1960s and well into the 1970s.

MODEL
Gretsch Chet Atkins Hollow Body (single cutway)

YEAR
1957

PRODUCTION
1955 to 1961

Even without the Chet Atkins signature signpost on the pickguard, this Custom Hollow Body is easily identifiable as some sort of an Atkins model.

The horseshoe inlay on the peghead is the same as that on Gretsch's Chet Atkins Hollow Body (Model 6120), having replaced the steer head in 1956. The body is the same size (15.75 inches wide) and shape as the Chet model. The Bigsby and metal bar bridge are features that Atkins specified on all his models.

This guitar not only has Atkins features, it was made for Atkins himself. Its most unusual feature is the addition of pickup polepieces under the bass strings in the upper register of the fingerboard. They were designed to run a signal through an octave effect to enhance the bass tones. The innovative electronics did not take, but the simulated f-holes of inlaid gold-sparkle material were precursors of the f-hole inlays (and the painted f-holes) that would appear in 1961 on the earliest versions of the Chet Atkins Country Gentleman model.

MODEL
Gretsch Hollow Body Custom

YEAR
1956

PRODUCTION
1956

293

The Gretsch Clipper was quite a "plain Jane" in the midst of large-bodied White Falcons, Cadillac Green Country Clubs and Amber Red Chet Atkins guitars, but the single-pickup, thinbody model held its own against Gretch's leading ladies for over a decade.

The Clipper's success was simple – it was a bona fide Gretsch, but without the frills and without the added expense. After starting in 1956 with just a sunburst finish and a cheap pickup (probably made by Harmony), the Clipper got an optional natural finish in 1959 and Gretsch's standard single-coil HiLo'Tron pickup in 1960. The natural finish was quickly discontinued, but the sunburst Model 6186 thrived at the bottom of the line. It was never deemed worthy of the "neo-classic" thumbprint inlays or even the zero fret that other Gretsches had, although for a short time, it had a palm-operated vibrato that was unavailable on any of the higher models.

In 1972 Gretsch discontinued the original Clipper but replaced it with a two-pickup Clipper that lived on as the entry-level Gretsch until 1975.

294

MODEL
**Gretsch Clipper
(single pickup)**

YEAR
1957

PRODUCTION
1956 to 1971

Within a year after Gretsch introduced the Chet Atkins Hollow Body, Atkins had a Top 20 pop hit with "Mr. Sandman." In 1957, Gretsch capitalized on Atkins's fast-growing fame by creating a new model and naming it after another Atkins recording whose title fit the man playing the guitar – Country Gentleman.

Aside from the rural signpost on the pickguard, the Country Gentleman left all the Western appointments of the earlier Atkins model behind. It featured a larger, 17-inch body, and most early examples had simulated f-holes that were actually black plastic inlays (later examples had paint or inlaid binding material to simulate the holes). Gretsch was close behind Gibson in developing double-coil "humbucking" pickups, and the Country Gentleman was fitted with these new units, called Filter'Trons because, according to Gretsch literature, they filtered out *all* electronic hum.

With a rich mahogany-stained finish, gold-plated hardware and a small plaque on the headstock with the model name and serial number, it looked expensive, and was – second only to the White Falcon.

MODEL
Gretsch Chet Atkins Country Gentleman (single cutaway)

YEAR
1961

PRODUCTION
1957 to 1961

GRETSCH

News that Gretsch was working on a double-coil humbucking pickup spurred Gibson to speed up their own development of a humbucker, and Gibson beat Gretsch to the market in 1957. However, Gretsch one-upped Gibson a year later when the Country Club appeared with not only new humbuckers, but with split coils for stereo capability.

Guitarist Jimmie Webster introduced the "Project-o-sonic" Country Club in a flyer that proclaimed "The biggest guitar news since electrification." The two Filter'Tron pickups had only three polepieces, with one set of polepieces under the bass strings and the other under the treble strings. With a click of the three-way "closing switch," the player got "Stereophonic Bi-Aural sound disbursement," with the treble strings going to one amplifier and the bass strings to another.

The system required a special cord and jack box, plus an extra amplifier, and it was only well-suited for players whose style effectively split the guitar into a three-stringed treble instrument and a three-stringed bass instrument. While basic Country Clubs continued to sell well, the stereo version did not last five years.

MODEL
Gretsch Country Club Stereo

YEAR
1958

PRODUCTION
1958 to 1960

In 1958, following Gretsch's introduction of the Country Gentlemen as the high-end Chet Atkisn model, the company balanced out the Atkins line expansion with a plainer model called the Tennessean.

With a body width of 16 inches, the Tennessean was the same size as the original Atkins Hollow Body (Model 6120), but it only had one pickup – a Filter'Tron humbucker mounted in the bridge position. It had open f-holes until 1961, after which they became simulated with paint or binding, just like those on the Country Gentleman. Like all Atkins models of the era, the Tennessean had a metal nut and a Bigsby vibrato tailpiece. Most examples had a cherry or walnut stain finich, but a few sported the eye-catching orange more often identified with the 6120.

Curiously, the Tennessean did not change to a double-cutaway body when the higher Atkins models did in 1961, but it nevertheless remained a solid sales performer in the Gretsch Hollow Body line until Atkins ended his endorsement in 1980.

YEAR
Gretsch Tennessean 6119

YEAR
1958

PRODUCTION
1958 to 1979

GRETSCH

Gretsch celebrated its 75th anniversary in 1958 with an Anniversary model, available with one or two pickups. The 16-inch single-cutaway model was basically a renamed and renumbered Streamliner (which had been introduced in 1951) or, from another perspective, it was simply a Chet Atkins Hollow Body (6120) with a different finish.

Colorful finishes were Gretsch's calling card in the second half of the 1950s, and the Anniversary introduced a new color scheme – a two-tone Smoke Green that was lighter on the top and darker on the back (traditional sunburst was also available). With an unbound fingerboard and peghead it was less expensive than the fancier models, but its pickup was the same Filter'Tron humbucker (until 1960, at least) that Gretsch put on the more expensive models.

The Anniversary of 1958 was successful enough that Gretsch continued the "celebration party" indefinitely, making the Anniversary a permanent member of the Gretsch electric archtop line. The single-pickup version remained in production through 1971, and the double-pickup model lasted even longer.

MODEL
Gretsch Anniversary

YEAR
1958

PRODUCTION
1958 to 1971

298

The two pickups – not the anniversary – were the "double" element of Gretsch's Double Anniversary model of 1958. Along with a single-pickup version, it marked the company's 75th anniversary and then continued as a regular production model.

Initially fitted with Gretsch's Filter'Tron humbucking pickups, the Anniversary was curiously downgraded in 1960 to the weaker Hi-Lo'Trons. Further evidence that someone at Gretsch had lost the celebratory spirit came in 1961, when the Chet Atkins Hollow Body (Model 6120) – essentially the same guitar as the Anniversary but with a different finish – went to a double-cutaway body, along with other high-end models, while the Anniversary models stayed with the single-cutaway body.

At the same time, in a dubious gesture to offset the Anniversary's second-class status, Gretsch offered the Double Anniversary with stereo for several years (1961–63) and gave it a bound fingerboard. In the 1970s, Gretsch took away the model's identity by discontinuing the Smoke Green finish and eliminating the nameplate on the peghead, and in 1974, the 16-year-long Anniversary celebration finally came to an end.

MODEL
Gretsch Double Anniversary

YEAR
1961

PRODUCTION
1958 to 1974

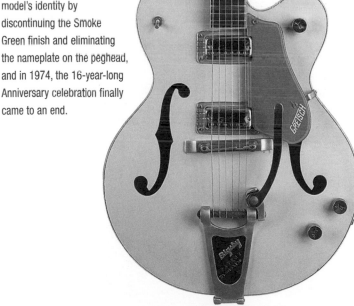

In 1958, Gretsch backed off a bit on the White Falcon's ornamentation but maintained its place at the top of the hollowbody electric line by offering it with stereo electronics.

The split-coil pickup, with apparent missing polepieces, was the telltale sign of stereo capability on the first stereo Falcons. Despite the more complicated choices offered by stereo, the controls were initially no more elaborate than on the non-stereo version. Instead of three knobs and two switches, the first stereo Falcon had two knobs and three switches.

In ormanenattion, a straight-across peghead logo replaced the Falcon's original vertical logo with gold wings, and engraved "humptop block" fingerboard inlays gave way to the "neo classic" (as Gretsch called them) or "thumbprint" (as everybody else called them) markers. It could be argued that the smaller inlays were more tasteful and that they allowed the ebony fingerboard to elegantly contrast with the white and gold, but the Falcon had always been about opulence, not elegance. The 1958 Falcon was still an eye-catcher, but it was a step down from the original.

MODEL

Gretsch White Falcon Stereo (first version)

YEAR

1958

PRODUCTION

1958 to 1959

Gibson introduced double-cutaway thinline electrics in 1958 with the ES-335 semi-hollow model, and Gretsch was not far behind. But rather than going through the expense of introducing and marketing an all-new model, in 1961 Gretsch simply began "upgrading" its top models from single-cutaway to double-cutaway.

By the time the Chet Atkins 6120 went to the double-cut body, it had lost most of its Western ornamentation. Even the rural signpost on the pickguard was gone, although the signature remained. The horseshoe on the peghead would last only until 1964 when the generic Hollow Body name was replaced with Nashville and a metal plate with the model name replaced the horseshoe.

In the meantime, the model acquired several new features, including Filter'Tron humbucking pickups (1958), a distinctive Gretsch version of the Bigsby vibrola, a foam-rubber string mute (just above the bridge), and a large, snap-on back pad. Discontinued when Atkins left Gretsch in 1980, the Nashville would be revived in both single- and double cutaway versions in the 1990s.

MODEL
Gretsch Chet Atkins Hollow Body (double cutaway)

YEAR
1962

PRODUCTION
1961 to 1980

GRETSCH

I n the first ten years of Chet Atkins's association with Gretsch, Atkins had gone from an up-and-coming country musician to one of the most influential figures in the music business. As a guitarist, his records were played by pop radio stations, and his distinctive finger-picking style was being copied by guitarists around the world. Moreover, he had begun producing records for RCA and was one of the architects of the Nashville Sound, the smooth, echo-laden productions that revived country music record sales in the early 1960s.

The growing notoriety of Gretsch's Chet Atkins line was pushed into overdrive in 1964, when The Beatles appeared on American TV, featuring George Harrison playing a double-cutaway Country Gentleman. His choice of an Atkins model was no coincidence, as evidenced by his Atkins-style solo in the middle of the Beatles hit "All My Loving."

Among vintage guitar collectors, the earlier single-cutaway of the Atkins Hollow Body (6120) is more popular than the double-cut, but thanks to The Beatles, the double-cutaway Country Gentleman is the most highly coveted version of that model.

MODEL
Gretsch Country Gentleman (double cutaway)

YEAR
1963

PRODUCTION
1961 to 1980

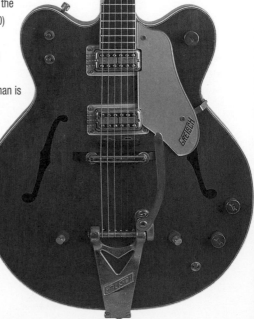

Gretsch changed its two top 17-inch models, the White Falcon and the Country Gentleman, from single-cutaway to double-cutaway bodies in 1961, but curiously, the Country Club was left with a single cutaway. That left a hole in the line that Gretsch filled with the double-cut Viking model in 1964.

The Viking had the standard appointments of a high-end guitar, including Gretsch's new Super'Tron humbucking pickups, a string mute, gold-plated hardware, and a nameplate on the peghead. But that was just a starting point. The new "T-Zone" fingerboard featured slightly slanted frets in the area of the dot inlays, which were designed to provide better intonation.

Perhaps the most bizarre Gretsch innovation was the "tuning fork" bridge – a floating piece of metal that extended into the body, where it was shaped like an actual tuning fork. The idea was presumably to create a resonance, but it would only be effective in keys related to the pitch of the tuning fork. Players who wanted better functionality from the Viking removed the tuning fork and repositioned the roller bridge.

MODEL
Gretsch Viking

YEAR
1967

PRODUCTION
1964 to 1974

GRETSCH

Lagging a bit behind Rickenbacker, Gibson, and Fender, who all introduced 12-string electrics in 1965, Gretsch jumped on the 12-string bandwagon in 1967.

The Gretsch was a hollowbody, different from the semi-hollow or solidbodies of its main competitors, but the Rickenbacker influence was evident in Gretsch's abbreviated triangular fingerboard inlays, which never appeared on another Gretsch, before or after the 12-string. Introduced just as Gretsch was being sold to the Baldwin company, the 12-string lacked the flair of a colorful finish (it was offered only in sunburst or natural). Moreover, the company seemed a little confused about its specifications, offering it with a 16-inch or 17-inch body, but under only one model number per finish color.

The model got an unexpected boost when, despite the existence of a Gretsch Monkees model, Monkees guitarist Mike Nesmith appeared on their TV show playing a natural-finish, 17-inch 12-string. Like The Monkees, whose show ended after the 1968 season, the electric 12-string proved to be only a passing attraction, and after 1972, Gretsch only offered the 12-string by special order.

MODEL
Gretsch 12-String

YEAR
1967

PRODUCTION
1967 to 1972

George Van Eps was the father of the seven-string guitar, and Gretsch was the only company to offer a seven-string jazz guitar as a regular catalog model.

Van Eps was the son of classical/ragtime five-string banjo player Fred Van Eps. He started his career as a swing guitarist, joining Benny Goodman's band in 1934. In 1938, he had Epiphone make a seven-string for him, and with the extra bass string he developed a unique style that featured a bass line, chordal support, and melody – all at the same time. He made a series of definitive recordings with the seven-string, beginning with *Mellow Guitar* in 1956.

Van Eps's seven-string style had a sizeable enough following for Gretsch to give him a signature model in 1968. The 17-inch cutaway archtop had a pair of Gretsch's Filter'Tron humbucking pickups with extra-heavy metal covers. It was also offered in a six-string version (Van Eps wrote instructionals and arrangements for six-string guitar as well). Gretsch continued to catalog the Van Eps model through 1979, and jazz players continue to play seven-strings today.

305

MODEL
Gretsch Van Eps

YEAR
1977

PRODUCTION
1968 to 1979

GRETSCH

Gretsch's Project-o-sonic stereo, which was available on the White Falcon in 1958, had initially been controlled with a simple two-knob, three-switch system, but within a year of Project-o-sonic's introduction, Gretsch's head designer Jimmie Webster couldn't resist making it better – or at least more complicated.

The Filter'Tron pickups with three missing polepieces were no longer a visual indication of stereo, having been replaced by standard-looking units, but a stereo guitar was now even more easily identifiable by the extra switches – five switches in all, along with two knobs. The 1959 version featured four switches on the upper bass bout; by 1965, they were moved to the lower treble bout.

Like the higher Chet Atkins Hollow Body and Country Gentleman, the White Falcon was "modernized" with a double cutaway body in the early 1960s. By the early 1970s, however, there was enough demand for the original single-cutaway that Gretsch reintroduced it, and the White Falcon became the only Gretsch model offered in single- and double-cutaway versions at the same time.

MODEL

Gretsch White Falcon Stereo (double cutaway)

YEAR
1980

PRODUCTION
1972 to 1980

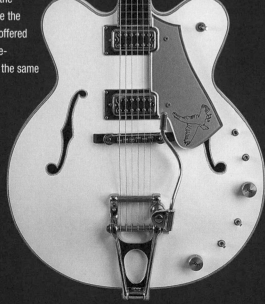

Although Chet Atkins's influence continued to be as strong through the 1970s as it was in earlier periods, Gretsch's quality was falling, and one of the most successful endorsement relationships in guitar history (second only to Gibson and Les Paul) ended in 1980.

Ownership of Gretsch had left the Gretsch family in 1967, when the company was sold to the Baldwin piano company, and Gretsch changed hands again in 1980, after which production slowed to a trickle. Fred Gretsch, great-grandson of the founder, reacquired his family's company in 1985 and began offering new, Japanese-made models in 1990.

Gretsch revived the Atkins models – the foundation of Gretsch's success a generation earlier – without the Atkins signature or model name, and the Country Gentleman (Model 6122) became the Country Classic. The Country Classic II was the double-cutaway with 1962 styling, eventually becoming model G6122–1962, while the single-cut 1958 version was dubbed the Country Classic I. After Atkins's death in 2001, his estate returned his endorsement to Gretsch, and this model is once again called the Chet Atkins Country Gentleman.

MODEL
Gretsch Country
Classic G6122-1962

YEAR
1993

PRODUCTION
1990 to current

Gretsch refrained from jumping into the doubleneck arena with Gibson in the 1960s or with Rickenbacker in the 1970s, but if Gretsch had made a doubleneck electric back then, it might have looked like the Nashville G6120-6/12.

Introduced in 1997, the six-string and 12-string model took its inspiration – like most of the guitars in the modern Gretsch line – from a tried-and-true model dating back to Gretsch's glory years of the late 1950s and early 1960s. The horseshoe on the pegheads, the orange-stain finish, and the Gretsch/Bigsby vibrola were all lifted directly from the Chet Atkins Hollow Body, aka Model 6120. The attempt to incorporate the single-cutaway body shape the early 6120s, however, left the doubleneck with an awkward bulge on the upper bass bout.

Chet Atkins's endorsement was not available at the time the 6120-6/12 was introduced, so the doubleneck, like other 6120-styled models in the new Gretsch line, was named Nashville – which has been Gretsch's name for the 6120 from 1964 to current times.

MODEL
Gretsch Nashville Double Neck G6120-6/12

YEAR
1997

PRODUCTION
1997 to current

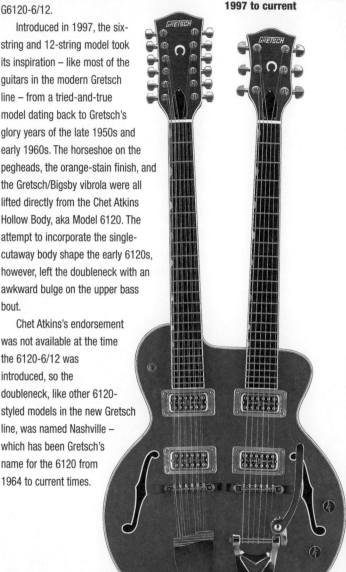

Brian Setzer's signature Gretsch models played a vital role in the 1990s in reviving Gretsch's reputation and promoting the company's new line of high-quality, Japanese-made guitars.

As front man for the Stray Cats, Setzer had led a rockabilly revival in the early 1980s, playing hot guitar licks on his 1959 Gretsch Chet Atkins 6120. In the 1990s, he reinvented himself in a swing band setting, and the Brian Setzer Orchestra led a new wave of interest in big band music with their remake of "Jump, Jive an' Wail."

Gretsch took advantage of Setzer's second round of fame by giving him a signature model in 1994 that was based on his vintage 6120. The Brian Setzer Hot Rod followed in 1999, featuring vintage-style "trestle" top bracing along with such Setzer specs as oversized soundholes, locking tuners, and custom-wound humbucking pickups (or, as an option, pickups made by TV Jones). In the best Gretsch tradition, the Hot Rod was offered in an array of flashy finish colors ranging from Lime Gold to Purple to Tangerine.

MODEL
Gretsch Setzer Hot Rod G6120SH

YEAR
2003

PRODUCTION
1999 to current

The neck-position pickup looks out of place among the vintage style appointments of this reissue of the 1957 Chet Atkins Hollow Body (Model 6120). It's actually a Gibson-style P-90, and it's on this Gretsch because rockabilly star Eddie Cochran put one on his Gretsch 6120 in the 1950s.

Cochran hit the Top Ten in 1958 with "Summertime Blues" and appeared in three rock'n'roll movies before he died in a London traffic accident in 1960. Along with instrumental star Duane Eddy (whose "twangy guitar" was a Gretsch 6120 before it was a Guild), Cochran helped build Gretsch's reputation as the home of the rockabilly guitar – a reputation that continues today with Brian Setzer's endorsement.

Gretsch's press announcement for the model in 2001 was headlined "Rockabilly Legend Eddie Cochran Remembered with G6120W-1957 Model," but before long, Gretsch seemed to forget. The current promotional pitch for the model known as the 1957 Chet Atkins Hollow Body begins with "C'mon Everybody," the title of one of Cochran's singles, but Cochran's name is no longer mentioned.

MODEL
Gretsch Nashville 1957 Western G6120W-1957

YEAR
2003

PRODUCTION
2001 to current

Despite having 1959 in its model name, this Country Classic was not a reissue of a 1959 Chet Atkins Country Gentleman (Model 6122). It was actually a custom-design model from guitarist Paul Yandell, who performed with Atkins for decades and was instrumental in convincing Atkins's estate to bring the Atkins endorsement back to Gretsch after Atkins's death In 2001.

When Chet Atkins left Gretsch in 1980, after a quarter-century of endorsement support, Gretsch tried to continue the Country Gentleman under the new name of Southern Belle, but the company was in such deep financial trouble that only a few were assembled in Mexico from leftover parts. In the 1990s, with Atkins firmly established as a Gibson endorser, new owner Fred Gretsch (great-grandson of the founder) introduced Japanese-made reissues of the 1958 single-cutaway Country Gent and the 1962 double-cutaway version under the model name Country Classic.

When Fender took over development and distribution of Gretsch In 2003, the Yandell-designed Country Classic 1959 appeared, featuring a slightly wider neck, custom TV Jones pickups, and a tubular-arm Bigsby vibrato.

MODEL
Gretsch Country Classic 1959 G6122-1959

YEAR
2003

PRODUCTION
2003 to current

GRETSCH

Although Gretsch's standard 1990s line of Japanese-made guitars already capitalized on the vintage appeal of the company's classic 1950s models, when Gretsch came under Fender's management control in 2003, Fender created a higher echelon of historic reissues, made in the Gretsch (Fender) Custom Shop in Corona, California.

The White Falcon G6136CST (CST for Custom Shop) featured all the trimmings of the original Falcon, including the "Cadillac" tailpiece, red rhinestones in the control knobs, pickups recreated by renowned vintage pickup maker Seymour Duncan, engraved pearl inlays, Melita bridge, gold sparkle binding, vintage-style body and neck construction, and even a nitrocellulose lacquer finish.

The original White Falcon of 1955 was the highest-priced model in the Gretsch line and, in the 21st century, the Custom Shop version maintained that position. Its list price of $11,000 was more than twice that of Gretsch's most expensive regular-production model, and it paved the way for a Custom Shop Chet Atkins Hollow Body and other limited-run models to follow.

MODEL

Gretsch White Falcon G6136CST

YEAR

2004

PRODUCTION

2004 to current

In the late 1950s, before restrictions on imports were lifted, London-based Emile Grimshaw made some of the highest-quality guitars available to British players. Grimshaw and his father, Emile Sr. (who died in 1943), had been making banjos and guitars since 1934, and his electrics combined quality with unique designs.

The deep cutaway of this Electric Deluxe model stood out like a sore thumb, but its most unusual feature was its electronic configuration. The controls were housed in the pickguard (which had its own unusual, meandering shape), but the pickups were not the "floating" type that were typically found with pickguard-mounted controls. The humbucking pickup in the bridge position was clearly mounted in the top, and there was a second pickup concealed in the fingerboard extension – a concept borrowed from Gibson's J-160E electric flat-top model.

Grimshaw found some success in the 1960s making copies of Gibson Les Pauls at a time when Gibson did not offer the model, but ultimately, Japanese makers did it at a lower cost and drove Grimshaw out of business by the end of the decade.

313

MODEL
Grimshaw Electric Deluxe

YEAR
Late 1950s

PRODUCTION
Late 1950s to early 1960s

GUILD

The six pushbuttons on Guild's Stratford X-350 of 1953 looked remarkably like the pickup selector system on Epiphone's Zephyr Emperor Regent model, and the similarity was no coincidence. Guild was formed with key employees from Epiphone who had stayed in New York when Epi production was moved to Philadelphia.

Guild made a huge splash with its debut line in 1953, which included seven large-bodied (17 inches wide) electric archtops – five with cutaways and two non-cutaways. Despite the X-350's upscale appointments – including block inlays, gold-plated hardware, three pickups, and the pushbutton system – it was only a midline model.

It went through a number of changes, among them a laminated maple top (the original was laminated spruce), a shorter scale length (from 25.5 to 24.75 inches), and humbucking pickups, but like Gibson's three-pickup ES-5, it succumbed in the 1960s, as the Folk Boom switched Guild's focus to acoustics and electric players began to realize that, for most performance situations, two pickups were enough.

MODEL

Guild Stratford X-350

YEAR

1954

PRODUCTION

1953 to 1964

In carrying on the Epiphone tradition with ex-Epiphone employees, Guild borrowed the signature inlay of high-end Epi models – a mother-of-pearl block with abalone V-wedge – for the top model in the Guild line, the Stuart X-550.

Guild initially gave natural-finish guitars a higher model number than the sunburst equivalent, so the sunburst version was the X-500. Around 1960 that disparity was eliminated when the X-550 became the X-500B (B for Blond finish). Beyond the name adjustment, the model went through few changes, receiving humbucking pickups in 1963 and a master volume control around 1961.

Although most high-end guitars did not sell as well as lower-priced models, the Stuart remained the flagship of Guild's archtop electric line through folk, rock, disco, metal and every other kind of music in the second half of the 20th century, while its fellow 1950s models fell by the wayside (most of them in the 1960s). The Stuart X-500 finally met its end in 1994 when it was upgraded, ironically, to a version with a solid spruce top called the X-700.

MODEL
Guild Stuart X-550

YEAR
1958

PRODUCTION
1953 to 1994

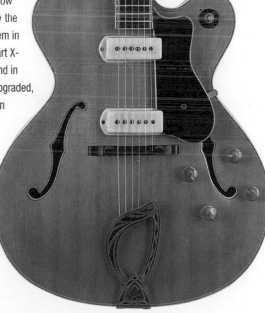

The Artist Award was Guild's Johnny Smith Award model, but only for a brief period.

Guild was founded in 1952, the same year Smith released "Moonlight in Vermont," the record that brought him fame for his lush "chord melody" jazz style. In 1955, Guild tapped him for a signature model, and the Johnny Smith Award debuted in 1956, by which time Smith was one of the most influential and respected guitarists in jazz (although he never considered himself a true jazz musician). Though not as flamboyant as Gibson's Les Paul, Smith brought an impeccable reputation to the Guild line.

Unfortunately, the Johnny Smith Award was not the guitar Smith had specified. Guild had altered it in order to make it easier to produce, and Guild's production head refused to change it back to Smith's specs. Smith ended the relationship, and Guild simply renamed the model the Artist Award. It remained the most prestigious model in Guild's archtop line through several Guild ownership changes but was finally discontinued – along with all other Guild electrics – in 2007.

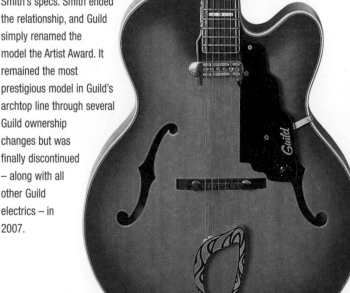

MODEL
Guild Artist Award

YEAR
1976

PRODUCTION
1956 to 2007

316

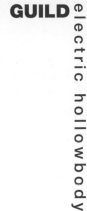

Guild introduced a pair of thin-bodied archtops with a pointed cutaway in 1958, so the Starfire models of 1960 were not really new – they were just better looking. Their cherry-stained "Starfire red" finishes set them apart from the traditional sunburst and natural finishes on every Guild that preceded them.

The Starfire I had a single pickup, the II had a pair of pickups, and the III featured two pickups plus a vibrato made by Bigsby. In 1963 the Starfires were further distanced from the more traditional thinline models when their single-coil pickups were replaced with humbuckers. By that time, all three Starfires were offered in such eye-catching finish colors as Emerald Green, Honey Amber and Ebony Grain.

The Starfire name worked well enough that Guild used it on a series of double-cutaway semi-hollow models – The Starfire IV, V, VI and XII – beginning in 1963. The single-cut Starfire III was discontinued in 1974 but Guild brought it back as a reissue from 1995–2005.

MODEL
Guild Starfire III

YEAR
1961

PRODUCTION
1960 to 1973

GUILD

Beginning in 1954, when Guild first put names with its original model numbers, the Stuart name signified the company's best electric archtop. The Stuart X-500 was one of the few consistencies in the model line as Guild underwent three ownership changes: to Avnet, an electronics company, in 1966; to an investment group, doing business as Guild Music Coproration, in 1986; and then in 1989, in the midst of a court-ordered financial restructuring, to FAAS Corporation, which became U.S. Music.

In 1994, Guild upgraded the Stuart model, as indicated by the change in model number from 500 to 700. The only significant change was the top – from laminated maple to solid, carved spruce.

The Stuart X-700 made it through yet another ownership change, when Fender bought Guild in 1995, and then received another upgrade in 1999 when famed archtop maker Bob Benedetto joined Fender and gave it a makeover. It continued simply as the Stuart model in the Benedetto series, and its long run ended when Benedetto left Fender/Guild in 2006.

MODEL

Guild Stuart X-700

YEAR

1995

PRODUCTION

1994 to 2000

Like virtually all Harmony guitars since the company's founding in the 1890s, the Meteor of the early 1960s was an "entry-level" instrument, a guitar designed for beginning players or musicians on a budget. As this rare left-handed Meteor shows, it had the same essential elements as a Gibson – two pickups, each with a tone and volume control. It wasn't until the guitar was played that the difference in quality – particularly the weak pickups – became apparent.

Not all guitarists viewed the low-level performance of the Meteor as a hindrance, however. Dave Davies of The Kinks put it to good use, pushing the Meteor's thick, distorted pickup sound through a small Elpico amplifier (with a cut speaker cone) to create the classic "hook" guitar lick that drove The Kinks' 1964 hit "You Really Got Me."

Another influential British guitarist, Peter Green, started out on a Meteor, but he didn't find it as useful as Davies did; it was the Meteor that Green traded in for the Les Paul that he played when he replaced Eric Clapton in John Mayall's Bluesbreakers.

319

MODEL
Harmony Meteor H70

YEAR
1965

PRODUCTION
Early 1960s 1967

HARMONY

Harmony capitalized on the dawn of the Space Age with such "buzz-word" model names as Meteor, Mars, Mercury, Jupiter and – the most popular of all – the Rocket.

Initially offered in sunburst finish only, the Rocket gained its more familiar red finish in 1963. Available as the Rocket I (single pickup), Rocket II (two pickups) and Rocket III (three pickups), it provided not just a cheaper alternative to Gibson's ES-125T, but an alternative with more features. The pickups, for example, were "GoldenTone Indox" units made by DeArmond. The "Ultra-Slim" neck featured a "Torque-Lok" adjustment feature. While these were high-class names for a low-end product, the H59 nevertheless sported three pickups, a feature that was only available in the Gibson archtop electric line on the ES-5, at several times the cost of the Harmony.

The Rocket was upgraded to a double-cutaway in 1968, and it eventually gained the dubious status of being offered in a build-it-yourself version marketed by the Heathkit eletronics company. It lasted in the line until 1970.

MODEL
Harmony Rocket III
H59 (single cutaway)

YEAR
Circa 1964

PRODUCTION
1960 to 1967

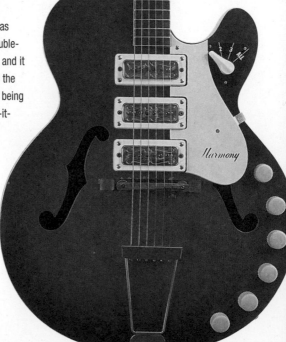

The H77 was about as fancy a guitar as could be expected from a budget brand. Harmony catalogs touted it as having "maximum electronics," and each of the three DeArmond pickups had its own tone and volume controls plus its own on/off switch – giving it more versatility than any Gibson three-pickup guitar ever had.

The H77 represented the last shining moment in Harmony's long history as one of America's leading makers of budget-priced instruments. The company has typically been grouped with Kay as a victim of cheap Japanese imports in the 1960s, but the turning point for Harmony was actually the death in 1968 of longtime owner Jay Kraus, who had bought Harmony from the giant Sears Roebuck catalog company in 1940.

After Kraus's death, the company bought several distributors in an attempt to secure its market base. Although sales of guitars remained respectable – even in the face of Japanese imports – the expansion attempt stretched the company's finances to breaking point. That point came in 1974, and Harmony's assets were sold at auction.

MODEL
Harmony H77

YEAR
1964

PRODUCTION
1963 to 1972

HOFNER

During the 1950s, when U.S. imports were banned in Britain, the German-based Hofner company offered some of the better-quality electric hollowbody models available to British guitarists. With the Hofner Club 50, guitarists had the appearance, at least, of a guitar comparable to Gibson's Les Paul.

Where the Gibson was a true solidbody, however, the Hofner's lack of soundholes belied a hollowbody underneath its solid spruce top. As with Hofner's more famous violin-body "Beatle bass," the small, hollowbody not only made it lighter in weight, it provided a unique sound.

The single-pickup Club 40, double-pickup Club 50 and fancy, maple-bodied Club 60 played a role in the early careers of some of Britain's best-known rock guitarists. John Lennon's first electric guitar was a Club 40. Ritchie Blackmore of Deep Purple started his career on a Club 50, but the boomy sound prompted him to trade it in towards a Gibson semi-hollowbody. The fancier, maple-bodied Club 60 helped along Moody Blues guitarist Justin Hayward and Pink Floyd's Dave Gilmour.

MODEL
Hofner Club 50

YEAR
Circa 1958

PRODUCTION
1954 to 1962

322

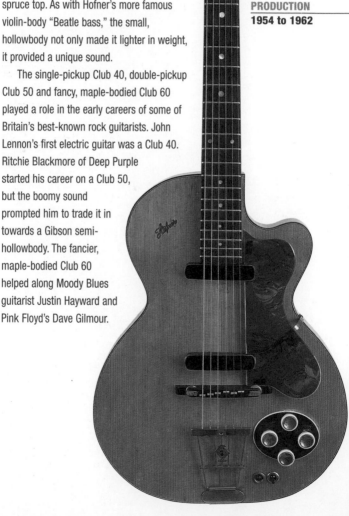

Hofner may have been an old-school German company with roots in the 1880s, but in the years after World War II, Hofner family members were well aware that the strongest market for their electric guitars was in the U.K. If British guitarists had felt any resistance to a German-made product, Hofner ingeniously dispelled it by creating a guitar that Brits could legitimately call their own.

Hofner called it the Committee because it was designed by a committee of British guitarists, including Frank Deniz, Ike Isaacs, Jack Llewellyn, Freddie Phillips, Roy Plummer and Bert Weedon.

Easily identifiable in its early years by its fancy peghead, the Committee got one of its biggest boosts from Denny Wright, a jazz guitarist who "moonlighted" in the recording studio with popular skiffle artists Lonnie Donegan and Johnny Duncan. The Committee was so important to Duncan's sound that, in later years, when session guitarist "Big Jim" Sullivan joined him in the studio, he made Sullivan put down his Les Paul and play a Committee.

MODEL
Hofner Committee

YEAR
1959

PRODUCTION
1956 to 1972

HOFNER

The President was the least expensive of Hofner's single-cutaway full-depth electrics, although the theme of American government continued down the line to the non-cutaway Senator and Congress models.

With a 16.25-inch body, the President was a bit smaller than the Committee, which varied between 17.5 and 18 inches. And the President had less binding, plainer inlay and a less ornate peghead. But when it came to performance the President started out with the same rosewood covered pickups as the Committee, and it moved right along with the more expensive model to the "toaster" style units and on up to double-coil humbuckers in the early 1960s.

The President, like most traditional archtop electrics, fell by the wayside in the 1970s, but Hofner revived the name in the 1990s for an updated version called the New President and an offshoot called the Vice President. In 2004, the political names took a curious turn toward the company's homeland when Hofner introduced a more expensive model called the Chancellor.

324

MODEL
Hofner President

YEAR
1959

PRODUCTION
1957 to 1973

In 1960, with the Committee well-established as one of the best electric guitars available in Britain, the German-based Hofner company topped it with an even bigger and fancier model called the Golden Hofner.

At 18 inches wide, the Golden model was larger than the Committee. It featured the same intricate peghead design and fingerboard inlay, but the neck was an 11-piece laminate. The body featured more binding, typically with an outer layer of pearloid. The most obvious identifying feature was the Golden Hofner's elaborately engraved, gold-plated "Escutcheon" tailpiece.

Hofner immodestly proclaimed the Golden to be "a masterpiece of guitar perfection." At a list price of 95 guineas (a guinea was a little over a pound), the Golden cost 50 per cent more than the Committee. It was either beyond the means of most guitarists, or else they realized they could get the same pickups and electronics on the Committee. After two years, Hofner had sold no more than 100 Goldens, and the last was made in 1962.

MODEL
Golden Hofner

YEAR
1961

PRODUCTION
1960 to 1962

Hofner's established models came in full-depth (3 inches or more) and thin (around 2 inches), but in 1960 the Hofner Verithin took it all the way down to 1.25 inches. The anorexic body was complemented by a thin "Slendaneck."

The influence of Gibson's ES-335 model, which had been introduced in 1958, was obvious in Verithin's double-cutaway shape – albeit with squashed-down horns. Unlike the semi-hollow 335, however, which had a laminated maple top and a solid block down the center of the body, the Verithin maintained elements of traditional archtop design with a fully hollow body and a braced spruce top.

The Verithin introduced a new look to the Hofner line with its full-width fingerboard markers of pearloid and tortoise, and the constrasting bars would become a Hofner signature look as they appeared on one new model after another in the 1960s. Hofner changed the Verithin's cutaways to a pointed shape in 1966, but it languished in the shadows of the more traditional archtops and disappeared in the early 1970s.

MODEL
Hofner Verithin

YEAR
1961

PRODUCTION
1960 to 1972

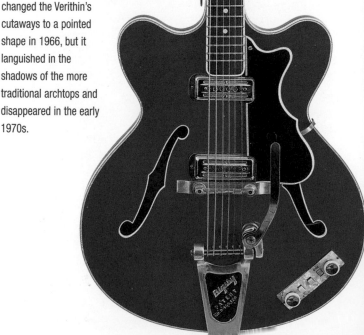

This guitar with a violin-shaped body was clearly modeled after Hofner's 500/1 bass guitar and intended to exploit the notoriety that the bass had gained in the hands of The Beatles' Paul McCartney. Although the violin-body guitar had a bolt-on neck rather than the set neck of the bass, the guitar had the upscale full-width fingerboard inlays while the bass only had pearl dots.

Hofner had previously used the model number on an unrelated, traditional archtop model. The new 459, introduced around 1965, was available in several variations. The VTZ version featured active electronics with treble boost and distortion control. The very rare 459/VTZ Super sported more elaborate ornamentation, gold-plated hardware and a natural finish (similar to Hofner's 500/5 violin bass).

McCartney had moved on from his Hofner bass to a Rickenbacker by the time the 459 guitar appeared, so the guitar never had much of a chance and was discontinued in 1970. Hofner's violin-body basses have become vintage classics, but the guitar version remains little more than an interesting footnote in Hofner history.

MODEL
Hofner 459/VTZ

YEAR
Circa 1965

PRODUCTION
1965 to 1970

HOPF

Caspar Hopf began putting his name on musical instruments in 1669, and the family business was passed down through a dozen generations before arriving at Dieter Hopf, who led the Hopf company into the electric guitar era in the 1950s. Working with designer Gustav Glassl, Hopf created some of the most modernistic guitars of the 1960s.

One of Hopf's signature features was cat's eye soundholes. Gretsch had introduced the smooth, tapered design on its high-end Synchromatic acoustic guitars in the late 1930s, but when Grestch dropped the cat's eye holes in the 1950s, Hopf picked them up and put them to good use.

The Saturn 63's body shape was inspired by Fender's solidbody Jazzmaster, but the double soundholes on the bass side – accentuated by metal binding – gave it a memorable look that was distinctive from a Jazzmaster or any other guitar, for that matter. Thanks in part to being featured in an ad for Star Club in Hamburg, the Saturn 63 was the most successful Hopf of the 1960s.

MODEL
Hopf Saturn 63

YEAR
Circa 1965

PRODUCTION
Mid 1960s

George Benson's Ibanez signature model of 1976 served as a wake-up call for American guitarmakers who had assumed that Japanese companies could never win over top American musicians.

Benson had been well-known as a versatile jazz guitarist since the 1960s, and his albums occasionally included a vocal track. In 1976, "This Masquerade" changed him from a great guitarist who could also sing to a great singer who could also play guitar, and the record went to No. 1 on the pop, jazz and R&B charts.

By the mid 1970s, Ibanez had gained a reputation for making better-quality copies of American guitars than the American makers were making, but Benson's model helped establish Ibanez as a maker with its own designs. The GB-10 body was smaller than the typical Gibson archtop – 14.75 inches rather than 16 – and the cutaway split the difference between a traditional rounded shape and the pointed horn of Gibson's ES-175. Through the years, Ibanez has offered seven different Benson guitars, and the GB-10 is its longest-running signature model.

MODEL

Ibanez George Benson GB-10

YEAR

1978

PRODUCTION

1977 to current

JACKSON

Although the Jackson name will forever be linked with the first hot-rodded "Super Strats" of the 1980s, the Charvel Surfcaster of the early 1990s was also memorable enough to be worthy of a revival at the end of the decade.

By this time both of the company's founders, Wayne Charvel and Grover Jackson were long gone. Charvel sold his parts business to Jackson in 1978, and Jackson left the company in the hands of a Texas-based distributor in 1989. The Japanese electronic instrument company Akai bought the brands in 1997 and brought back the Surfcaster a year later under the Jackson brand.

Where the basic Charvel Surfcaster of the early 1990s had a basswood body, or else a mahogany back with figured maple top, the later Jackson version had a mahogany top and back. Also, a more powerful, more appealing humbucker replaced the Charvel's cooler-looking "lipstick" single-coil bridge pickup. Like the original, the revived Surfcaster had a hip nostalgic appeal that wore off quickly, and it only lasted in production for three years.

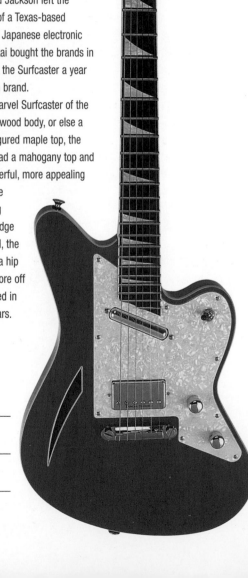

MODEL
Jackson Surfcaster

YEAR
1998

PRODUCTION
1998 to 2001

Blues artist Jimmy Reed, a major influence on The Rolling Stones, played an unusual Kay electric guitar with a flat top and no soundholes. He became so closely identified with it – Kay even pictured him in catalogs with the guitar – that it is widely known today as the Jimmy Reed model. Its official name, however, was the Kay Thin Twin.

The Kay company, based in Chicago, was named for its president Henry Kay Kuhrmeyer. It began as Groeschel (founded in 1890), which became Stromberg-Voisinet, the first company to market an electric guitar and also one of the first to make guitars with laminated wood bodies. Kuhrmeyer changed the company name to Kay in 1931, and made it an industry leader in budget-priced guitars.

The Thin Twin took its name from its body depth, which was only slightly thinner than a conventional acoustic guitar, and from its two pickups. The lack of soundholes gave the top enough stability to make the Thin Twin, along with a companion bass, one of the better performing Kay electrics of any era.

331

MODEL
Kay Thin Twin

YEAR
1954

PRODUCTION
1952 to 1959

Sidney Katz succeeded Hank Kuhrmeyer as president of Kay in 1955, and his first order of business was to elevate Kay's budget-brand reputation. To that end, he enlisted jazz guitarist Barney Kessell to endorse not just one but three Kay models. A Charlie Christian disciple, Kessell had made a name for himself in the Oscar Peterson trio and had just been featured prominently on Julie London's torchy 1955 pop hit "Cry Me a River."

The Artist was the middle model of Kessel's three Kay signature guitars, between the small, soundhole-less Pro and the fancier Special. All three featured what vintage guitar buffs today refer to as the "Kelvinator" peghead, nicknamed because it brings to mind 1950s-style appliances.

The Kessel models were a high-water mark for Kay, and the company reverted to budget-brand status in 1960 when Kessell moved his endorsement to Gibson. Kessell's career continued to rise, as he became a first-call studio musician, but Kay did not make it through the 1960s.

MODEL

Kay Barney Kessel Artist

YEAR

Circa 1958

PRODUCTION

1956 to 1960

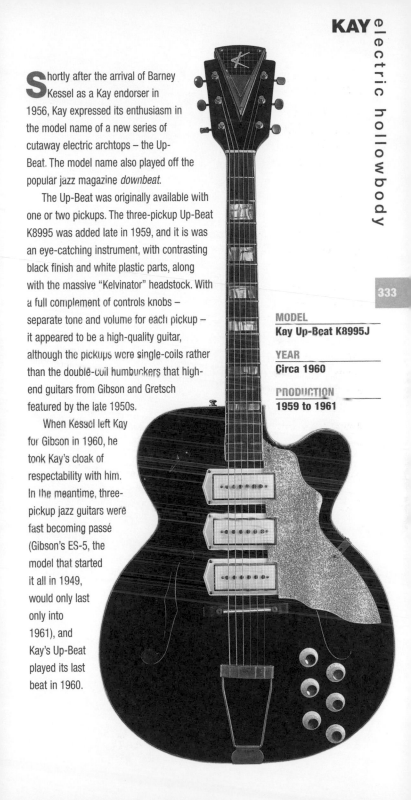

Shortly after the arrival of Barney Kessel as a Kay endorser in 1956, Kay expressed its enthusiasm in the model name of a new series of cutaway electric archtops – the Up-Beat. The model name also played off the popular jazz magazine *downbeat*.

The Up-Beat was originally available with one or two pickups. The three-pickup Up-Beat K8995 was added late in 1959, and it is was an eye-catching instrument, with contrasting black finish and white plastic parts, along with the massive "Kelvinator" headstock. With a full complement of controls knobs – separate tone and volume for each pickup – it appeared to be a high-quality guitar, although the pickups were single-coils rather than the double-coil humbuckers that high-end guitars from Gibson and Gretsch featured by the late 1950s.

When Kessel left Kay for Gibson in 1960, he took Kay's cloak of respectability with him. In the meantime, three-pickup jazz guitars were fast becoming passé (Gibson's ES-5, the model that started it all in 1949, would only last only into 1961), and Kay's Up-Beat played its last beat in 1960.

MODEL
Kay Up-Beat K8995J

YEAR
Circa 1960

PRODUCTION
1959 to 1961

KAY

Following the lead of Gibson's double-cutaway, thin-bodied ES-335 of 1958, Kay came with its own version in 1960 called the Jazz II.

Like many lower-quality guitars, this Kay was more style than substance. Its humbucker-sized pickups were actually single-coils, nicknamed "Kleenex box" style by vintage collectors. The fingerboard inlays took their quarter-circle design from the guitars of National, another Chicago-based maker of budget-priced instruments. And the "Slim-Lite" neck was bolted-on, a feature it shared with no high-quality jazz guitars.

Despite the model name, Kay's target for this guitar was questionable. It had a long, 26-inch scale at a time when the trend among some jazz players was toward the shorter scales lengths of Gibson's Byrdland and ES-350T models. The Jazz II became most famous, ironically, in blues-rock circles. Eric Clapton's grandmother bought him a Jazz II (or a similar model) for his birthday, and that was the instrument wielded by the future guitar god in 1963 when he joined his first band, The Roosters.

MODEL

Kay Jazz II K776

YEAR

1961

PRODUCTION

1960 to 1963

The K592 "Red Devil" brought the bold look of pointed horns to Kay's archtop line in the early 1960s, but it nevertheless represented the toning down of Kay models after the gaudy "Kelvinator" headstocks and "Kleenex box" pickups of the late 1950s. The earliest version of the model had a very simplified "Kelvinator" headstock, but by the time of this example, the peghead logo had been reduced to a stenciled letter K.

Kay had moved into a larger factory in suburban Chicago in 1964, which would suggest that the company was doing well, but model K592 proved to be a more accurate indicator – an early sign of troubled times, as the company consistently lost market share in competition with cheap Japanese imports.

The Seeburg jukebox company bought Kay in 1966 and then sold it a year later to the Chicago-based Valco company, which was struggling with its National and Supro brands. In 1968, Valco went bankrupt. The Kay name was bought at auction in 1969 and was used on cheap, Asian made guitars after that.

MODEL
Kay K592

YEAR
Circa 1964

PRODUCTION
Circa 1962 to circa 1964

KENT

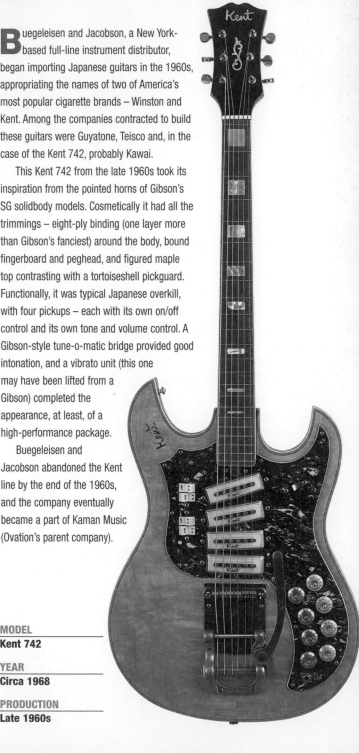

Buegeleisen and Jacobson, a New York-based full-line instrument distributor, began importing Japanese guitars in the 1960s, appropriating the names of two of America's most popular cigarette brands – Winston and Kent. Among the companies contracted to build these guitars were Guyatone, Teisco and, in the case of the Kent 742, probably Kawai.

This Kent 742 from the late 1960s took its inspiration from the pointed horns of Gibson's SG solidbody models. Cosmetically it had all the trimmings – eight-ply binding (one layer more than Gibson's fanciest) around the body, bound fingerboard and peghead, and figured maple top contrasting with a tortoiseshell pickguard. Functionally, it was typical Japanese overkill, with four pickups – each with its own on/off control and its own tone and volume control. A Gibson-style tune-o-matic bridge provided good intonation, and a vibrato unit (this one may have been lifted from a Gibson) completed the appearance, at least, of a high-performance package.

Buegeleisen and Jacobson abandoned the Kent line by the end of the 1960s, and the company eventually became a part of Kaman Music (Ovation's parent company).

MODEL
Kent 742

YEAR
Circa 1968

PRODUCTION
Late 1960s

Dick Knight started as a banjo and clarinet player but a hand injury turned him to making instruments. After World War II he worked for Selmers music store in London, repairing and building instruments, and also with Selmers shop manager, Joe Van Stratten, building Stratten-brand guitars. When his wife became ill, he worked as a mill foreman until her death in 1963, when he began making guitars full-time.

Based in Surrey, England, Knight made all types of guitars but specialized in archtops such as the Imperial. Although it appeared to be a standard archtop jazz guitar with a floating pickup, the top bracing was actually carved and integral with the top. The neck construction was also a special Knight feature that he called the "billiard cue" design.

Knight suffered a heart attack in 1986 – about the same time this Imperial was made – and quit making guitars. He died in 1996, but his son-in-law Gordon Wells (who had been working with Knight since 1967) and Wells's son Rob carried on the business.

337

MODEL
Knight Imperial

YEAR
Circa 1986

PRODUCTION
Circa 1986

MICRO-FRETS

As if Micro-Frets' nuts, vibratos and body shapes were not innovative enough to grab the attention of electric guitarists, the company gave this Golden Melody model a glowing green sunburst finish called Moonscape. (A later version with darker green finish was called Martian Sunburst.)

Practically every feature of a Micro-Frets was a departure from conventional guitar deisgn. The front and back of early models were joined together by a plastic gasket (much like the molded fiberglass bodies of National's early-1960s models). The control knobs were tastefully incorporated into the edge of the pickguard. The soundhole had a shape that repeated the lines of the company's logo. The pickups, supplied by Gretsch, had actually been designed for Martin's short-lived electric model line.

The Golden Melody only lasted a few years before it evolved into the Spacetone and Stage II models, which featured more conventional, symmetrical body shapes, but it made a lasting impression. It was one of the five models revived by a new Micro-Frets company, founded by Will Meadors and Paul Rose in 2003.

MODEL
Micro-Frets Golden Melody

YEAR
Circa 1970

PRODUCTION
1967 to circa 1969

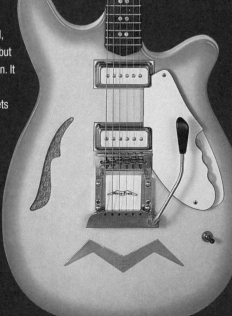

MICRO-FRETS electric hollowbody

The Huntington model was the standard-bearer of Micro-Frets' unorthodox body shapes throughout the company's brief existence in the late 1960s and early 1970s.

The Micro-Frets facility in Frederick, Maryland, was a hotbed of design ideas, but in 1973, founder Ralph Jones died. His partner and financial backer wanted to keep the company going, but Jones's widow did not, so after six years in business and a total output of no more than 3,000 guitars, Micro-Frets closed its doors in 1974. Some leftover parts appeared in the next few years on Diamond S guitars.

Although models such as the Huntington and Orbiter were attention grabbers, with their four body points and slightly bloated look, the more conventional, symmetrically shaped Micro-Frets designs were more widely seen. Mark Farner of Grand Funk Railroad played a Signature model, and Carl Perkins played a Calibra during the company's heyday. In the 1980s, long after the company's demise, Martin Gore of Depeche Mode kept the brand name in front of audiences, playing a Micro-Frets Spacetone.

MODEL
Micro-Frets Huntington

YEAR
Circa 1971

PRODUCTION
1967 to 1973

The double logo, like the pickups on this resonator guitar, represent the incongruous union the resulted when Semie Moseley, founder of Mosrite, acquired the Dobro brand in 1965.

Mosrite was riding a wave of success in the mid 1960s, thanks to a solidbody electric model endorsed by the popular rock instrumental group, The Ventures. The Dobro brand, named after the *Do*pyera *bro*thers, who founded the National company and invented the resonator guitar in the 1920s, had been virtually dormant since World War II.

Dobros were played almost exclusively in bluegrass by the 1960s and Mosrite models, such as the California, with its thin, double-cutaway body, sieve-like soundholes (the prewar Dobros had smaller soundholes covered by window screen), and electronics, were so far afield from traditional, bluegrass instruments that any advantage of brand recognition was also removed. In the meantime, Dopyera family members began producing instruments again, and when Mosrite's fortunes fell in the late 1960s, the Dopyeras reacquired the Dobro name and returned it to the headstocks of traditional-style resonator guitars.

MODEL
Mosrite California D-100

YEAR
Late 1960s

PRODUCTION
1965 to 1969

The fiberglass body of the Studio 66, along with its oyster-shell pickup shape and curvy pickguard, exemplified the modern, innovative flair of National's guitars in the early 1960s.

National had a reputation for innovation, going back to its origins in the late 1920s as the company that invented the resonator guitar. Founded in California, the company moved headquarters to Chicago in the mid 1930s and changed its name to Valco. One of the early players in the electric guitar arena, Valco had foreseen the rise of the electric guitar in the 1930s and in the postwar years focused almost exclusively on electrics.

By the end of the 1950s, National had a reputation for flashy but, for the most part, cheaply made instruments. In the early 1960s, buyers' concerns about quality were diverted by a series of new models with bodies of molded fiberglass. While the Studio 66 stood out visually from the guitar of any other maker, the company's financial troubles, along with the inferior performance quality of its instruments, doomed National's fiberglass models to a five-year lifespan.

341

MODEL
National Studio 66

YEAR
1961

PRODUCTION
1961 to 1964

NATIONAL

The transition of National's Studio 66 to the Varsity 66 accurately represented the falling fortunes of National's parent company, Valco, in the mid 1960s.

The Studio had introduced modern materials – such as the fiberglass body – and unconventional pickguard and pickup designs, but the Varsity seemed to remove all the flair. The single pickup looked as if it had been lifted off some budget-brand model from the 1950s, and the screwed-down pickguard had more in common with the ultra-cheap Danelectro/Silvertone models that Sears sold than with the stylish creations National was known for.

The offset cutaways gave the Varsity 66 the appearance of modern playability, and the black plastic headstock overlay had a beveled edge that simulated the binding on more expensive guitars, but with a plain, dot-inlaid fingerboard, a single pickup, and an almost homemade-looking pickguard, the Varsity 66 would have been more at home in Valco's budget-priced Supro line. Its performance was no better than its design, and it barely lasted a year before National discontinued it.

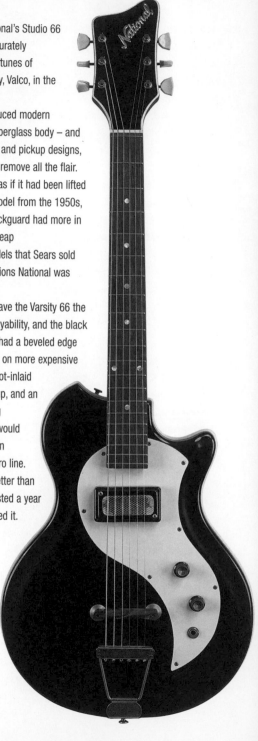

MODEL
National Varsity 66

YEAR
1964

PRODUCTION
1964 to 1965

National coined the term Res-o-glas for the fiberglass bodies of its early 1960s guitars and described the material as "polyester resins with threads of pure glass." National also claimed that its Res-o-glas was "more adaptable and workable than conventional wood," and the company seemed to prove that point in 1962 with the introduction of guitars with bodies resembling a map of the United States.

Res-o-glas was, in fact, easier to work with when it came to finishes. National sprayed the finish color into the mold for the body, then filled it with the fiberglas material, and the two body pieces came out of the mold already finished.

The map-shapes came in three groups of three models each. At the top were the Glenwoods, with model numbers in the 90s. Next came the Newports, with numbers in the 80s, followed by the wood-bodied Westwoods, with model numbers in the 70s. Within each series, models featured a variety of finish colors, electronic configurations and ornamentation. The Glenwood 95 had a pair of pickups, a "vermillion" finish, and flashy diamond-in-square fingerboard inlays.

MODEL
National Glenwood 95

YEAR
1964

PRODUCTION
1962 to 1964

ational's Newport 84 debuted in 1962 as
the Val-Pro 84, sporting an Arctic White
finish. A year later, with the name change to
Newport, the finish also changed to Sea
Foam Green.

Like all the higher models in the
map-shaped series, the Newport 84
featured, in addition to one or two
standard magnetic pickups, a unit that
picked up vibrations from the bridge rather
than directly from the strings. Although it
seemed to be a preview of the piezo pickups
that would be developed for acoustic guitars
later in the 1960s, it was actually a throwback
to late-1920s pickup designs. It produced a
weak signal, as did National's conventional
pickups.

Weak pickups were not the only problem
with the Glenwood and Newport map-shaped
models. Their bodies were hollow, with two
pieces of molded fiberglass held together by a
vinyl gasket. Res-o-glas, as
National called it, was
anything but resonant, and
that, coupled with the weak
pickups, made these guitars
more enjoyable to look at
than to play.

MODEL
National Newport 84

YEAR
1964

PRODUCTION
1963 to 1964

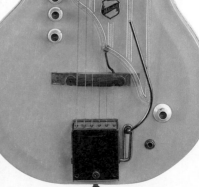

The Newport 82 was the lowest of the three models in the Newport model family of map-shaped guitars. It was initially called the Val-Pro 82 (a play on the name of National's parent company, Valco), but a year after its introduction, National decided that Newport – a beach town in California as well as a seaport in Rhode Island – would have more appeal. The finish changed, too, but only nominally, from Scarlet to Pepper Red.

National claimed that Res-o-glas (its term for fiberglass) was easier to work with than wood, and that was probably true. Bodies were produced in a mold, and the finish color could be sprayed into the mold, so skilled work – shaping, sanding, finishing – was minimized. Unfortunately, though, fiberglass guitars were still not any cheaper to make than wood-bodied instruments.

The rise of cheap Japanese imports pushed National's parent company, Valco, into financial trouble by the mid 1960s. In 1967, Valco somehow managed to buy Kay – a long-established budget brand that was in even worse shape – and the whole ship went down a year later.

MODEL
National Newport 82

YEAR
1964

PRODUCTION
1963 to 1965

PRS

Ted McCarty's name was legendary by the 1980s as the man who led Gibson through a golden age of electric guitar innovation in the 1950s. As president of the company from 1948–66, he brought Les Paul to Gibson and was personally responsible for the invention of the semi-hollowbody guitar (Gibson's ES-335).

Paul Reed Smith's guitars, introduced in 1985, were inspired in part by the solidbody Gibsons of the McCarty era, and in 1986 Smith contacted McCarty for advice on production issues. McCarty became a friend and mentor, as well as a PRS consultant, and Smith thanked him by creating a PRS McCarty line in 1994.

The first McCarty models were solid, but appropriate to McCarty's history with the company that invented the archtop guitar, Smith introduced PRS's first hollow models under the McCarty name. The McCarty Hollowbody of 1998 wasn't fully hollow; the routed mahogany back came up to meet the top under the bridge – an important feature that negated the need for a trapeze tailpiece as well as any tendency for the guitar to feed back.

MODEL

Paul Reed Smith McCarty Hollowbody I (Private Stock #62)

YEAR

1998

PRODUCTION

1998 to 2003 (continues as Hollowbody I)

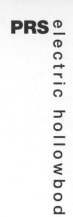

Along with the McCarty Hollowbody of 1998, PRS introduced a deeper-bodied model called the PRS McCarty Archtop. And topping the Archtop was the super high-end, special-order Archtop Artist, with Brazilian rosewood fingerboard, bird inlays with gold-inlaid outlines, gold-plated hardware, and an abalone peghead signature.

The Archtop design come from PRS master luthier Joe Knaggs, who created PRS's first archtops for their Guitar of the Month and Private Stock programs. As a self-described ex-jazz guitarist, Knaggs felt that the wide bodies of traditional jazz guitars — a carryover from the pre-electric era, when a guitar had to be big to be heard — were simply uncomfortable to play, and he wanted to capture the performance of a Gibson L-5CES, for example, in a smaller-bodied instrument.

With a depth of 2.75 inches at the rim and a full 4 inches in the center of the body, the PRS McCarty Archtop was substantially deeper than the standard PRS or a typical "thinline" guitar, but it still had the compact, easy-to-play body of a solid model.

MODEL

Paul Reed Smith McCarty Archtop Artist

YEAR

1998

PRODUCTION

1998 to 2001

RICKENBACKER

In contrast to Gibson's haphazard model naming scheme (which would appear to place the L-5 below the ES-175) and Gretsch's confusing array of models and finish colors, Rickenbacker's Capri line was refreshingly easy to understand.

The Capris were organized into three basic model groups: a short-scale model with plain ornamentation, a standard-scale with plain trim, and a fance standard-scale model. Model groupings started with numbers 310, 330, and 360, and model numbers increased by 5 with each upgrade, starting with two-pickups (the 310, 330, and 360), then two pickups with vibrato (315, 335, and 365), then three pickups, finally three pickups with vibrato.

The 330 was the basic two-pickup model and the least expensive full-scale Capri model, and consequently, it became the most popular and the most enduring of all Rickenbacker models. Although it had no frills – no binding on the body or neck, simple dot inlays on the fingerboard – it still had an elegant look that distinguished it from the designs of any other maker.

MODEL
Rickenbacker 330

YEAR
1958

PRODUCTION
1958 to current

Rickenbacker's Roger Rossmeisl was the most successful of any guitar designer at bringing together elegance, modernism, and functionality. The proof was in the Capri series that Rickenbacker introduced in 1958.

The 360 was the basic two-pickup, no-vibrato model of the Capri series' high-end model grouping. Its "sweeping crescent" double-cutaway style was not only highly modernistic – Gibson introduced its first double-cutaway archtop, the ES-335, the same year, but it had more traditional rounded horns – it also provided more accessibility to the upper-register (all 21 frets were clear of the body) than any other guitar on the market. The rout for the tailpiece made the guitar aesthetically less bottom-heavy, and it also increased the angle of the "string break" across the bridge for better performance.

The elongated gold logo plate on the peghead (which doubled as a truss-rod cover), the gold split-level pickguard, the triangular fingerboard inlays, the slash soundhole, the large diamond-pattern knobs – every element of the 360 was new and elegantly designed, setting the Capris apart from the era's traditional Gibsons and gaudy Gretsches.

349

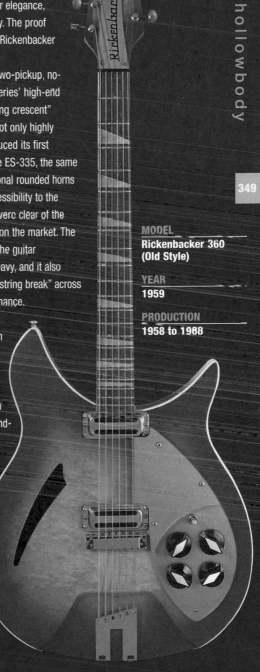

MODEL
**Rickenbacker 360
(Old Style)**

YEAR
1959

PRODUCTION
1958 to 1968

RICKENBACKER

For Rickenbacker's F-series models of 1959, designer Roger Rossmeisl seemed to take a step back from the sweeping cutaway shapes and "German carve" body contours of his earlier Rickenbackers. The new semi-hollow models, known by the seemingly contradictory term "Thin Full-body" because of their thin depth and full-size width, featured a traditional rounded cutaway and were the most conventional-looking electric models of Rickenbacker's modern era (which began with F.C. Hall's acquisition of the company in 1953).

Rickenbacker appropriated the orderly model numbering system of the Capri-series for the F-series. Like the 360, the 360F was the basic two-pickup model with fancy trim – triangular fingerboard inlays and body binding. Model numbers increased when a vibrato and/or a third pickup were added. The 330F was the plainer model, with dot inlays and no body binding. The short-scale Capris (models 310-325), were not offered in the "full-thin" F-series.

Although the Capris had only been introduced a year earlier, their modern styling set an aesthetic standard for Rickenbackers that the Thin-Full models couldn't live up to. The F-series lingered into the 1970s but never really found a market.

MODEL
Rickenbacker 360F

YEAR
1959

PRODUCTION
1959 to 1972

In Rickenbacker's "Thin Full-Body" (thin depth, full width) F-series, as in the Capri series, number 375 signified the top model. The 375F came with all the trimmings, including three pickups, a vibrato, triangular fingerboard inlays, and body binding.

The F-series models featured Rickenbacker's most traditional design, but on the vibrato-equipped models, the side-pull Kauffman unit went beyond tradition, and not in a good way. Invented by Clayton Orr "Doc" Kaufmann, Leo Fender's original partner (they made electric Hawaiians and amps under the K&F brand in 1946), the Kauffman vibrato had appeared on Rickenbackers as early as 1935. Compared to the Bigsby units that Gibsons and Gretsches sported in the early 1950s, or the Fender unit that debuted on Stratocasters in 1954, the Kauffman was an ancient relic.

Even with more modern vibratos, the F-series guitars, with their single-cutaway design, failed to inspire guitar buyers. Production totals show less than 40 of the plainer 330F family, the last of which were made in 1963. The fancier models lasted a decade longer but never sold in respectable numbers.

MODEL
Rickenbacker 375F

YEAR
1964

PRODUCTION
1959 to 1972

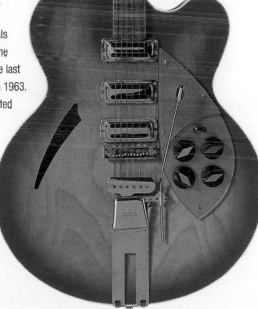

RICKENBACKER

When The Beatles arrived in New York in February 1964 to make their American debut on the Ed Sullivan TV show, Rickenbacker president F.C. Hall was waiting for them, with a special room set up to demonstrate guitars at the Savoy Hilton hotel.

Among the guitars Hall brought with him was a prototype for a 12-string based on Rickenbacker's two-pickup, fancy-trimmed Capri 360 model. Harrison was sick with the flu in his hotel room, but Lennon played the 360/12 and suggested that they take it to Harrison to try out.

Harrison used the Rick 12-string for the broad opening chord of "A Hard Day's Night," and its octave effect enhanced his solo in the middle of that record. When he appeared with the 360/12 in the Beatles movie *A Hard Day's Night*, California folkie Roger McGuinn saw it and was so moved that he traded in his acoustic 12-string for a guitar like Harrison's. McGuinn went on to make the Rick 12-string a vital part of The Byrds' sound as they brought folk and rock music together.

352

MODEL
Rickenbacker – 360/12

YEAR
1964

PRODUCTION
1964 to 1989

Rickenbacker started the electric guitar era in 1932, but under the ownership of Adolph Rickenbacker (a machinist – not a musician, instrument designer or salesman) the company fell well behind Gibson, Fender, and Epiphone by the early 1950s. Rickenbacker sold his company in 1953 and new owner F.C. Hall hired German-born designer Roger Rossmeisl. New solidbodies appeared immediately, and in 1958 Rossemeisl hit his stride with the elegant new Capri series, identifiable by the sweeping curve of their cutaway bouts.

In Britain, Rick distributor Rose, Morris & Co., Ltd., offered a limited selection of Capris, all with a traditional f-hole rather than the "slash" hole (or, in the case of the short-scale models, no soundhole at all), and Rose, Morris's Model 1996 corresponded to the short-scale 325 model.

John Lennon's 1958 Rickenbacker 325 had no soundhole because he bought it when The Beatles were playing in Hamburg, Germany, in 1960. Rickenbacker later offered a Lennon signature model, but the more accurate reissue of Lennon's first Rick was the 325V59 Hamburg, introduced in 1984 and still in production.

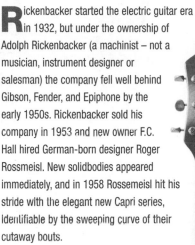

353

MODEL
Rickenbacker 1996

YEAR
1964

PRODUCTION
1964 to 1969

RICKENBACKER

When Rickenbacker owner F.C. Hall gave George Harrison a 12-string in February 1964, Beatles manager Brian Epstein shrewdly snagged a second one for one of his other artists, Gerry Marsden, front man for Gerry and the Pacemakers.

In the hands of those two gutiarists, the Rickenbacker 12-string was assured a warm welcome in Britain, and distributor Rose, Morris promptly began importing a model. Like all of the models Rickenbacker made for export to Britain, Model 1993 featured a conventional f-hole rather than Rickenbacker's trademark "slash" soundhole. It had a bound top, which the standard Rickenbacker 330 did not have, but for all practical purposes it was a 330/12.

Instead of the typical, crowded, six-in-a-row tuner configuration of typical 12-strings, Rickenbacker came up with an innovative design that combined slot-head and solid-peghead configurations so that half the tuner posts pointed to the back of guitar (as they do on a slot-head) and half were at a right-angle to the peghead. Consequently the tuners were not only in their familiar places, they were also easily paired with their proper counterparts.

MODEL
Rickenbacker 1993

YEAR
1964

PRODUCTION
1964 to 1969

It was not an optical illusion or a special effect from a computer designer – the frets really were mounted at an angle on this Rickenbacker 360/SF (SF for Slanted Frets).

Gretsch was the first major company to introduce the concept of slanted frets; its T-Zone fingerboard had frets in the upper register mounted at a slight angle (the opposite angle of Rickenbacker's slant) to provide better intonation. However, Rickenbacker's goal for slanted frets was simply to match the natural angle of the fingers of the left hand, to make the guitar more comfortable to play. The pickups seem to have fallen under the influence of the frets, too, as they were mounted at an angle.

While the slanted frets may have helped playability, they hurt the aesthetic of this model. The triangular fingerboard inlays that distinguished the 360 from lower models would not have lined up with these frets, and the dot inlays showed that Rickenbacker didn't have enough confidence in the SF to redesign its high-end inlays. Players felt the same way.

355

MODEL
Rickenbacker 360/SF

YEAR
1968

PRODUCTION
1968 to 1970

RICKENBACKER

Rickenbacker's 381 V69 (initially called V68) was a reissue of a 1969 model, which itself was a reissue of the original 381 made from 1958–63.

The 381 was part of a proposed series – few of which were ever produced – that featured what was a radical idea for Rickenbacker: a full-depth body. The deep body gave Rickenbacker designer Roger Rossmeisl plenty of room to exercise his "German carve" – the pronounced lip around the top edge that he brought to Rickenbacker from his native Germany.

The first version of the 381 attracted few converts, but the second, offered from 1969–73 found its way into the hands of John Kay, leader of the band Steppenwolf ("Magic Carpet Ride," "Born to Be Wild"). In 1988, Rickenbacker and Kay created a limited-edition signature model, the 381JK. At the same time, Rickenbacker offered the signature-less version as the 381 V69. It took ten years for Rickenbacker to sell out the run of 250 Kay models, and when the 381JK was retired, so was the 381 V69.

MODEL
Rickenbacker 381 V69

YEAR
1990

PRODUCTION
1987 to 1997

The Who's Pete Townshend bought his first Rickenbacker in 1964, after seeing John Lennon playing a Capri 325 with The Beatles, but unlike Lennon's guitar, Townshend's Model 1998 (the model number used by British importer Rose, Morris) didn't last out the year before he destroyed it in a club performance. He tried to take better care of future Rickenbackers, reserving his more easily repairable solidbodies for smashing, and he used a 1998 on the group's recording of "My Generation" in 1965

Townshend's guitar had an f-hole rather than a slash but was otherwise the equivalent of Rickenbacker's 345, with regular-scale, dot inlays, three pickup, and a vibrato. For his signature reissue, however, Towshend substituted the *R* tailpiece for the vibrato.

The pickguard on the 1998PT featured Townshend's name in block letters – ironic on a signature model – and an image of him with arm raised in the middle of his trademark windmill assault on the strings. Rickenbacker introduced the model in 1987, and the limited run of 250 sold out in a year.

357

MODEL
Rickenbacker 1998PT

YEAR
1998

PRODUCTION
1987 to 1988

RICKENBACKER

In 1987, Rickenbacker dressed up the 360/12 with an eye-catching black-and-white color scheme known as the Tuxedo finish. The company produced, appropriately, only 12 of these "formal" 12-strings.

The body and neck – including the fingerboard – were white, while the plastic and metal parts were all black. The binding was black, too, but on this "New Style" body with curved top edges (introduced on the Capri 360 series late in 1964), only the back of the body was bound.

Rickenbacker 12-strings had a different sound than those of other makers, and the secret was in the stringing. From the days of the first acoustic 12-strings, the octave pairs had been strung so that the player's downstroke hit the high string first and then the low string. Conversely, the upstroke hit the low string first, emphasising the low octave, and the result was an accented off-beat when players alternated up- and downstrokes. Rickenbacker reversed the pairings, so that the low octave was struck first, giving greater power and depth on downstrokes and relieving the "wrong foot" sound of conventionally strung 12-strings.

MODEL
Rickenbacker 360/12 Tuxedo

YEAR
1987

PRODUCTION
1987

Roger McGuinn of The Byrds wasn't the first rock guitarist to play an electric 12-string, but his opening lick on the group's 1965 hit "Mr. Tambourine Man" immediately established the 12-string as a rock'n'roll instrument.

McGuinn's guitar was a Rickenbacker 360/12, with two pickups and the rounded-top "new style" construction (one of only six made in 1964). He had seen George Harrison playing one in the Beatles film *A Hard Day's Night*, and he immediately traded in a banjo and an acoustic 12-string to one for himself. Early in 1966, he sent it back to the factory for a third pickup, making it a 370/12. It disappeared shortly thereafter, and McGuinn acquired another 360/12.

In 1988, Rickenbacker honored McGuinn's contributions to the company's success with a limited-edition signature version of the 370/12, offered in Mapleglo (natural, like McGuinn's original), Fireglo (red sunburst) or Jetglo (black). After the production run of 1,000 sold out, Rickenbacker continued to offer the 370/12 without McGuinn's signature and custom circuitry.

MODEL

Rickenbacker 370/12 RM

YEAR

1988

PRODUCTION

1988

RICKENBACKER

In February 1964, during The Beatles' first trip to America, Rickenbacker president F.C. Hall presented John Lennon with a new Jetglo 325 to replace Lennon's well-worn 1958 model. At the same time, Hall gave George Harrison one of the prototype Rick 12-strings and, later that same year, Lennon custom-ordered his own 12-string, based on his Rick 325, with three pickups and short scale length.

As the 325/12 model name would suggest, Lennon's guitar originally had a vibrato, but it didn't work well, and F.C. Hall removed it before sending it to Lennon. In 1985, five years after Lennon was killed by a fan, Rickenbacker began offering the 325/12 as a regular model (still without the vibrato and technically a 320/12). In 1989, the company officially teamed up with Lennon's estate to create the limited-edition 325JL and, a year later, the 325/12JL.

The limited-edition 12-string featured vintage-style "chrome bar" (aka "toaster top") pickups, five-knob control configuration, Lennon's signature and self-portrait drawing on the pickguard, and the same flat, non-vibrato tailpiece found on Lennon's original guitar.

MODEL
Rickenbacker 325/12JL

YEAR
1990

PRODUCTION
1990 to 1991

The German-made Roger guitars were *not* made by famed guitar designer Roger Rossmeisl; they were named *for* him. It was his father, Wenzel Rossmeisl, who started using the Roger brand as a guitar distributor in the late 1930s.

Rossmeisl began building jazz guitars in Berlin shortly after World War II. At the request of jazz guitarist Coco Shumann, and with the help of his then-teenaged son, Rossmeisl made what may have been the first electric guitar ever built in Germany. In the early 1950s, Roger Rossmeisl left for America, where he enjoyed a successful career designing guitars for Rickenbacker and Fender. Wenzel continued making mostly acoustic jazz guitars under the Roger brand.

This semi-hollow Model 54 was one of his few true electrics, but with a spruce top and a pickguard that appeared to be housing the electronics, it showed that Rossmeisl's heart was still with the acoustic guitar. The letter R in the tailpiece design of this 1960 Roger 54 no doubt inspired the "R" tailpieces that appeared on Rickenbackers in 1963.

MODEL
Roger 54

YEAR
1960

PRODUCTION
1960 to 1962

The "Duo" in the name of Vega's Duo-Tron models referred to its dual capability – it could be played as an acoustic or as an electric – thanks to its "floating" pickup.

The concept of a pickup suspended off the top of the guitar wasn't new in the late 1940s, but Vega did one-up DeArmond, Gibson, and other makers of add-on pickups by offering the Duo-Tron with two and even three floating pickups (the E-400 and E-500, respectively). Vega's tailpiece-mounted controls were also unique.

Based in Boston, Vega was a well-known name in the banjo world, starting in the classical banjo era of the 1890s and continuing through the Jazz Age of the 1920s and on into the folk era of the 1960s, but like most of the great banjo makers (Epiphone being a notable exception), Vega was never quite able to make a successful transition to guitars. Vega touted the Duo-Tron as "the finest guitar built in America or the world over today," but few guitarists ventured to find out if the claim was true.

MODEL
Vega Duo-Tron E-300

YEAR
1951

PRODUCTION
Late 1940s to early 1950s

"Stereo" was the buzzword in the recording industry in the 1950s, and the idea of splitting a sound into two separate channels caught the imagination of guitar makers, too, but this Vega 1200 Stereo model took it to a bizarre extreme.

Gibson's stereo guitars simply separated the bridge pickup from the neck pickup so that each could be played through its own amplifier. Gretsch's stereo system split the pickups so that treble strings were in one channel and bass strings in the other. Vega went the extra mile – or the extra ten miles – with the 1200, which featured 12 pickups (two for each and every string) and what appeared to be a woefully inadequate control system for so many pickups.

The 1200 Stereo proved to be a dubious high point in the history of Vega electric guitars, which quickly faded into the shadow of the company's banjos. The brand continued to be known for banjos, under the ownership of Martin in the 1970s and most recently as a part of the Deering banjo company.

363

MODEL
Vega 1200 Stereo

YEAR
Circa 1959

PRODUCTION
Late 1950s

Vox's Starstream XII was the hollowbody version of the teardrop-shaped Mk VI solidbody that Rolling Stones guitarist Brian Jones made famous. It was symbolic of the parent-company JMI's seemingly overnight change from one of the most promising companies of the mid 1960s – whose guitars, amps and combo organs were pervasive among the British Invasion Groups – to an importer of increasingly bizarre Italian instruments.

Introduced at the same time Vox had outfitted a guitar with organ electronics, the Starstream XII was overloaded with features, including a built-in tuner, distortion effects, treble and bass boost, percussion generators and even a hand-operated wah-wah – not to mention its 12 strings.

Vox's fall was even faster than its rise. In 1964, unable to produce enough instruments to meet the surging demand, owner Tom Jennings outsourced instruments to the Italian-based Eko company. At the same time, he sold a controlling interest to Royston, a British holding company. Guitar designs veered toward style rather than substance, and when Royston folded in 1969, that was the end of Vox guitars.

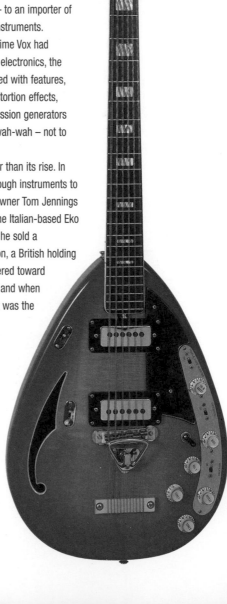

MODEL
Vox Starstream XII

YEAR
Circa 1967

PRODUCTION
1967 to 1968

The guitars of Willi Wilkanowski are among the most easily identifiable by any maker because their "rolled" edges make them look like violins.

Wilkanowski was born in Poland in 1886 and came to the U.S. around 1920, settling in Boston, where he made violins for the Oliver Ditson Co. Around 1938 he relocated to New York to work for the Gretsch company and, by 1939, he had opened his own shop in the New York borough of Brooklyn. Although he lived until around 1960, he only made guitars for a short period.

Most of Wilkanoswki's guitars had the squat, non-cutaway shape of this Airway model, with body points off the upper bouts. The rosewood pickguard was not his typical shape, but it was no doubt altered to accept the floating pickup. This example was unusual in that it sported modern "slash" soundholes (probably inspired by the "cat's eye" soundholes that appeared on Gretsch archtops in 1939) rather than Wilkanowski's typical violin-style f-holes.

MODEL
Wilkanowski Airway

YEAR
1940

PRODUCTION
Circa 1939 to early 1940s

YAMAHA

amaha is one of the oldest companies in the music business, founded in 1887, but its electric guitars of the late 1960s – exemplified by the SA-15 – looked like anything *but* the product of a long-established musical instrument company.

The SA-15 appeared to come from two different design teams, as if the first team got half of the way to creating a Rickenbacker and then the second team took over. The upper part of the body was actually a smoothed-down version of the infamous Yamaha solidbody SG-5A, better known as the Flying Samurai, which did in fact look like a reversed Rickenbacker; the lower body half was traditionally symmetrical. Also like the Rickenbacker, the Yamaha had a semi-hollow body with a soundhole, but again, the design inspiration appeared to be split between a Rickenbacker slash-hole on the upper half and a traditional (though reversed) f-hole on the lower half.

Despite its shaky start in the 1960s, Yamaha would go on to contribute popular and enduring designs to the electric guitar world in the last quarter of the 20th century.

MODEL
Yamaha SA-15

YEAR
1968

PRODUCTION
1966 to late 1960s

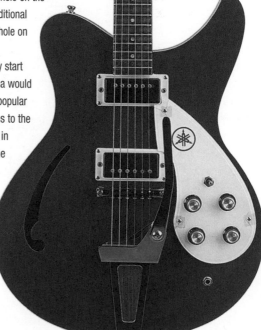

Although Yamaha stood apart from many Japanese companies in the "copy era" of the 1970s, establishing itself as a company with its own recognisable and successful designs, Gibson's ES-335 – the original semi-hollowbody model – was simply too tempting for Yamaha to resist copying in the late 1980s.

The SA-1100 had ever-so-slightly narrower horns than the ES-335, and the headstock had two dips in the top rather than Gibson's trademarked single-dip "dove-wing" shape, but it was unashamedly a copy of the legendary Gibson semi-hollow model. Actually, when it came to performance, the SA-1100 did the Gibson one better, by way of a coil-tap control (which the 335 had from 1977–81).

The SA-1100 was supplanted in the Yamaha line in the early 1990s by the SA-2200, which featured highly figured wood. Gibson did not fight back until 2000, when the company's import division released its own dot-neck ES-335 copy, called the Epiphone Dot. Still, the SA-2200 maintained enough attention that it carries on the 335-style guitars in today's Yamaha offering.

367

MODEL
Yamaha SA-1100

YEAR
1990

PRODUCTION
Late 1980s to 1993